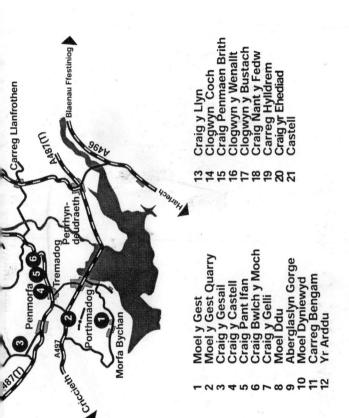

1  Moel y Gest
2  Moel y Gest Quarry
3  Craig y Gesail
4  Craig y Castell
5  Craig Pant Ifan
6  Craig Bwlch y Moch
7  Craig y Gelli
8  Moel Ddu
9  Aberglaslyn Gorge
10 Moel Dyniewyd
11 Carreg Bengam
12 Yr Arddu

13 Craig y Llyn
14 Clogwyn Coch
15 Craig Penmaen Brith
16 Clogwyn y Wenallt
17 Clogwyn y Bustach
18 Craig Nant y Fedw
19 Carreg Hylldrem
20 Craig yr Ehediad
21 Castell

Unknown climbers on *The Plum* E1 and *Micah Eliminate* Hard Severe, Craig Bwlch y Moch. Photo: Dave Wilkinson

**Climbers' Club Guides**

**Edited by Ian Smith**

# Tremadog

by
**Dave Ferguson**
**Iwan Arfon Jones**
**Pat Littlejohn**

Assistant Editor Artwork **Simon Cardy**
Maps by **Tim Hall**
Crag photos by **Alan Leary and Simon Cardy**

 Published by The Climbers' Club

*Snowdon South* — First Edition 1960
by Trevor Jones and John Neill

*Snowdon South* — Second Edition 1966
by Trevor Jones and John Neill

*Snowdon South* — Third Edition 1970
by Trevor Jones and Les Holliwell

*Tremadog and The Moelwyns* — Fourth Edition 1978
by Mike Mortimer

*Tremadog* — Fifth Edition 1983
by Leigh McGinley

*Tremadog and Cwm Silyn* — Sixth Edition 1989
by Mark Pretty, Geoff Milburn and Dave Farrant

*Tremadog* — Seventh Edition 2000
by Dave Ferguson, Iwan Arfon Jones and Pat Littlejohn


Front Cover: Percy Bishton on *Spare Rib* E4, Craig Pant Ifan.
Photo: David Simmonite.
Rear Cover: Ali Thomas climbing *Bovine* HVS, Clogwyn y
Wenallt. Photo: Ray Wood.
Frontispiece: Martin Crook on the highly technical *Honorary Grit*
E5, Craig y Llyn. Photo: Ray Wood.

Ferguson D,  Jones I A,  Littlejohn, P

Tremadog

(Climbers' Club Guides)

British Library Cataloguing in Publication Data

A catalogue record for this book is available from the British
Library

796.522

ISBN 0-901-601-65-9

Prepared for printing by the Editor
Produced by The Ernest Press, Glasgow
Distributed by Cordee, 3a De Montfort Street, Leicester LE1 7HD
© The Climbers' Club 2000

# Contents

# Maps and photodiagrams

# Climbers' Club Guides

## The Climbers' Club

The publisher of this guidebook is the Climbers' Club, which was founded in 1898 from origins in Snowdonia and is now one of the foremost mountaineering clubs in Great Britain. Its objects are to encourage mountaineering and rock-climbing, and to promote the general interest of mountaineers and the mountain environment.

It is a truly national club with widespread membership, and currently owns huts in Cornwall, Pembrokeshire, Derbyshire, and Snowdonia. Besides managing six huts, the Climbers' Club produces an annual Journal and runs a full programme of climbing meets, dinners, and social events. Club members may also use the huts of other clubs through reciprocal arrangements. The Club publishes climbing guidebooks (currently 18 in number) to cover most of Wales and Southern England. The Club is a founder member of, and is affiliated to, the British Mountaineering Council; it makes annual contributions to the BMC's Access Fund, as well as to volunteer cliff and mountain rescue organisations. In 1999 the Climbers' Club Colin Kirkus Guidebook Fund was set up as a means of distributing some of the profits the Club makes from guidebooks to assist climbing-related projects in keeping with the aims of the Club. Typical projects include ground erosion work and they need not be confined to the Club's guidebook areas.

Membership fluctuates around 1,000 and at present there are no limits on growth. Members of two years' standing may propose a competent candidate for membership and, provided that adequate support is obtained from other members, the Committee may elect him or her to full membership; there is no probationary period.

## Climbing Style

The following policy statement on climbing style was agreed in principle at The Climbers' Club Annual General Meeting on 25th February 1990:

The Climbers' Club supports the tradition of using natural protection and is opposed to actions which are against the best interest of climbers and users of the crags. This applies particularly to irreversible acts which could affect the crags and their environs.

Such acts could include: the placing of bolts on mountain and natural crags; retrospective placing of bolts; chiselling, hammering, or altering the rock appearance or structure; excessive removal of vegetation and interference with trees, flowers and fauna.

# TREMADOG AREA SOUTH

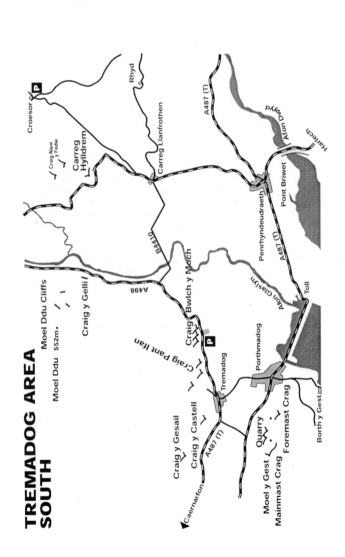

The Climbers' Club policy is that guidebooks are written to reflect the best style matched to the ethos and traditions of British climbing.

## Guidebook Disclaimer

This guidebook attempts to provide a definitive record of all existing climbs and is compiled from information from a variety of sources. The inclusion of any route does not imply that it remains in the condition described. Climbs can change unpredictably; rock can deteriorate and the existence and condition of *in-situ* protection can alter. All climbers must rely on their own ability and experience to gauge the difficulty and seriousness of any climb. Climbing is an inherently dangerous activity.

Neither The Climbers' Club nor the authors and editor of this guidebook accept any liability whatsoever for injury or damage caused to (or by) climbers, third parties, or property, arising from its use. Whilst the content of the guide is believed to be accurate, no responsibility is accepted for any errror, omission, or mis-statement. Users must rely on their own judgement and are recommended to insure against injury to person and property and third party risks.

**The inclusion in this guidebook of a crag or routes upon it does not mean that any member of the public has a right of access to the crag or the right to climb upon it.**

Information on all climbing in the area is made available regardless of the access position: for historical purposes; for the sake of completeness; and so that the facts are available if access is permitted in the future.

Before climbing on the crag in this guidebook please read any appropriate access and conservation notes.

# TREMADOG AREA NORTH

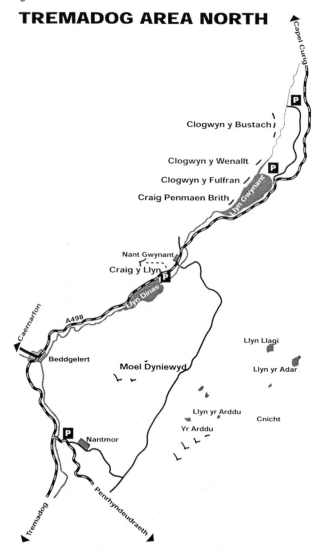

Capel Curig

P

Clogwyn y Bustach

Clogwyn y Wenallt

Clogwyn y Fulfran

Craig Penmaen Brith

P

Llyn Gwynant

Nant Gwynant

Craig y Llyn

P

Llyn Dinas

Caernarfon

A498

Beddgelert

Moel Dyniewyd

Llyn Llagi

Llyn yr Adar

Llyn yr Arddu

Cnicht

Yr Arddu

P

Nantmor

Tremadog

Penrhyndeudraeth

# Editor's Note & Acknowledgements

The Tremadog area is now firmly established as one of the finest and most popular climbing areas in North Wales. It is very important to The Climbers' Club and a new *Tremadog* guide is particularly special, this edition is our seventh in 40 years. As Editor it has been a pleasure to work on the scripts supplied by the three authors who have done tremendous work to produce this edition, in particular, they have:

a) Taken enormous trouble to sort out the complexities, regarding routes on the Tremadog crags, caused by the difficulties of describing rockfall-affected and re-vegetated routes and also clarifying the somewhat complex histories behind other routes.

b) Rediscovered climbing areas that have been written up in the past but not previously recorded in CC guides, an example is the easier routes of the flanks of Moel y Gest.

c) Catalogued the modern developments on the smaller, but nontheless high quality, crags that have been discovered in the area such as those around Nantmor and in the Gwynant.

Thanks should also go to a host of others who have helped in a number of ways: to Simon Cardy for his work as Assistant Editor Artwork and printer of the excellent crag photographs, and Alan Leary who took more than three quarters of them. The photographers who have offered photos for inclusion; Dave Wilkinson, Dave Kendall, Mike Lewis, Terry Gifford, Keith Robertson, Glenn Robbins and, in particular, Harold Morris, Alan Leary, Carl Ryan, David Simmonite and Ray Wood. Thanks to Dave Ferguson and Vivienne Smith for updating and amending Geoff Milburn's Historical from the 1989 guide. Tim Hall created the maps based on the work of Iwan Jones. Dave Turnbull and Barbara Jones supplied the important access and conservation notes. A number of people read and commented on the script: Kelvin Neal, Neil Foster, Graham Sutton, Nick Dixon, Dai Lampard, Keith Robertson, Toby Keep, Martin Crook and Mike Lewis. Bob Moulton and Mike Vetterlein did a great job of checking and proof reading, my thanks to them, not just for this guide but for their support in many other ways. My apologies to anybody I may have inadvertently missed.

The authors wish to add: particular thanks should go to the following for a tremendous amount of help: Martin Crook, Dai Lampard, Glanfor Williams and Mike Lewis. Also thanks to: Ian Abbot, John Appleby, John Cousins, Noel Craine, Ian 'Danny' Dutton, Cefin Edwards, Alex Ekins, Charlie Greatwich, Dave Green, Jon 'Spike' Green, Dick Griffiths, Mel Griffiths, Fred Hall, Perry Hawkins, Gwion Hughes, Glenda Huxter, Elfyn 'Chang' Jones, Eric Jones, Paul Jenkinson, Charlie Jordan, Toby Keep, Gill Lovick, Leigh McGinley, Steve Mayers, Tony Morley, Andy Newton, Chris Parkin, Iain Peter, Dave Powell, Mick Poynton, Keith Robertson, Morgan Rowlands, Doug Shaw, George Smith, Chris Slinn, Tom Thomos, Mike 'Twid' Turner, Bob Wightman, Bruce Woodley.

# Introduction

## Tremadog, Nantmor and Nant Gwynant

Almost more than any other part of the country, rock-climbing in North Wales continues to progress and expand, both in style, variety and acceptance of what is fitting to be climbed. Due to this continued expansion and development, it has been necessary to divide the previous guide into more manageable guidebooks rather than to create a hugely obese opus. This particular book concentrates on the generally low level cliffs to be found in the upper and lower reaches of the Glaslyn. The upper area is generally known as Nant Gwynant, while those cliffs overlooking the reclaimed estuary of the Glaslyn are collectively recognised as being Tremadog. To these two areas can be added a further area which one could possibly term as being the Nantmor area.

To many, Tremadog is, simply, the best climbing in Britain, holding as it does an almost unrivalled concentration of high quality routes at all grades. What is certain is that the ease of accessibility, sunny aspect and diversity of climbing styles make it one of the most popular climbing venues in the country.

One of the most versatile cliffs at Tremadog is Bwlch y Moch, whatever your particular bent, these rough dolerite cliffs will probably have it. Although dominated by the beefy Vector Buttress, the other sections provide the bulk of the classics. However, some ascribe the popularity of climbing there to the closeness of the cafe, this certainly is an important consideration on those drizzly dog days of winter.

Pant Ifan is made up of two main sections, contrasting in style but synonymous in availability of top-notch routes. The left-hand section with its slabs, arêtes and overhangs provides some of the best lines found at Tremadog; the steeper right-hand section has a clutch of power routes.

Craig y Castell, with is imposing position above the village of Tremadog itself, has the benefit of openness. The climbing is as varied as Bwlch y Moch with the benefit of greater solitude. The newer routes on its western flank are worth a visit, particularly, for jaded locals and adventurous newcomers.

Craig y Gesail, the most westerly cliff is fairly broken in comparison to the main Tremadog crags. However, the quality of the climbing makes up for the occasional brush with vegetation. All the routes on Moel y Gest, the offshoot, have now been included, quarried warts and all.

The Gwynant valley has an almost timeless air. Although stunningly beautiful, the valley seems to be a bit of a climbing backwater. This misnomer belies the fact there is a fine collection of classic routes and modern test pieces to be found. Clogwyn y Wenallt is a sheer little crag with a fine sunny location, the climbing is on generally sound rock with sharp incut holds, making for some quite sensationally steep routes. Although not as steep, the slabs of Craig y Llyn have long had a reputation of sorting out the men from the boys. A little more traffic would allow a few more youths through. Clogwyn y Bustach is the largest cliff in the upper valley, however, its broken nature and some rather friable routes have helped to put off a great many.

The Nantmor crags, pronounced and sometimes spelt Nanmor by the locals, are in a kind of halfway area between Tremadog and Nant Gwynant. Hylldrem is a well-known arena, some of the steepest and most outrageous routes in the area can be found there. It also boasts the best girdle in the area and a short bouldering wall. The newer addition, Craig Nant y Fedw sports some highly technical offerings and makes up for its lack of height with ridiculous amounts of lean. Both Moel y Dyniewyd and Yr Arddu areas cater for those with a hankering for seclusion and long walks in, this has an added benefit of some tremendous scenery. Forgotten classics and modern fierceness abound, as well as acres of craggy hillside in which to lose yourself on a bouldery summer afternoon.

# Important note regarding 'stars'

The commonly used 'star' system which has been established in Climbers' Club guidebooks for many years has been discontinued for this edition. It may be no coincidence that the recent *Lliwedd* guide is also 'starless'. Now, there is little comparison between the moody *Lliwedd* and the more jovial crags of Snowdon South but the arguments against a star system remain persuasive.

The rock at Tremadog in particular, a fairly coarse dolerite, is beginning to suffer from overuse in some areas. These unsurprisingly tend to be the ★★★ routes from previous guides. Now it would be nonsense to expect climbers to avoid these, they are after all some of the best routes in the guide and *Creagh Dhu Wall*, *Christmas Curry* and *Vector* would stand nationally as major routes. Many would say the damage has been done, these and many other routes are very polished, with worn nut placements and usually a trail of chalk to follow, so why bother? Lets sacrifice these to the masses and let other more discerning climbers enjoy the rest.

The argument against stars is to reduce the impact of the 'honeypot' mentality, lessen the queues, which can be frustrating and dangerous for all involved and, finally, to incite climbers to think a little bit more about their choice of route.

Many excellent routes are becoming overgrown and therefore less attractive through reduced traffic. A quick glance any weekend will see queues of climbers on maybe 10 routes on Bwlch y Moch while a stone's throw away a couple of brambles seem to prohibit access. Stars are after all very subjective, examples abound. *Striptease* is now a polished horror at the grade whilst *G String*, 10 feet right is a fine route, much neglected. Very few routes are not worth climbing, they all have a move or two to stretch the aspirant at the grade, many require route finding ability and cunning use of protection. All will provide an experience whether good or bad to reflect on, which is after all what makes an experienced climber experienced.

We have attempted to highlight the good and bad routes in the text, those described as neither good nor bad are just that. This is very much an experiment for the Climbers' Club and the decision was by no means unanimous, there are strong arguments both ways, it is up to you, the users of this guide to decide — we welcome all feedback, whether positive or negative. I'm sure the debate will continue long into the night.

## Route symbols

† as usual indicates that the route is not known to have had a second ascent in a style comparable with, or better than, the first.

†† indicates that the route has suffered a substantial rockfall since the last known ascent which will almost certainly have affected the grade and/or description.

‡ indicates that the route, or an important part of it, has become revegetated and that it may thus not be climbable as described without prior top-rope cleaning.

Climbers interested in routes in either of the last two catergories as strongly advised to inspect by abseil and carry out any necessary work first.

## Access and Environment

The Tremadog crags form part of a larger stretch of south-facing cliffs and woodland extending along the northern edge of the Glaslyn Estuary and are located about one mile east of Tremadog village. Base-rich dolerite rocks outcrop to form cliffs and screes which are steep enough to have restricted the heavy sheep grazing affecting so much woodland regeneration elsewhere in Snowdonia. The flora varies from woodland with a luxuriant growth of herbs and mosses to diverse communities of cliff and scree vegetation. The woodland is less disturbed than most other woods in North Wales and is generally healthy with a good structure and adequate regeneration. The main tree species are oak and ash, with some introduced beech and sycamore together with a shrub layer of hazel, rowan, holly and hawthorn. The rock faces and screes support a number of uncommon plant species dependant on the shallow soils in crevices and on ledges. These are fragile vegetation communities and some of the ledges have suffered from erosion in the past. Most climbing on Tremadog cliffs avoids the more vegetated areas, however, if future impacts are minimised in these sections, then conservation and climbing can continue to co-exist at this special site.

## Guidebooks
Details on the availability and prices of a wide range of guidebooks, including Climbers' Club guides, can be found on the web site of Cordee at www.cordee.co.uk

# Historical

After Geoff Milburn
Updated and amended by Dave Ferguson and Vivienne Smith

---

Exploration of this area occurred later than the more mountainous crags of Wales. The great pioneer W P Haskett Smith claimed the Aberglaslyn Gorge was a good place for 'practice climbs'. Other exploration began very late in the history of rock-climbing, apart from the early adventurers who were prepared to trudge down Nant Gwynant for short boulder problems such as *The Gwynant Crack*. The only route of merit for many years was *Lockwood's Chimney*, then known as The Great Chimney, first climbed in 1909. Clogwyn y Bustach later was to give such reputable climbers as W R Reade some early routes, forcing their way through the inevitable undergrowth.

The Tremadog cliffs had been noticed on occasions by passing climbers and P L Roberts (of *Main Wall*, Cyrn Las fame) found a minor route on Craig Pant Ifan. Menlove Edwards also had a look at the possibilities but failed to finish a line when he visited Craig y Castell. Elsewhere climbers were scrambling in a variety of areas, notably Yr Arddu where the good, clean rock with fine, incut holds must have given good sport. One can only surmise at what was climbed as such minor offerings were not recorded at the time.

During the Second World War there were two incidents of note: a tremendous fall of rock from the Avalanche Buttress region of Pant Ifan, which swept across the road into the fields on the other side and the accidental re-discovery of the cliffs by Dave Thomas, who flashed by at a low level while flying a bomber. He returned by a more conventional means of transport. Nothing happened in the next few years but by the early early 50s, Paul Work had explored the crags of the Aberglaslyn Pass and Nantmor. Local climbers from Porthmadog and the Midland Association of Mountaineers recorded a few routes on Moel y Gest and a guide by Showell Styles was published in 1951. The area enjoyed a brief spell of popularity and the local climbing club, Clwb Dringo, held an annual Boxing Day meet there for many years.

The first noteworthy Tremadog climb was to be *Hound's Head Buttress* on Craig Pant Ifan. Top-roped by local climbers it had to wait for Tony Moulam and Geoff Sutton to lead it in 1951. Over the next few years Moulam was to lead fine routes such as *Shadrach*, *Scratch*, *Christmas Curry*, *Merlin* and *W.O.B.* Also in 1951, John Cunningham, Bill Smith and Pat Vaughan discovered the classics of *Creagh Dhu Wall* and *Valerie's Rib*. The Gwynant Valley also began to receive more attention at this time and on Clogwyn y Bustach Menlove Edwards climbed what were most likely his last two new routes prior to his mental decline. Further down the valley John Lees made a foray on to Clogwyn y Wenallt, which resulted in the fine route of *Oxo*. His second on that route, G D Roberts, returned later in the year for *Carol Crack*. Moulam teamed up with gritstone ace Peter Harding to produce *Gash Wall* on Craig y Dyniewyd, the hardest route in the area for quite a while.

The ascent of *Clutch*, by Moulam, was the first route in the area on which pitons were utilised for direct aid. The use or overuse of pitons at Tremadog has always been a delicate subject but nevertheless is one which cannot be avoided. During this era pitons were considered by many to be fair game on gritstone quarries and limestone outcrops. At this stage Tremadog was undoubtedly thought of as a mere outcrop of no great significance. The CC Guidebook Editor, Wilfred Noyce, was even reluctant to include it in the 1956 supplement and John Neill, the compiler, commented 'climbing at Tremadog has little connection with mountaineering'.

Tremadog was, however, appreciated as a wet weather crag with plenty of very technical problems. In addition to the 'outcrop' attitude that prevailed, it must also be remembered that most of the cliffs were festooned in dense vegetation and pegs were needed to help the extensive gardening operations. One curious ethic was the use of top ropes for parts of some routes on Craig y Gesail.

During the 50s quite a few aid routes were to appear, including *Niobe*, *Anniversary Waltz*, *Pincushion* and *The Barbarian* and also a number of routes that no longer exist: *Lucretia*, *Cottage Buttress* and *The Bastion*. The aid on the routes in the former category was gradually reduced over the years, whereas in the latter category the climbs were overtaken by rockfall, vegetation and 'improved' lines. At the time of the original ascents the aid used was freely admitted and there was no great issue about its use.

Several keen activists in the 1950s were creating free routes as well as using aid. Harry Smith, a member of the Cave and Crag Club, which took over the Pant Ifan farmhouse in 1954, created *Grim Wall* and *Stromboli*. One of the first free routes to obtain a really fierce reputation was the intimidating chimney of *Strapiombo* which was climbed by Don Whillans in 1955; years later it is still being avoided by many climbers. Other notable additions were Hugh Banner's *Aquila* on Craig y Llyn and the unique *Gallop Step* by John Disley and a young Denise Morin. After some embryonic pegging Trevor Jones was to create, in his typically enthusiastic fashion, many excellent routes between 1956 and 1969, including *Great Western*, *The Brothers*, *One Step in the Clouds* and *Kestrel*

*Cracks.* Jack Longland had also been active around this time, his finest contribution being *Helsinki Wall*, his other more esoteric offerings have, perhaps fortunately, been lost to the vegetation. Claude Davies's ascent of *Bovine* on Clogwyn y Wenallt in 1957 produced a fine route, whose top pitch achieved an early and deserved reputation for quality.

Enter Joe Brown, fresh from several years of success on Cloggy and in the Pass. His first two lines, *Ferdinand* and *Torero* on the Wenallt marked a huge leap in standards on a relatively undeveloped crag. Following ascents of *Leg Slip*, *First Slip* and *The Wasp* it was *Vector* which marked a change of attitude towards the area. This climb with 'big atmosphere' soon developed a reputation for technical difficulty and thus a testpiece against which hard men could be measured. Many came and failed, which only served to increase its reputation. Brown also opened up the crazily overhanging crag, Carreg Hylldrem, with *Primus*, *Hardd* and the *Hylldrem Girdle*. *Hardd* in particular was considered a very vicious proposition and defeated many competent leaders.

As might be expected, the 1960 guidebook revealed several gaps and Brown was quick to fill them, going for the most obvious challenges: *Striptease*, *The Grasper*, *The Fang*, *The Neb*, *Nimbus*, *The Toit*, *Tensor* and *Pellagra*, one good route after another. In most cases Brown kept pegs to a bare minimum and used them for aid only as a last resort, the maxim two pegs per pitch was not exceeded due to judicious use of chockstones and slings on *The Wasp* and *The Grasper*. Other good routes included Ron James's *Meshach*; Bas Ingle's *Scratch Arête* and *The Struggler* and Ingle and Hugh Banner's *Mangoletsi*. Rowland Edwards arrived on the scene in 1964 with *Toreador* and followed this up later with a succession of hard routes including *Sisyphus*, *Castell High Girdle*, *Geireagle* and *Erebus*. At the same time, local guide 'Scotty' Dwyer discovered Snowdon's answer to Napes Needle beside Llyn Gwynant.

In addition to the odd peg and slings threaded round chockstones for protection, drilled nuts were being widely used by the early 60s. It was, therefore, rather surprising when, following Brown's hard free routes which clearly set the standard, several new artificial routes were to appear: *Vulcan*, *Falcon*, *Tiros* and *Victimisation*. Pete Crew was to comment in 1964 'The controversies which arise through the use of pitons, nuts and aid are now commonplace... It is a pity that the older traditions and ethics of climbing admirably adhered to by Brown and his contemporaries, have gone by the wayside in this upsurge of youthful disregard'. One answer to such controversy was action, such as when John Clements freed *Falcon* within two years of the first ascent.

Other climbers were actively seeking out routes on the smaller cliffs, such as local climbers from Clwb Dringo. In 1963 Showell Styles published a guide to climbs on Yr Arddu, 'Offering nothing to the tiger and much to the rabbit'. The routes described had been climbed upon for many years, Herbert Carr mentions climbs there in his guide of 1926, and so first ascent details are unfortunately not available. In 1963 the fine pinnacle of *Hound's Head Buttress* was destroyed in a blasting operation owing to the fact that it was thought to be unsafe. Although this seemed an act of vandalism at the time later rockfalls were to indicate the concern that gave rise to this drastic course of action.

As mobility increased, and the need to work on Saturdays decreased, more people were able to visit Wales for the weekend. The popularity of the Tremadog cliffs grew, Trevor Jones could confidently state, 'Incredibly, Llanberis seems now to be a fallen idol; and Tremadog, which was the wet weather alternative, has now attained seniority as a major climbing ground for both tigers and apprentice hard men'. Of course, the Pass had by no means been deserted and both Martin Boysen and the Crew/Ingle team were hard at work developing fine lines on the south side. Significantly Crew did not take to Tremadog and apart from repeating many of the harder established lines he only added one major new line when, somewhat surprisingly, he resorted to seven points of aid on the top pitch of *Zukator*. His second, Al Harris, wore a cow gown and winklepickers for the occasion.

It is interesting to note that this route was not given an artificial grade six years later in Crew's guidebook (when the aid had been reduced to four points) despite the fact that routes with a similar aid, such as *The Croaker*, were. Clearly the aid controversy was by no means settled at that time. Crew's attitude to the cliffs gave rise to one classic quip, 'Dismantle Vector Buttress stone by stone and rebuild it in the Pass and you could blow up the rest of Tremadog for all the good it is'. By this time Tremadog was passing out of favour and the sea cliffs of Gogarth were offering greater promise.

Yet by 1966 the Tremadog cliffs had become sufficiently popular for Jones and Neill to produce an updated guidebook to the area. This guide was not to see major development following its publication. There were some notable exceptions, the Holliwell brothers, Les and Laurie, did their first Tremadog new route, *Itch*, and later followed it with the serious *Poker* on Carreg Hylldrem. The brothers also blitzed the loose and unpopular Moel y Gest Quarry a year later, but most climbers gave this a wide berth. Also on Hylldrem a young Ray Evans was creating a couple of very steep routes; *The Burner* and *The Prow* were both impressive leads for the time. 1966 saw the last of the controversial aid routes, *Via Nimbus*. The Clwb

Dringo members explored the cliffs west of Craig y Castell, *Gestiana* being a particularly fine addition.

Apart from notable solo ascents of *The Grasper* by Eric Jones in 1968 and *Vector* by Richard McHardy in 1969, things then went quiet for several years until 1970 when the Climbers' Club was faced with guidebook competition. Grumbles within the climbing world voiced the opinion that the CC was not producing up-to-date guidebooks fast enough. Consequently Trevor Jones wrote one guide for the CC while Crew and Harris produced another guide for a commercial firm. This reflected the continued popularity of the cliffs, least of all for their proximity close to the road and a cafe.

As techniques and equipment developed during the 1970s climbers were able to turn their attention to the vicious-looking cracks, walls and routes that had previously been ascended with aid. Regular training on climbing walls and the growing popularity of chalk as an acceptable free-climbing ethic enabled many of these problems to succumb. Ray Evans's brute thuggery on *King Kong,* Hank Pasquill's superb *Silly Arête* on Pant Ifan and Brian Wyvill's *Samurai Groove.* Tom Leppert and Dave Cook were also active on the Bustach attacking the steep wall below the second pitch of *Gallop Step* to produce two difficult routes.

The smooth and imposing walls of Tremadog offered ample challenges to the new generation of super-fit rock athletes who had developed finger strength and stamina through training. Tremadog became the place to be, although this era was not dominated by one man as the 1960s had been. Alec Sharp ascended *Vulture,* a really steep and imposing crack climb and Rowland Edwards climbed *Void,* a spectacular line up the *Vector* headwall. On *Fingerlicker* Livesey was forced to use yo-yoing tactics to make his ascent, but the result was a superb finger crack, a real testpiece. Following this, Livesey freed *Zukator* of its aid to produce a very technical groove pitch. He also teamed up with Ron Fawcett and alternated leads on *Cream,* which has an exciting finish on the *Vector* headwall. A third Yorkshireman, Ian Edwards, added his own testpiece, *Venom.* Jim Moran produced *Steelfingers, Scarecrow* and *Tall Dwarves* on Pant Ifan, whilst Pete Gomersall added the impressive *Pippikin* to the right of *Vulcan.* The magnificent corner of *Vulcan* itself was free climbed in 1977 by Ron Fawcett, to give one of the best pitches in Wales. Fawcett also added *Marathon Man,* a serious pitch for the time up the groove to the right of *Zukator.* Gomersall invited controversy by leading *Mongoose* on the edge of the Vector Buttress, having top-roped the route, he then climbed it with side runners in *Void.*

Moving to Nant Gwynant Stuart Cathcart opened up the scary slabs of Craig y Llyn with his ascent of *The Moon*. 1977 was also the year when a serious rockfall in the area between Pant Ifan and Bwlch y Moch caused extensive damage to a house and seriously injured a lady resident. This event raised again the question of the stability of the cliffs as a whole and climbing was barred on Pant Ifan. Activity continued with the development of the vegetated area of rock right of *Belshazzar* by Rowland Edwards, Paul Williams and Dave Roberts. Eventually a number of good climbs were un-earthed, including *Daddy Cool*. Edwards and Roberts also shared leads to produce the fierce *Groove of Horror* on Pant Ifan, which was to be freed the same year by Brian Hannon. Livesey returned that year and added the bold *Wailing Wall* to Craig y Llyn and Leigh McGinley pulled out all the stops with his ascent of *Curved Air*.

Such activity and popularity meant that a new guidebook was badly needed. Mike Mortimer's 1979 book led to further exploration of an area many had considered more or less worked out. *One Step in the Crowds* by Al Evans proved to be a good addition to Craig y Castell. Within a year Paul Williams and Chris Shorter added *The Weaver*, an instant classic, to Vector Buttress, whilst John Red-head climbed *The Atomic Finger Flake* on the back side of the Ochre Slab. Redhead also opened up the buttress to the right of *Stromboli* with *Sexual Salami*, a serious and technical route. Steve Haston was also very active in 1981 on a crag which suited his climbing style, Carreg Hylldrem. He solved the direct start to *Hardd* with *Wildebeest* and also produced the strenuous *Weirpig*.

Meanwhile Fawcett had been making numerous attempts at the obvious but impossible-looking crack to the left of *Cream*. He man-aged to get within 10 feet of the top after two days of effort, but had to concede defeat. He then returned the following weekend and, after abseiling down and pre-placing his runners and ropes at the high point of the previous weekend, completed the route in one push; in effect leading only the last 10 feet. This, like *Vector* before it, became a testpiece of its time. Jerry Moffatt repeated *Strawber-ries*, the name Fawcett had given to this route but in no better style than Fawcett had managed. The best ascent managed in 1982 was by Johnny Woodward but the route had to wait until 1987 for a 'flashed' ascent by visiting star Stefan Glowacz. A certain amount of debate has gone on as to who should be credited with the first ascent to the point that the route was almost left out of the 1983 guide.

The area continued to attract top climbers who competed to pro-duce the hardest and the best. Redhead took a line up the flake arête above *The Croaker*, unzipping *Bananas* with a technical grade of 7a, though this was quickly shot down by other protagonists.

Redhead also added a superb girdle to the Vector Buttress, *Sultans of Swing* and, with Fawcett, the somewhat pointedly-named *Penicillin*. Fawcett went on to free climb *Poacher* on Clogwyn y Wenallt, to give a very technical groove pitch, certainly the hardest in the valley at the time. *Hitler's Buttock*, a climb to the left of and harder than *Sexual Salami*, was also added by Redhead. Not to be out-done Jerry Moffat finally succeeded in climbing the highly technical wall to the left of *Vulcan* to give *Psyche 'n' Burn*.

Leigh McGinley's guide was published in 1983 and was well-received. Up until then routes, especially at Tremadog, had been gradually whittled down to only include the 'worthwhile' lines, the vegetated ones or those deemed worthless were left out following CC policy at the time. Less frantic activity was to follow this publication although Tremadog still attracted the important climbers of the day. Andy Pollitt added a couple of excellent pitches with *Blade Runner*, a classic arête and *The Unreal Finish* which gave a technical finish to the Lee brothers' route, *Surreal*. *Emotional Crisis* by Andy Andrews and *Pwyll* by Mike Lewis showed that routes were still to be found.

Over on Carreg Hylldrem the full body pump was in evidence when Mel Griffiths made the free ascent of *The Prow* to give *Raging Bull*. Pat Littlejohn then climbed the obvious roof crack left of this; *Raving Lunatic* will probably have few repeats. *Limited Editions* and *The Sandbagger* were two hard eliminates by Pete Gomersall but it was Martin Atkinson who stole the limelight with his ascent, over several days, of the direct finish to *Strawberries*, *Dream Topping*. On Clogwyn y Wenallt, John Redhead climbed *Fishbox* and back at Tremadog Martin Crook added the eliminate, but hard, *Iron in the Soul*. 1986 drew Craig Smith to Tremadog to climb *Quite Easy for Bigheads* but it was Johnny Dawes who stole the show with his *Honorary Grit* on Craig y Llyn, 'the best move in Wales'. Dawes was active again the next year succeeding on another 'last great problem', the wall left of *Strawberries*; *Llanberries* is wildly exposed and although initially overgraded sees few repeats. Down the road at Carreg Hylldrem Dick Griffiths solved the oft-eyed problem, left of *Wildebeest*, to give *Gwyddbwyll* while George Smith undertook some spacewalking practice up the wild scoop right of *Raging Bull* to give *Total Bull*.

The hasty publication of a new guidebook to the area in 1989 did not necessarily spur teams into action, the general feeling of many was that the area was fully developed. This view was reflected in the final paragraph of that guidebook's Historical section 'The future development of the area would appear to lie on the small, previously overlooked crags... whilst down at Tremadog there is little prospect of anything particularly outstanding being climbed'.

This has been borne out in the subsequent 10 years where new routes have been few and far between. A number of new climbs were ascended in the broken area to the left of Craig y Castell. A few of the routes claimed had been recorded previously, however, the quality of climbing on such routes as *Pleasure Cruise* and *California Dreaming* were good despite some initial over-grading. The routes served to remind one of the possibilities still available in the area. George Smith amazed ordinary mortals with his hangout on the underside of the Ochre Slab, *Swift Undercut* was the spectacular result. On Pant Ifan, Steve Mayers was getting fed up with the profusion of bars and produced the fingery *No Holds Barred*. Covering some amazing territory, the route still hasn't seen a second ascent. Whilst on Bwlch y Moch, Fred Hall sorted out some logical additions to the area to the left of the *Slips* and George was aping it up with *The Chimp in Me*. Mike Lewis has continued to develop some reasonable routes in obscure surroundings including *Trivial Pursuits* as well as getting to the *Root of Things* on *Extraction*.

The major developments since the 1989 guidebook have been in the Glaslyn and Gwynant areas where Martin Crook and other local climbers became a driving force in new route development. Martin sprang into action with the discovery of a steep little cliff of perfect rock on the slopes of Yr Arddu, putting up a fine set of climbs — *Zeitgeist* and *Wild Orchid* being among the best. His efforts on Craig y Llyn were even more impressive, with *Get Weaving* being overshadowed, technically, by the difficult *The Thing of Shapes to Come*. A year later, Pat Littlejohn began to show interest in Clogwyn y Wenallt and he weighed in with two bold routes, *Sharky* and *The Hanging Tree*.

However, probably *the* find was the amazing Craig Nant y Fedw. Discovered by the Carson brothers, their first route was *Wagtail*, a bold route up the slabby left-hand area of rock; their next route *Chute Up or Chute Off*, ascended the ridiculously steep section of cliff to the right. This part of the cliff, that is somewhat reminiscent of a frozen wave, is an area of rock also breached by *The Hayward Slot*, tackling this eponymous weakness requires strength and determination. In 1991 the Carson brothers returned to Craig Nant y Fedw and produced a couple of desperates in *Cracking Up* and *Cookie Munster*. Gwion Hughes put up *Caleb*, a companion slab route to *Wagtail*, however, the history behind Ben Pritchard's *Sad Cow* is rather more disappointing with chipped holds appearing from persons unknown. George Smith on the other hand, was hanging out on his *Big Fin Reef Squid* on Hylldrem and a year later his *Fin Bar* on the same crag proved to be a technical offering.

On Craig Nant y Fedw, Owain Hayward continued his quest for big E numbers with *Ripcurl*. Higher up the valley, the offset walls of

Clogwyn y Wenallt continued to give surprisingly good routes. *Alt Statzione* and *Don't Look Now*, by Paul Jenkinson and Pat Littlejohn respectively, both provide steep technical climbing in great situations. A little later, Pat had his own *Personal Problems* with the technical intricacies of the multicoloured right wall of Clogwyn y Fulfran. Meanwhile, back at the Bustach), George rode in to scatter the herd with his *Stampede*. A supplement to the new routes west of Castell was published privately at this time and gave local climbers a brief rest from the hordes. In Nant Gwynant, the pinnacle of Martin Crook's achievements in the area was his fine upstanding effort of climbing *Priapic Worship*.

1995 was another quiet year all round, although fun names were in vogue, Adam Wainwright's *Liposuchfun* on Clogwyn y Fulfran proving to be the best offering. Al Leary and Sam Sturgess developed a small buttress, Craig Cors y Celyn, on the long overlooked northern slopes of Nant Gwynant in 1996. Sturgess's *Braveheart* is probably the best contribution. Leary also brought in Glenda Huxter to sample the delights of the valley; *False Destiny* on the Bustach being an exceptional line. After *Trout Fishing in America*, John Appleby went on to poach a number of lower grade routes in some obscure areas. Although short one-pitch affairs, the quality of the climbing on all these Gwynant cliffs has astounded some. Also in this particular year, Dai Lampard's steady progression through all the climbs on Craig y Llyn allowed him to spot the vacant area now taken by *Eclipse*. In 1997, Al Leary's explorations on the Bustach led him past, although well below, the oft espied 'good wall' of Craig Cwm Dyli; this wall gave a trio of routes. Martin Crook continued to put up routes of 'stature', *Power Snob* on Craig y Llyn being a fine example.

There was a minor explosion in new route activity prompted by work starting on a new guidebook with over 30 climbs being established. Pat Littlejohn continued to uncover little gems in Nant Gwynant: *Wizard*, *Eloquence* and *Heddwch* probably being the best. Other teams scoured the faces of Moel Dyniewyd, each contributing enjoyable lines. The Appleby team were also active on the delightful facets of Yr Arddu; *Punky's Dilemma* being a fine little climb. Terry Taylor also came upon the area and ascended some harder additions on the steep white block of Y Graig Wen. With the guidebook publication fast approaching, Moel y Gest received a visit, with a number of short but entertaining climbs being made.

It seems presumptuous to suggest that the Tremadog cliffs are worked out, there are still lines to be completed. However the future for the area lies in the acceptance of a half-hour walk for quality micro routes and the flanks of Yr Arddu and Moel Meirch have yet to give up all their secrets, good hunting.

# Tremadog

## Craig y Gesail (Crag of the Recess) OS Ref 545 411

Craig y Gesail is the most westerly of the Tremadog crags and is reached from Penmorfa on the A487. At the upper end of the village turn right onto a lane signposted Yr Hen Lon, follow this for a quarter of a mile to the gate of Tyddyn Deucwm Isaf. There is room inside the gate on the left for two or three cars but please do not block access to the fields. A faint path, which has been waymarked by the National Park Wardens and the BMC leads up to the left of the farm, on up to a scree slope and so to the crag. This route has been agreed to by the landowner and is not a right of way, please do nothing to aggravate the good relations which presently exist. If the parking spaces are full, or the field muddy, park with consideration near the Carazim Chapel (not the one on the main road) in Penmorfa and walk back up the lane (5 minutes).

The crag consists of a number of buttresses, the lower parts of which can be quite vegetated. The gullies in between are steep and unpleasant and should not be used in descent. On the extreme left is the steep and impressive area of rock taken by *The Castle*, this is the first notable buttress. To the right is the prominent rib of *Bramble Buttress* which forms the left edge of the *Sheerline* buttress. Backstairs Gully separates *Sheerline* from *Princess* buttress, whose large area of slabs is a prominent landmark. The area to the right of the dividing gully is known as Midas Buttress, which has several pleasant climbs.

There are two easy descents: one to the right of Midas Buttress, the other to the left of the crag involving quite a long walk. Descending by Backstairs Gully is steep and unpleasant and is thus not recommended.

Craig y Gesail has always been looked upon as the poor relation to the other Tremadog cliffs. There may not be the concentration of harder routes or the classic quality associated with Bwlch y Moch but the routes are nevertheless worthwhile and provide a pleasant change for those who wish to escape from the crowds at the other crags. Most of the routes are in the middle grades and for the VS leader tired of fighting for space on *One Step...* or *Merlin*, this is the ideal location to relax and enjoy an uninterrupted day's cragging. It is possible, especially on Sheerline and Midas Buttresses, to fix an abseil point at the top of the crag so avoiding the vegetated starts to some of the routes. Just make sure you are in the right place.

The first route takes a line up the left-hand side of *The Castle* buttress and is reached by a scramble up vegetation via a path of sorts.

**Perilous Journey**  160 feet  E2                              (1979)
This route takes a line on the left of the steep headwall of *The Castle*, the top pitch being quite steep and exposed. Start as for *The Chateau*, a few feet left of a broken arête.
**1** 100 feet. 4b. Climb the arête until a traverse left is possible to another arête. This leads to large ledge below the headwall. Pitch 1 of *The Chateau*.
**2** 60 feet. 5c. Climb a short groove on the left side of the steep headwall to a short rightward rising groove. Climb this and move left to make an awkward move up, continue with less difficulty to the top.

A poor variation to the next route **The Rampart** (4.84) scrambled horizontally left from the second pitch of *The Chateau* to climb easy slabs way out left.

**The Chateau**  170 feet  Very Severe              (Easter 1966)
A fairly direct ascent of *The Castle* buttress giving good climbing in an exposed position. Start directly below the summit, a few feet left of a broken arête.
**1** 100 feet. 4b. Climb the arête until a traverse left is possible to another arête. This leads more easily to a large ledge below the overhanging final wall.
**2** 70 feet. 4c. Move right into a scoop in the overhanging wall. Swing right to the arête and climb it, followed by the steep wall, direct to the top.
Variation
**2a** 60 feet. Climb over a block at the left-hand end of the ledge. Step up into a short groove and traverse below the obvious smooth ramp until it is possible to pull up onto a large ledge. Finish easily up steep rock.

**The Castle**  90 feet  Very Severe 4c                    (4.9.54)
This route takes a line up the right flank of the buttress and has an impressive finish. Start by scrambling up a grassy wall and ledges to a stance in a small bay about 20 feet below an obvious pinnacle in a niche on the right-hand flank of the buttress. Climb the right-hand groove to the top of the pinnacle. Ascend the corner above and pull into the niche on the left. Swing left and climb an exposed wall to finish.

**Astonall**  95 feet  Very Severe 4c                      (24.4.66)
A gymnastic and entertaining climb which feels stiff for the grade. Start as for *The Castle*. Climb a line of flakes up the wall on the

right to gain a slight niche below a steep wall. A thin crack on
the right leads to a small ledge at the base of a steep crack.
Climb this and the wall above to finish — a high quality pitch.
A variation finish has been claimed climbing out to the right from
the line of flakes, but it is very much an eliminate and covers little
new ground, **Paradise Lost** VS 1980?

**Bramble Buttress**   190 feet   Very Difficult        (13.12.53)
One of the few good lower-grade routes at Tremadog. It follows
the rib on the left side of the *Sheerline* buttress throughout and
improves steadily to give an excellent finish. Start at the foot of
the rib.
**1** 70 feet. Climb a series of little walls just to the left of the rib to
the foot of a small corner at 30 feet. Climb the corner and move
right onto the crest of the rib and go up this to the top of a
pinnacle. Belay in the gap behind the pinnacle.
**2** 60 feet. Move left into a groove, then go back right and up the
edge. Continue easily through the trees to the foot of the final
tower.
**3** 60 feet. Climb the final tower in an impressive position,
starting on the left and trending right to finish.

**The Jewel in the Crown**   110 feet   E1 5b        (2.10.87)
A good climb taking the wall to the left of *Clutch* and starting
from the same ledge as for that climb reached by a vegetated
scramble. From the left-hand end of the ledge climb into a small
niche and step left into the obvious groove. Climb this until forced
to traverse left over a large detached block. Finish up the left-
hand edge of the buttress.

**Non Stop**   100 feet   E3 6a        (24.4.83)
An even better route which takes 'the' line, steep, with one very
hard move. Quite eliminate as it possible to step into *Clutch* from
the crux. Climb the obvious groove as for *The Jewel in the Crown*
but, instead of traversing left, move up right to gain the crack in
the headwall which is followed with great difficulty past a peg.
Move slightly left and finish up the centre of the wall.

**Clutch**   100 feet   Very Severe 4c        (20.12.53)
An enjoyable pitch up the obvious groove in the centre of the
*Sheerline* buttress. Start by a steep and unpleasant scramble to
reach a grassy ledge below and to the right of the groove. Move
up left to reach the groove and climb it direct until forced onto the
right rib about 10 feet below the top of the groove. Continue up
to a flake and finish up the short wall.

**Plumbline**   100 feet   Very Severe 4c        (7.4.65)
Excellent climbing on steep rock taking the obvious sentry-box

and wall above. Start by scrambling up steep and unpleasant vegetation to reach the start of *Clutch*. Climb the short wall and move right to the sentry-box, climb this until it is possible to pull up left into a crack. Step back right above the sentry-box then climb straight up to finish as for *Clutch*.

**Sheerline**   100 feet   Very Severe 4c                  (20.12.53)
Another good quality route taking the steep wall right of *Plumb-line*. Start from a grassy ledge below an obvious flake, which is reached by a vegetated scramble (right of the approach to *Clutch* and *Plumbline*). Climb onto the top of the flake and then follow the obvious crack to reach the top of another flake. Step off the top of the flake onto a steep wall and ascend this to the top. An easier variation (Hard Severe) traverses into the sentry-box of *Plumbline* and moves up and right to the top of the second flake.

**Backstairs**   105 feet   Very Difficult  ‡              (13.12.53)
This route begins with a battle up vegetation in Backstairs Gully to then traverse onto the *Sheerline* buttress in an exposed position. Start halfway up the grassy gully at an obvious weakness in the left wall.
**1** 85 feet. The weakness leads up left to a thorny platform on the crest of the buttress. Keep moving diagonally left up a gangway to the summit of the flake/pinnacle; exposed stance.
**2** 20 feet. Climb the final steep wall above, taking it slightly on the left.

**Wow Factor**   50 feet   E4 6b  †                        (31.5.99)
Takes the steep little buttress high up in Backstairs Gully. Abseil to a grass ledge to start. Hard moves through the overhangs (peg runner) lead to a steep wall. Climb this swinging right onto a flake and a final step up left.

**Caravansoreye**   180 feet   Hard Severe  ‡              (24.4.74)
A climb which has never cleaned up despite the first ascensionist's pleas. Start in the trees just right of the foot of Backstairs Gully.
**1** 120 feet. Traverse out across an awkward wall to reach a groove. Follow this with a step right to avoid a bulge, to a flat-topped pinnacle. Step onto a slab, and go up to a ledge and block belay.
**2** 60 feet. Climb up behind the belay; traverse right and climb awkwardly rightwards over a bulge to reach good holds and an easy finish.

**Ace High**   150 feet   E2                               (12.4.80)
A good, sustained route up the buttress left of *Javelin*. Start at the bottom left-hand end of the buttress. A large oak tree directly

behind the start is a distinguishing feature

**1** 90 feet. 5b. Climb up rightwards to reach some slabs. Pull round the overhang on the right and follow the steep wall above over two small overlaps to an awkward finishing move. Climb up to easy ground and move right to a tree below the top pitch of *Javelin*.

**2** 60 feet. 5a. Climb the wall directly behind the tree to reach a V-shaped overhang. Pull over this and move rightwards to finish up some cracks.

**Food for Thought**   165 feet   E2   †   (3.4.88)

Eliminate in nature and a little bit dirty. Start 20 feet right of *Ace High* at a leaning block.

**1** 90 feet. 5c. Climb the leaning block to a grassy ledge. Continue up the slab until it steepens and make some difficult moves to gain the small arête (peg runner). Continue in the same line to a tree and a large ledge (junction with *Javelin*).

**2** 75 feet. 4c. Climb *Javelin* and move right after 10 feet into the next corner and go right again to a ledge. Move right over a flake to gain a blunt rib and follow this and the wall above.

**Assegai**   200 feet   Very Severe   ‡   (15.6.72)

An obvious corner-groove left of the arête of *Javelin* gives the line of the first pitch. Start just left of the lower slabs of the *Princess* buttress. The whole route is now pretty overgrown.

**1** 100 feet. 4c. Climb a 15-foot chimney or the crack just to the left. Follow the slab above until a projecting block in the groove can be gained. Bridge steeply up and step right onto a rib. Climb this to a pinnacle stance.

**2** 100 feet. 4b. Scramble up to a short arête and climb up and step right into a groove. A short delicate traverse right gives access to a scoop and possible belay. A narrow slab right of the blocks is climbed to a steep corner. Step right and traverse airily across the main slab to the edge; follow this to the top.

Variation   40 feet   Very Severe   (1972)

**2a** 40 feet. 4c. From the scoop and possible belay climb the narrow slab and continue up the awkward corner above.

**Javelin**   210 feet   Hard Very Severe   (16.9.56)

A worthwhile climb whose poorly-protected first pitch takes the pillar of rock just left of the *Princess* slabs; very popular. Start from a ledge above a small tree.

**1** 100 feet. 5a. Climb the slabs just left of a small overlap, moving left to reach a large block under an overhang. Step off the block and climb the wall to reach a sharp rib. Climb this on the right and continue along a horizontal knife-edge to belay in a gap at the foot of the wall.

**2** 110 feet. 4c. Climb the wall and then trend left up grass to a ledge below the final wall. Follow the left-hand groove and then a short wall to a finish up a pleasant open crack.

**Muscles**   120 feet   E1 5b                              (18.6.81)
This takes a line to the right of the tower right of the final pitch of *Javelin* and gives good quality climbing in an exposed position. It is best approached by abseil from the top. Start at the bottom right-hand side of the tower. Climb up through some overhangs and ascend the crack above. Climb the right-hand of two grooves and at the top make a hard move right to the arête and climb direct to the top.

**Princess**   240 feet   Hard Severe                      (19.12.53)
At the lowest point of the right-hand side of the slab is a rib about 25 feet left of an ivy-covered pinnacle. Start at the foot of the rib.
**1**  130 feet. Climb up the rib for 35 feet to a ledge and groove. Step up and traverse right, using holds on the lip of an overhang, to gain a large slabby groove. Climb this to a ledge and make steep moves left to a vegetated bay and belay; an interesting pitch.
**2**  110 feet. Follow slabs and a rib on the left to a big ledge on the edge of the buttress. Climb up to a spike on the rib, step right and climb a crack to a ledge. Continue up cracks, which lead to another ledge. Either continue direct up a steep crack, or take the original, and marginally harder, finish across to the edge on the right to finish up a small corner.
Variation   110 feet   Severe
A more direct, though easier, line which follows the slabs just left of the ivy-filled bay at the base of the *Princess* buttress. Climb the slabs for 35 feet, move right to a corner. Climb this and then go leftwards to a weakness in the wall which leads to the belay of pitch one.

A vegetated V Diff, **Dryad** (21.7.72) climbed the centre of the recessed slab above the saplings in the middle of the *Princess* buttress, starting from Backstairs Gully and traversing right to below the slab. Vegetated and obscure if you like that sort of thing.

**Acropolis**   210 feet   Hard Severe                     (4.60)
Worth doing for the top pitch. Start as for *Princess*.
**1**  70 feet. Climb the rib for 35 feet to a ledge and groove, step up and traverse right to gain a large slabby groove. Climb this to a ledge and belay.
**2**  60 feet. The wall on the right is climbed to a ledge. Move up a grassy diagonal crack to reach a leftward-sloping ramp, which is taken to a tree belay.
**3**  80 feet. 4b. Step up onto the wall on the right to an earthy ledge and continue up a small groove. Traverse delicately right descend-

ing slightly to the edge of the buttress and climb straight up to a ledge. Move left and climb direct into a short V-groove to finish.

The next three routes are approached via a gangway leading left-wards across the front face of the *Princess* buttress. Ascend the steep slope right of the buttress to the start of the ramp.

**Sphincter**   110 feet   Very Severe   (10.61)
An exciting route up the right-bounding wall of the *Princess* buttress giving good quality climbing at the upper end of the grade. The blocks on pitch 2, however, are not attached to much. Start at the beginning of the ramp.
**1** 60 feet. 4c. Climb the steep slab and move right until a further step right leads into a groove below a cracked bulge. Pull over this to a stance just right of a large overhang.
**2** 50 feet. 4c. Climb up to the top of a leaning spike above the belay. Step right to the foot of the steep diagonal cracks and climb these, exposed, to finish over large detached blocks.
Variation
**Sphinx**   Very Severe   (26.6.80)
**2a** 50 feet. 4b. Climb up and left to a cracked block on the edge of the buttress; follow the arête to the top in a superb position.

The original line up this part of the cliff was provided by **Oakway** (9.6.57) but this has been superseded by *Sphincter*, which gives a more direct and enjoyable line.

**Tachyphouse**   120 feet   E1   (4.77)
Technically quite interesting but an artificial line. Start in the groove just right of the steep slab of *Sphincter*.
**1** 80 feet. 5b. Climb the groove until it is possible to step left onto the slabby wall and cross *Sphincter*. A further awkward move left leads to a flake-crack and so to a sloping ledge underneath the prominent roof. Traverse left again to a thin diagonal crack, which is climbed with difficulty to a small stance and thread belay in a groove.
**2** 40 feet. 4b. Climb up behind the stance to reach a large vegetated ledge. Traverse left and climb easy rock to finish.

**Wild Horses**   120 feet   E2 5b   (27.2.88)
Interesting climbing with a couple of precarious moves. Start at the foot of a gangway as for *Sphincter*. Go easily up the gangway for 20 feet to a leftward-facing corner. Climb this and the overhang above. Move diagonally right to cross the overlap via a small niche. Continue in the same line to a small ledge on the edge of the buttress and climb the awkward crack to continue up the arête to the top.

A steep gully separates *Princess* buttress from the next area of rock, Midas Buttress.

## Midas Buttress

**Turnterror**   75 feet   Hard Very Severe 5a   ‡        (1979)
Thrutchy in places this route takes the steep, vegetated chimney line and is now a battle of the brambles. Start just right of the gully at the start of Midas Buttress. Climb the wide crack to a steep section and continue up the corner above to the top.
Variation
**Tumbledown Variation**   30 feet   Hard Very Severe 5a   ‡
(5.6.88)
A minor deviation. Start 10 feet right of the big chimney. Climb a rib and step left to join the normal route; continue up the corner.

**Jumble Tumble**   75 feet   Hard Very Severe 5a   ‡   (25.12.87)
Not a very good route. Start 20 feet right of the gully that separates the *Princess* buttress from Midas Buttress at the left-hand end of a small overhang. Climb diagonally right below the overhang. Pull through to a ledge on the right. Climb the wall to a large detached block and pass this by its right-hand edge. Continue in the same line to the top. Rather overgrown.

**Golfball**   80 feet   E1 5b   ‡        (5.6.88)
A very eliminate line just right of *Jumble Tumble*. Start as for that route. Traverse right to a short crack. Climb this then move right below the obvious block in the centre of the wall. Continue to the ledge. Climb the left side of the wall for a few feet and make a difficult step right to gain the flaky crack. Climb this moving left at the top.

The next few routes all start from a grassy area directly below the main pillar of Midas Buttress, up which *Touch and Go* weaves its way.

**Klondyke Meic**   90 feet   Very Severe 4c   ‡        (13.1.71)
A few good moves but now increasingly affected by vegetation. One of the most prominent features of Midas Buttress is a central V-groove capped by a roof. About 30 feet left of this groove is another overhang-capped groove; start below this. Climb up to the overhang and move left immediately to gain the slab, climb the left edge to a good ledge. Move up left onto the wall. Climb this moving towards the right edge at the top then climb the front of the large block to a belay.
Variation
**2a** 60 feet. 5a. An optional second pitch. Having moved left from the belay and gained the wall above move immediately

right below a small overhang. Climb this and continue up the arête to the same belay.

**Foul Touch**   90 feet   Very Severe 4c                                    (11.57)
The top section needs a little cunning to protect adequately. Start at the foot of the groove of *Klondyke Meic*. Climb the groove turning the overhang on the right and follow the wall above to a good ledge below a recessed slab. Continue up the corner on the right-hand side of the slab.

**Touch Up**   100 feet   E1 5b                                              (7.70)
A quality route up the wall between the two grooves. The hard climbing is well-protected with small wires; start at a flake. Step off the flake and climb the wall to a short shallow groove. Awkward moves up this lead to a step right into another groove, move up this and hand-traverse right along an obvious ledge (the traverse of *Touch and Go* in reverse). Step up to a ledge below a small niche and climb straight up the wall into a shallow groove, which is followed with difficulty to the top. This route supersedes an earlier climb (**Ek Borge** HVS 1961) which took a line a little to the right of *Touch Up* to finish up a small slab right of the pinnacle on *Touch and Go*.

**Avalon**   120 feet   Very Severe 4c                                        (4.60)
A tricky route, the first pitch is a bit prickly. Start below the central groove. Climb into the groove and immediately step left to a diagonal crack. Climb this past two gorse bushes and pull onto the ledge on the left; possible belay. Climb a short corner which leads to a ledge at the foot of the recessed slab. The thin crack up the centre of the slab eases in difficulty towards the top.

**Touch and Go**   120 feet   Very Severe                                    (11.57)
This popular route gives excellent climbing with a gymnastic top pitch. It does weave around a little but the quality of the climbing makes up for this; high in its grade. Start as for *Avalon* at the foot of the central groove.
**1** 70 feet. 4c. Climb the groove to an overhang (thread). A delicate traverse left leads to a good ledge. Continue easily up to another ledge a little higher.
**2** 50 feet. 4c. Above and to the right is a short groove between a wall and a flake. Pull into this groove with difficulty or traverse across the base of the flake until its right edge can be reached. Either way leads to the top of the flake and a finish up the steep wall.

A more direct variation on *Touch and Go* has been climbed eliminating the traverse (**Touche** HVS, 1965) but somehow misses the point.

**Right Touch**   120 feet   Very Severe 4c                    (11.57)
A poor route which traverses the wall right of the main pillar of
Midas Buttress. Follow the groove as for *Touch and Go* to the
thread below the roof. Step right and follow a long traverse line
right for 30 feet until it is possible to gain and climb a crack on
the right edge of the wall. A belay may be required on the
traverse to reduce rope drag.

**Soft Touch**   100 feet   E1 5b                          (1976)
Good climbing with a couple of moves that feel stiff for the
grade. Just right of *Touch and Go* is a groove capped by a
cracked bulge. A hard start leads to the steep groove. Pull round
the bulge on the right to gain a small ledge below an obvious
left-slanting overlap. Climb up to this and go left with difficulty to
join a groove which is taken to the top. This groove can be
reached direct from the V-groove of *Touch and Go*.

**Touched in the Head**   100 feet   Hard Very Severe 5a
                                                       (20.4.74)
A bold pitch taking the wall to the right of *Soft Touch*. Start 20
feet right of *Touch and Go* behind a tree very close to the rock.
Climb straight up for 35 feet to the traverse of *Right Touch*. Move
slightly right to a slight crack and continue up on very small, flaky
fingerholds to a weird mantelshelf near a spike. Follow easy rock
to the top.

**Lysergic Touch**   100 feet   E1 5b                      (1979)
Yet another line squeezed into this part of the wall. Start just right
of the tree and make bold moves up the wall to the bottom of a
shallow groove system just right of *Touched in the Head*. Climb
this with a couple of awkward moves to the top.

Thirty yards right of Midas Buttress is a short wall. The smooth left-
hand side of the wall taking the overhang on the left was climbed
by **The Kitten** (HVS) but has since been overgrown by ivy.

**Overcome**   60 feet   Very Severe 4c
A short route, but clean, with positive climbing. Climb the corner-
crack to the right finishing through a roof.

**Puki**   100 feet   Severe                              (23.4.67)
Just to the right a rib runs down to form a rocky scoop bounded
by grass slopes on either side. Start at the foot of the rib. Climb a
short wall and a groove to an overhang, move left and up a short
rib to a grass ledge and fence.

Above: Glanfor Williams climbing *The Gwynant Crack* in the 1950s. Left: Bob Davies and Peredur Lloyd in the *Hail Bebe* area of Tremadog in the 50s. Below: Glanfor Williams, Harold Morris and Peredur Lloyd, Tremadog activists of the 50s. Photos: Harold Morris collection.

Peredur Lloyd (right) and Jeremy Trumper (below) on the artificial version of *Basin Street* in the 1950s.
Photos: Harold Morris collection

# Craig y Carlwm (Crag of the Stoat)

This is a small crag 300 yards east of Craig y Gesail. There is some very loose rock and the brambles make the approach to the crag rather painful. The cliff is in two sections, the left-hand consisting of three buttress separated by two corners, *Carlwm Corner* takes the left-hand one. It is probably best reached from the eastern end of Craig y Gesail via an old quarry level, passing a ruined building, to its termination at a level area overgrown with trees. The crag is directly above.

**Carlwm Corner**  110 feet  Very Severe  ‡      (11.6.66)
Below the left-hand section of the cliff about five yards left of the obvious easy angled groove, a steep corner splits the upper part of the face. Go up the wall and rib to the foot of the corner and climb it directly over three slight bulges.
Variation
**The Fox**  Very Difficult      (9.2.64)
The original line which avoided the corner via a traverse left to regain the rib.

**Carlwm Arête**  110 feet  E3  †      (10.1.99)
The steep right arête of *Carlwm Corner* with a hard but well-protected crux.
**1** 70 feet. As for *Carlwm Corner* to a spike belay.
**2** 40 feet. 5c. From the foot of the arête swing up right to a good hold. Reach up left to a finger slot and climb the arête moving out right at the top into a short corner.

**Biolet**  130 feet  Severe  ‡      (10.9.64)
Takes a line up the arête on the right-hand buttress on the left-hand part of the cliff. Start at the foot of the rib. Climb up the right-hand side of the face to a step right onto the arête. Step back left onto the face and go up this to the top.

**The Fly**  120 feet  Very Difficult  ‡      (18.7.64)
Towards the right-hand end of the cliff is an area of black rock. Start at the left edge of the area left of the overhangs at an indefinite leftward-slanting groove.
**1** 90 feet. Climb straight up the face to a large dead tree.
**2** 30 feet. Go left to the corner, round the rib and so to the top.

# Craig y Castell (Crag of the Castle) OS Ref 557 403

This crag boasts a selection of some of the best climbs at Tremadog. Although not as extensive as the crags nearer the cafe there are some good quality routes on fine, sound rock. The addition of the routes west of the main cliff will be of interest to those who have climbed extensively elsewhere at Tremadog, or who despair of the crowds at weekends.

Craig y Castell, also known as Craig y Dre (Town Crag) is within a National Nature Reserve (NNR) and a Site of Special Scientific Interest (SSSI) and can be reached by parking in Tremadog village square or on the main A487 running west from the village. Near the junction of the A4085 and A498 there is a short lane which leads to the school. Follow this and go through a kissing gate to take a track to a ruined building on the right. Fifty yards further on are two slate gateposts; go through these and cross a field to the scree. Head straight up for Creigiau Cra'r Neidr or slant up rightwards over boulders to Craig y Castell itself. On no account should one park on the lane up to the school.

## Allt Wen (White Bluff)

The first three routes are best described as esoteric and lie about 400 yards left of the main crags of Creigiau Cra'r Neidr. The buttress is situated at the top of a wire fence running up the scree. Approach along the track from the school, past the old building and stone wall which mark the approach to the other climbs. Follow the old railway track to a small gate from which the wire fence runs up the hill. Two large boulders mark the correct place to start up the scree.

**Jude the Obscure**   110 feet   Very Severe 4b   †   (20.1.97)
Certainly obscure and not particularly well-protected. Start 30 feet left of the top of the fence, underneath the obvious rib. Climb the rib for 70 feet to an overlap. An awkward move over this leads onto the final slab.

**Far From the Madding Crowd**   80 feet E1 5b †   (30.3.97)
Esoteric but with some good moves. Start 20 feet right of the fence. Climb up to the large overhang, move right, climb up and then hand-traverse left onto the front of the buttress. A couple of reachy moves up the crest lead to a tree belay.

**Jess**   100 feet   Hard Very Severe 5a   †        (30.3.97)
A worrying line with some loose rock. Start 40 feet right of the fence at some perched blocks. Step left off the blocks and climb up to the foot of a corner. Ascend the corner and take a deep breath before traversing right above some large dubious-looking blocks. Move through the overhang and climb the crack to the top.

## Creigiau Cra'r Neidr (Viper's Garlic Crags)

These are the collection of outcrops just to the west of Craig y Castell. They share the same approach as far as the scree where a direct ascent up scree and a mossy gully leads to Craig Cra'r Neidr. The climbs have been developed sporadically over the years and the area was 'rediscovered' in 1990 when new routes were climbed and older routes claimed again. Some routes are vegetated and quite eliminate, while others offer good climbing on sound rock. Definitely worth a visit for those who tire of the crowds on the more popular crags. Descent can at times be awkward as the paths are not well-worn, the main descent lies between Souvenir Buttress and Craig Cra'r Neidr. It is best to identify each craglet from the track as you walk in; confusion reigns when in the jungle.

## Rwdlan Buttress

This craglet can be identified from the walk-in as a short wall of rock poking out from the trees just left of, and at a slightly higher level than, a rightward-slanting pillar with a crack in it (Souvenir Buttress). It is situated about 130 yards west of Craig Cra'r Neidr and can be approached as for this crag by following a faint track up through the dense woodland; descent as for Craig Cra'r Neidr. An isolated route lies at the top left of the scree slope above and left of the buttress. A tortuous approach leads to:

**Y Dewin Dwl**  100 feet  E1 5c  †                    (13.3.93)
Hard for its grade and unlikely to become popular. A sustained initial section leads to a bulge. Climb this and then easier ground to the top of the rib.

The first route on the buttress proper starts at the left-hand side beneath some overhangs.

**Mursen**  65 feet  E1 5b                              (22.5.93)
Harder than it looks. Start on top of an undercut pedestal beneath overhangs on the left side of the crag. Climb up to the overhangs moving slightly left to the obvious break. Climb this awkwardly and continue up the rib on the right.

**Rala Rwdins**  50 feet  E2 5c                         (22.5.93)
A good technical little problem. To the right is a wall with a groove on its left-hand side and a diagonal crack running up the middle; this route takes the groove. Climb up to the groove and climb it to the top.

**Rwdlan**  50 feet  Hard Very Severe 5a                (9.5.93)
Right of the above is the arête bounding the end of this stretch of rock; a fun route. Swing onto the arête from the left and move up to an obvious V-corner. Climb this awkwardly, moving out left at the top.

## Souvenir Buttress

This Buttress can be identified as a rightward-slanting pillar of rock
with an obvious crack running up the middle. It is on the far left-
hand side as viewed from the approach track. Approach as for
Craig Cra'r Neidr and walk 100 yards up and left. A peg on *California Dreaming* identifies the correct piece of rock.

**Souvenir**  80 feet  Hard Very Severe 5a  (1.9.90)
A remote but entertaining pitch with a superb crack near the top.
Start below the Buttress at an overhanging niche. Climb the
centre of the niche to gain a ledge. Move up and left to gain a
slim groove that leads to a roof. Go over this via a crack which
leads to a tree belay.

**California Dreaming**  80 feet  E1 5c  (23.9.90)
A baffling sequence provides the meat of the route; high in its
grade. Start as for the previous route. Climb up slightly right to
gain a blunt rib and follow this to a peg and make some hard
moves to gain the upper slab. Move left across the crack of
*Souvenir* to the arête, which is followed to the top.

## Craig Cra'r Neidr

This, the most extensive of these outcrops, lies directly above the
ruined building on the approach track from the school, where one
crosses the field to the scree. An approach can be made directly up
the scree followed by a mossy gully, this allows one to bear right
onto more scree. A track can now be followed left to below the
crag. The base of the crag can be identified by a band of sloping
shale, the obvious groove-line in the centre of the crag is taken by
*Brass*. Although well-cleaned a few years ago the crag is beginning to become a little overgrown again. A little more traffic will
quickly resolve this.

**Shadow Play**  50 feet  Hard Severe 4b  (25.8.90)
The first route is over to the left and is not really worthwhile being
short and dirty. Start approximately 30 yards left of the main
buttress, slightly up and right of the descent gully. Awkwardly
gain a ledge at 12 feet. Step right onto a large hold on the arête,
which is followed to the top.

**Sourveld**  110 feet  E1 5b  (8.9.90)
Pleasant but not as good as the routes further right. Start on the
left-hand side of the crag below an overhang and a vegetated
groove. Climb the wall below the overhangs moving right to pass
them into a groove above. Follow this until forced left onto the
easy slabs which are followed to gain a smooth corner below
overhangs. Climb the corner, moving right through the overhangs,
to finish up an easy slab.

**Pleasure Cruise**   110 feet   Hard Very Severe 5a   (11.4.90)
Enjoyable moves up the arête provide the fun. Start at the left-hand side of the crag beneath a hanging arête. Climb the slabby wall to a corner below and left of an arête. Follow this until it is possible to step right onto the arête. Climb the arête to a ledge and continue up a short wall and blunt rib to the top.

**Gestiana**   100 feet   E1 5b   (10.67)
A very good route and sustained at the grade. Start as for *Pleasure Cruise* below the hanging arête. Climb the slabby wall moving right below the overlap into a corner-groove. Follow this and take the overlap above direct. Step right and take the next overlap using undercuts to make a long reach for good holds. Follow a crack in the headwall to the top.

**Jill the Thrill**   120 feet   Hard Very Severe 5a   (13.3.82)
This route takes the series of overlaps just left of the central groove-line and gives good sustained climbing. Start below the central groove at some slatey rock and just right of a forked oak tree. Climb direct to gain the overlaps and move left through these into a shallow groove on the front of the buttress. Follow the groove until it becomes a shattered crack leading to a break below the steep headwall which is climbed, via a small groove, to the top.

**Holly Tree Variation**   120 feet   E1 5b   (13.3.82)
An eliminate, not particularly worthwhile. From the ledge at 10 feet move round left into a short groove. Ascend this for a few feet to move round into the left-hand groove (*Gestiana*). Climb up this until easier climbing leads leftwards below a holly tree on the prow. Climb up to the left of the holly to finish up slabs and a short bulge.

**Brass**   110 feet   Hard Very Severe 5a   (13.3.82)
A good sustained pitch, well-protected with small wires. Start below the central groove. Gain the bottom of the obvious central groove-line and follow this with interest to the top.

**Cheap Trick**   110 feet   E2 5c   (30.11.80)
Good climbing, but hard for the short. Start below a large overhang 20 feet right of the central groove line. Climb up to and make a long reach to pull through the overhang. Continue up the wall to a small overlap and move up right to the base of a short corner. Finish up this.

**Carbonara**   100 feet   E2 5c   (14.2.93)
Start as for the previous route. Very much an eliminate, but with some good moves. Move up and right to the tree with a jammed

block at its base. Take a direct line up the slab to the overlap. Cross this and continue more easily up a shallow corner moving left across the groove of *Brass* to a finish up the headwall just right of a blade peg.

**Helix**   110 feet   Hard Very Severe 5a                    (25.8.90)
This takes the groove-line right of *Cheap Trick*, start as for that route. Move up right through vegetation and past the tree with the jammed block to gain the obvious left-facing corner. Climb this and cross the overlap above on the left. Continue up the slabs on the left to the top.

**Cawod**   120 feet   Hard Very Severe 5a   ‡              (10.67)
Although a little dirty at present, it should clean up to give a reasonable route. Start 20 feet right again at a short V-groove. Ascend the groove to a ledge. Climb the bulge directly above and step left onto the rib. Follow this to a slab and climb up the centre of this to finish.

**Whirlwind**   130 feet   Hard Severe   ‡              (9.12.63)
The first route on the buttress but, unfortunately, not the best; rather overgrown. Start just right of *Cawod* below a small oak tree which is some way up the crag.
**1** 35 feet. Climb straight up vegetated rock to a stance next to the oak tree.
**2** 95 feet. 4b. Step up right and then climb straight up, keeping left of a detached flake. At about 60 feet traverse left into a groove. Climb this and continue up the arête to the top.

**Blas y Cynfyd**   120 feet   Hard Very Severe              (10.67)
The top corner is good and sustained but the start is a little dirty. Start at a short white wall on the right-hand side of the crag, just left of a blunt white rib with a block forming its top. Climb up left past a pointed spike to a small ledge. Swing out right and move up until a move left leads to a wide ramp. Climb this to below the big open book corner and finish up this.

**Ribidires**   75 feet   Hard Severe 4b   ‡              (10.67)
Takes the white, ivy-covered arête 10 feet right of the white rib with the jammed block. Climb the arête direct to a tree and short corner. Finish up behind the tree; now very overgrown.

## Lonely Edge Buttress
This is just right of the *Cheap Trick* buttress and is separated from it by an impenetrable vegetated gully. A good landmark is a gnarled tree trunk growing horizontally over the path at the bottom of the crag.

**Trick or Treat**   100 feet   E2 6a                                     (1990)
A short, sharp crux. Start at a niche just up from the arête of
*Lonely Edge*. Climb up into the niche then move right onto the
steep slab. Make some hard moves (crux) to gain a ledge and
continue up the slabs to the left of *Lonely Edge*.

**Lonely Edge**   100 feet   E2 5c                                   (15.3.81)
A good climb which feels quite bold near the top, high in the
grade. Start at the lowest point of the arête. Climb the arête until
a spike is reached, peg on the right. Continue up the arête to an
overhang. Pull over this on the right and move back left to ledges.
Move up and make a committing move right onto the arête which
provides a gripping finish.

**Corniog**   165 feet   Very Severe   ‡                           (14.1.61)
A long-forgotten route, now sadly overgrown at the start but
providing a good quality finish. Start 20 feet right of *Lonely Edge*
at a slightly lower level. A rib of yellowish rock with a wide
irregular crack starting 15 feet up is a distinguishing feature.
**1** 50 feet. 4a. Climb to the crack and ascend this direct, taking
the left edge of the slab above. Walk right to belay.
**2** 35 feet. 4b. The corner-chimney above and its right-hand
continuation groove lead to a ledge with large blocks.
**3** 80 feet. 4c. Gain a thin crack in the wall above with difficulty.
Traverse left below a small roof and climb up a groove to a good
ledge. The short wall above is climbed to finish between the two
capstones.
Variation   60 feet   Hard Very Severe 5a                            (1990)
**3a** Climb the slab making some awkward moves to gain a
corner, which is followed until one is forced right onto the arête to
finish. The arête between this and the original route can also be
climbed at 5b.

## Pert Buttress

This is situated up and right of *Corniog* and can be distinguished
by a roof at 20 feet with a tree growing very close to the right wall.
Short grey slabs lie just left of the roof.

**Pert**   170 feet   E3                                            (14.2.82)
A good top pitch which feels very committing. Start at the base of
the lower buttress with a roof at 20 feet and a tree close to the
right wall.
**1** 90 feet. 5a. Climb the wall left of the tree to gain the gully on
the right. Move right onto a wall and follow this to a small roof
which is passed by moving right again onto the upper wall.
Belay just above, below the final arête.
**2** 80 feet. 5c. The obvious arête is followed until a step right to a

good foothold; *in-situ* thread. Step back left and continue boldly up the arête to the top.

## Pwyll Buttress

Situated up and right of *Pert*, this buttress can be reached via the first pitch of *Pryderi*.

**Pryderi**   175 feet   E1                              (22.4.83)
The first pitch provides access to the main area of rock above. Start directly below Pwyll Buttress, best identified from the walk in.
**1** 75 feet. 4c. Climb a short slab and the isolated rib above to a tree belay. Scramble up to the base of the buttress proper.
**2** 100 feet. 5b. Climb the easy cracks to gain the rib and follow this stepping left into an open groove. At the top of this move left and climb the crack with the jammed flake to the top.

**September Blue**   100 feet   E1 5b                    (1.9.90)
Pleasant climbing; start as for the second pitch of *Pryderi*. Climb the crack and gain the rib on the second pitch of *Pryderi*. Move left and hand-traverse the ledge to the left edge of the buttress. Climb the short wall (tricky) to gain the corner which is followed to the exit crack with the jammed block.

**Knight on the Tiles**   100 feet   E3 5c               (3.11.90)
This route is based on the arête on the left-hand side of the buttress; some good climbing. Start as for the previous route. Climb the crack and rib of *Pryderi* pitch 2 to the foot of the open groove. Move left onto the steep slab under the arête and make blind moves up left to a ledge before moving back right to gain the arête proper. Follow the arête with difficulty but good gear to the foot of the final crack on *September Blue*.

**Pwyll**   100 feet   E2 5c                             (22.4.83)
The first route on the buttress and probably the best. Start just right of the second pitch of *Pryderi*. Climb a short wall to gain a left-facing corner. Climb this until forced right onto the slab above. Follow the obvious traverse right into a short corner and climb this and the crack above to reach steep slabs. Continue up these directly to the top.

The buttress right of *Pwll* has been climbed via a groove and ledges overlooking the gully. The top 30 feet is dangerously loose and can therefore not be recommended.

Another poor route, **Mimsy** (Very Difficult) lies between Pwyll Buttress and Craig y Castell. It was overgrown and vegetated in 1955, it is a horticulturist's delight now and best forgotten.

# The Main Cliff

This is the major outcrop in the vicinity and is situated directly above Tremadog school. It contains some high quality climbing including probably the best Hard Severe at Tremadog. The cliff is less popular than the crags closer to the cafe and this is an added attraction. Approach as for the previous routes but slant right up the scree. There is vague path but it is hard to find from the bottom.

The crag has a slabby left-hand flank capped by overhangs. The main buttress is bounded on the right by a prominent groove whilst right again are prominent overhangs capping the fine *Tantalus* slab. Right again are smaller buttresses before the cliff fades into vegetation. A steep path on the right-hand side of the cliff gives the safest descent.

**Iolyn**   180 feet   Severe                                    (24.5.64)
This route climbs the first overhang on the left and follows pleasant slabs before battling through some unsavoury vegetation towards the top. Start at the left-hand side of the crag, just right of the vegetation.
**1** 90 feet. Climb up diagonally left and take the overhang on its left side. Step right to a ledge and continue bearing rightwards up the clean slab to a ledge. Continue up slabs to a niche and belay.
**2** 90 feet. Climb up, trending left, to beneath overhangs. An awkward step left leads to scrambling up broken rock and vegetation. A better, but harder, finish is to traverse to the tree of *Tiercel* and finish up this.

**Pulsar**   180 feet   Hard Very Severe                         (10.79)
The hard section is short but not well-protected.
**1** 70 feet. 5a. As for *Iolyn* to the overhang then move right between the overlaps to make a bold move up to gain the arête. Pull over the overhang onto a slab above and climb it via the right-hand edge to a tree belay.
**2** 110 feet. 4c. Ascend an easy slab on the left, move under a roof and go left to a small holly tree. Move up right via a loose spike onto the wall and climb this and a steep slab to finish.

**Tiercel**   180 feet   Hard Severe                             (23.8.58)
Not particularly worthwhile. Start about five yards right of *Iolyn*, below a square-cut overhang.
**1** 130 feet. Climb up slabs to the overhang. Go left and then up to a small ledge. Pull through the overhang to a ledge continuing up the clean slab and on to a tree. Climb up through trees until a belay can be taken at a tree below the final steep wall.
**2** 50 feet. Climb the tree and fall into the left-hand of two grooves. Ascend this stepping left to finish at a large ledge.

**Salix**   160 feet   Hard Very Severe                              (5.64)
An excellent and technical first pitch with a final pitch which is
serious for the grade with virtually no protection. Start at a steep,
cracked wall beneath and right of a steep rib.
**1** 120 feet. 5a. Climb diagonally right to a thin crack. Climb this
with difficulty and go over a bulge and then left to a rib. Climb
this for a few feet, go left and diagonally back right to a small
ledge. Continue up to the tree belay of *Tiercel.*
**2** 40 feet. 4c. Ascend the tree (traditional and the last runner)
and step right onto rock, or climb the overhang direct. Go right
again to gain the nose which gives a thrilling finish.

**Jackdaw on the Edge of Time**   170 feet   E1      (30.5.81)
Some good climbing though rather disjointed; it traverses quite a
long way on the first pitch. Start below and left of *Creagh Dhu
Wall.*
**1** 70 feet. 5b. An easy open groove leads to an overhang. Move
left across a slab to join *Salix* at its crux. Pull up and over the
next overlap to a small stance.
**2** 100 feet. 4c. Traverse right to gain and climb a fine flaky
groove to finish up *Creagh Dhu Wall.*

**One Step in the Crowds**   170 feet   E1      (1.6.79)
A good, enjoyable route which takes the large overhang just left
of *Creagh Dhu Wall.* Start at the open corner of *Creagh Dhu
Wall.*
**1** 90 feet. 5b. Climb up the corner and step left into a steep
groove. Ascend this via a flake until below an overhang. Step
right onto a rib then make difficult moves to gain a sloping ledge;
possible belay. Use the diagonal, quartzy crack in the overhang
to gain a jutting rib on the left. Pull up to another crack and
follow this round the roof to better holds on the right. Step left into
a shallow groove and climb this to belay on a small ledge.
**2** 80 feet. 5b. Continue up the groove and crack system until
reaching the overhang. Pull over this on the right and step round
the arête on the left. Make a thin move up a slabby wall to an
exciting finish.
Variation
**Iron in the Soul**   80 feet   E3 6b   †      (9.84)
A direct start to *One Step in the Crowds* gives a fierce well-
protected problem. Climb the thin crack left of the original start to
the roof. Pull over this direct into the groove above and join the
original route at the overhang. Finish up this.

**Creagh Dhu Wall**   200 feet   Hard Severe      (12.7.51)
An all-time classic which is a must for any visitor to Tremadog
giving varied climbing on superb rock. Now, sadly, showing
signs of wear. Start below the large corner with a block on the

left. The starting ledges are very polished.

**1** 90 feet. 4b. Scramble up slightly on the left to the foot of the corner. Climb the corner and a slanting quartz-filled crack to reach another slanting crack which leads right to the arête. Step down to the right and carefully foot-traverse right until a crack is reached which leads to a large ledge and tree belay.

**2** 110 feet. 4b. Step down and hand-traverse out left on the flake in a very exposed position to gain the crest of the buttress. Continue up via cracks to a small ledge and possible belay at a hollow block. Move up left to make a difficult entry into a sloping polished groove (crux) to finish right of a small overhang.

### Creagh Dhu Wall Direct   140 feet   Very Severe   (2.6.57/ 11.57)

These two variations on the parent route combine to give one of the best Very Severes in the area. Start as for the previous route.

**1** 110 feet. 5a. Climb the corner to a bulge and make an awkward move left across the steep wall to reach a diagonal crack. Ascend this to join the ordinary route on the slabby nose and climb this to the stance at the hollow block.

**3** 30 feet. 4c. Climb the slabby groove directly behind the stance. An excellent pitch with just adequate protection.

### Rombold   225 feet   Very Severe   (11.57)

A circuitous route which although one of the first climbs on the crag has been superseded by better, more continuous, lines. Start as for *Creagh Dhu Wall*.

**1** 90 feet. 4b. Move up left and climb into the base of the corner. Follow this for 20 feet and move right to the arête. Make a descending traverse to the foot of the prominent crack. Climb this until a hand- and toe-traverse left (*Creagh Dhu Wall* in reverse) leads to a stance in the groove.

**2** 95 feet. 5a. An awkward pull across the left wall leads to a diagonal crack high on the left. Pull round and traverse left to a thin crack. Ascend this to within a few feet of the overhang and step right to a stance in an exposed position.

**3** 40 feet. 4c. Step right and then go across to a groove which is climbed to the top. This is right of *Creagh Dhu Wall Direct*.

### Bigger Bug   170 feet   E4   ††   (19.4.81)

A difficult eliminate giving some worthwhile climbing. Start 15 feet right of *Creagh Dhu Wall*.

**1** 80 feet. 5a. Start as for *Creagh Dubh Wall*, climb up to the large roof then traverse delicately right across the slab to a corner; cross the roof using a short ramp. From the base of the wide groove above step right onto the arête and follow this to the terrace.

**2** 90 feet. 6a. Climb a thin crack in the slab between *The Wasp* and *Pellagra* (peg) to a large roof. Climb this and finish direct.

**Craig y Castell**

1. Salix HVS
2. One Step in the Crowds
3. Creagh Dhu Wall HS

4. The Wasp E2
5. Pellagra E3
6. Tensor E2
7. Tantalus HVS
8. Niobe VS
9. Mensor VS

Just to the right is the fine *Tantalus* slab.

**Sisyphus**  180 feet  E2                                    (17.10.65)
Though an eliminate this route offers some interesting, and quite difficult, climbing in an airy position. Start below a large corner at the bottom left-hand corner of the *Tantalus* slab; initially rather vegetated.
**1** 90 feet. 5c. Climb the corner until a traverse left can be made to a large ash tree. Go left again with difficulty to a groove. Climb this to a stance at the left end of a large ledge. A harder variation is to move out to the arête almost immediately and boldly climb it to join the normal route.
**2** 90 feet. 5c. Go up the obvious corner for 15 feet (as for *The Wasp*). Pull out left to a good handhold on the arête. Continue left with difficulty to a resting place. Climb the slabby buttress and a short groove to finish.

**The Wasp**  170 feet  E2                                    (9.60)
A really enjoyable route with two excellent and contrasting pitches. A tiring crack is followed by a technical groove. Start as for *Sisyphus*.
**1** 90 feet. 5c. Go up the corner for 30 feet until a tree is reached. Traverse left to a pinnacle below an overhanging crack. Climb this with difficulty to a large ledge.
**2** 80 feet. 5c. The prominent corner at the left-hand edge of the ledge is climbed direct moving left at the top.
Variation Start                                               (15.11.85)
**1a** 5b. From the foot of the crack move left onto the wall and mantel onto a sloping ledge. Continue up to the large ledge below the start of the second pitch.

**Pellagra**  180 feet  E3                                    (5.64)
A really excellent route giving technical climbing with a particularly awkward first pitch. Start as for *The Wasp*.
**1** 90 feet. 6a. Ascend the corner, past the tree, to a bulge. Pull over this to the right and make a difficult traverse on layaways underneath a big roof to emerge onto the big ledge of *The Wasp*.
**2** 90 feet. 5c. Above the right-hand end of the ledge is a bulge. Pull over this and another bulge to reach the large roof. Traverse left under the roof to join the last few feet of *The Wasp* or finish direct over the roof. An excellent sustained pitch.

**Tensor**  220 feet  E2                                    (3.64)
A spectacular route which climbs through the overhangs above the *Tantalus* slab. The crux is a long reach for the tall or a very technical sequence on slopers for the short; well-protected. Start at the foot of the slab.

**1** 90 feet. 4b. Climb the slab in a direct line until a step right into a short groove is possible. Ascend this to reach a belay on a small ledge. The first pitch of *Titanium Man* would give a more fitting start.
**2** 100 feet. 6a. Move down then traverse left across a slab below the overhang until it is possible to move up to the overhang. Move left and pull into a shallow corner and climb this to a niche. Step right, make difficult moves over the overhang and pull up into a groove and follow this to a belay.
**3** 30 feet. Climb up into an easy groove to finish.

**Cruel Tone**   80 feet   E3 5c                    (24.6.79)
An eliminate giving bold climbing if one does not deviate. The slab left of *Tantalus* leads past a tiny overlap to the roof. Traverse right to belay; poorly protected.

The line between *Tensor* and *Titanium Man* through the three large overhangs has been climbed with some aid. A free ascent will provide somebody with a fantastic pitch; three pegs mark the way.

**Tantalus**   220 feet   Hard Very Severe            (3.7.55)
A good route at the upper end of the grade. Start at the foot of the slab.
**1** 90 feet. 4b. Climb the slab more or less direct with a step right into a short groove to finish on a small ledge.
**2** 100 feet. 5b. Climb up ribs and grooves on the right until it is possible to move left onto the wall. A hard move to reach the arête is followed by thin moves across a slab to bring better holds and a stance above the roof of *Tensor*.
**3** 30 feet. Finish up the easy groove as for *Tensor*.

**Titanium Man**   180 feet   E3                    (1978)
Good climbing, this climb provides a direct variant to *Tantalus*. Start in the centre of the slab, below a brown streak.
**1** 80 feet. 5b. The faint, brown streak right of *Tantalus* is followed to the belay ledge of *Tantalus*. Adequately protected with small wires.
**2** 100 feet. 6a. Behind the stance is a corner. Climb this and pull left through an overhang, strenuous. Continue up a steep groove to a junction with *Tantalus*. Finish direct up an arête and groove.

**Tarantula**   180 feet   E1                    (14.5.66)
The right edge of the *Tantalus* slab gives a poorly protected pitch. Start below an overhang on the right-hand side of the slab.
**1** 90 feet. 5b. Go up to the overhang and make a difficult step onto the slab above. Move across to the right edge and follow this to the *Tantalus* belay ledge.
**2** 90 feet. 4c. To the right is a groove capped by a triangular

overhang. Go up towards the overhang and move left onto a rib, follow this moving right to finish.

The pitches of *Tantalus* and *Tarantula* can be interchanged at will giving routes of a more sustained standard.

**Niobe**   150 feet   Very Severe                              (26.6.55)
The corner right of *Tantalus* gives a tricky pitch which can provide problems for the unwary. Start below the corner.
**1** 100 feet. 4c. Move rightwards onto the rib and then move back left into the corner. Climb this, awkward, with a move left near the top to reach a tree belay.
**2** 50 feet. Continue up broken ground to the top.

A poor and wandering route (**Whittington** Severe 11.6.55) started up *Niobe* crossing *Mensor* and finishing through the jungle right of *Sorry Sally*. Black spot tickers can follow their nose.

**Mensor**   160 feet   Very Severe                            (25.4.64)
A really delightful route giving superb, satisfying climbing. Start just right of *Niobe* below an obvious pinnacle.
**1** 70 feet. 4b. Climb the left side of the pinnacle to below an overhang. Step left and go up a steep wall, moving right to a sloping stance.
**2** 90 feet. 4c. Pull up into a shallow groove and continue rightwards to the rib. Climb a steep wall, with difficulty, then continue more easily to the top.

**Sorry Sally**   150 feet   E1                               (31.5.79)
A filler-in but with some good climbing, particularly on the second pitch. Start 15 feet right of *Mensor* at a wide crack splitting the flake.
**1** 95 feet. 5a. Climb the crack to a ledge, move up right to the top of the flake. Step down and go across an easy ledge on the right to a smaller flake/pinnacle. Ascend this and bulges above to a steep corner. Go left and up to join the traverse of the second pitch of *Mensor*. Traverse 15 feet right to belay.
**2** 55 feet. 5b. Move up left from the ledge and then go back right to the foot of a steep crack. Pull into it with difficulty and continue up it, past a good resting ledge, moving left at the top to finish.

**Castell High Girdle**   350 feet   E2                       (9.2.66)
An excellent right-to-left girdle giving good, exposed climbing. Start as for *Tarantula*.
**1** 90 feet. 5b. Pitch 1 of *Tarantula*.
**2** 90 feet. 5c. The sandwich slab to the left has a niche at its bottom right-hand corner. Ascend this to gain the slab then

traverse along this into the groove of *Tensor*. A difficult move up leads to a roof. Traverse left along a slab to join *Pellagra*. Follow this to a tiny belay under the roof.
**3** 70 feet. 5c. Continue into *The Wasp*. Reverse this until the good hold on *Sisyphus* can be reached. Continue as for *Sisyphus* and on to *Creagh Dhu Wall*.
**4** 40 feet. Go down a little and across to the tree of *Salix*.
**5** 60 feet. 5b. Go left into a bottomless chimney and ascend this; move right at the top to finish.

**Castell Lower Girdle Traverse**   440 feet   Very Severe   ‡
(16.11.58)
This climb is curiously uninteresting, perhaps because it keeps moving away from the interesting parts of the crag. Really not worth the effort.
**1** 90 feet. 4b. Pitch 1 of *Tiercel*.
**2** 120 feet. 4b. Follow *Tiercel* until the grooves peter out in vegetation. Traverse horizontally right along small footholds to the edge and *Creagh Dhu Wall*. Down-climb this a few feet until level with the hand-traverse.
**3** 30 feet. 4b. Reverse the hand-traverse to belay on the large ledge as for *The Wasp* et al.
**4** 40 feet. Abseil to the oak tree in the corner of *Tantalus*.
**5** 70 feet. 4b. Follow *Tantalus* pitch 1 to the belay ledge.
**6** 90 feet. 4c. Finish up the top pitch of *Tarantula*. (Originally finished up *Tantalus* in its entirety.)

# Craig Pant Ifan (Crag of Ifan's Hollow)

OS Ref 569 406

The cliffs of Craig Pant Ifan form a rock scarp along the top of the hillside extending almost all the way from Tremadog to Bwlch y Moch. The most important, and certainly the most impressive, section of this scarp is that of Peuterey Buttress. This is seen from Bwlch y Moch Cafe as a steep smooth wall and a slabby buttress cut by overhangs rising above the trees high up to the west. Beyond and out of sight to the left are a series of isolated buttresses, the most distant of which is Two Face or Stromboli Buttress

Two Face Buttress is so-called because of the characteristic 'Easter Island' faces formed by the slabs and overhangs. This is bounded on its left by *Helsinki Wall*. The smooth central slab is followed by *Olympic Slab* and *Stromboli* finds its way through the overhangs on the right. The Upper Tier is the small crag seen just above and behind Two Face Buttress and contains a number of good, short routes on excellent rock.

The buttresses to the right of Two Face Buttress are almost lost in the trees and form the least distinguished part of Pant Ifan. However, some of the routes there provide plenty of interest. They are separated from the main crag by Porker's Gully, a good descent provided with wooden steps. The long vegetated rib bounding Porker's Gully on the right is climbed by *Krakatoa*.

The main part of the crag starts with the prominent tower of Peuterey Buttress, cut in its upper part by the deep chimney of *Strapiombo*. The slab on the right of the tower is climbed by *Poor Man's Peuterey*. The buttress continues to the right as three smooth, massive, overlapping slabs separated by two fine clean-cut corners. *Pincushion* climbs the left-hand slab with *Silly Arête* magnificently situated on the right edge overlooking the obvious deep corner of *Barbarian*. *Mangoletsi* traverses the central slab to finish just right of *Barbarian*, whilst *Scratch* climbs the second corner to finish on the right-hand slab. Finally *Scratch Arête* gives clear definition to the right edge of the buttress.

A small buttress to the right of Peuterey Buttress possesses a prominent rib, *Integral*, a fierce overhang, *The Toit,* and an unpleasant vegetated gully. Across the gully Avalanche Buttress gives a large area of broken slabs, the scene of a huge rockfall during the Second World War. Right again, a fine wall, Strangeways Buttress, rises above the trees and merges into the long wall of Hogmanay Buttress. The latter wall is split by a steep smooth corner, *Vulcan,* and three cracks: *Falcon, Scarecrow* and *Steelfingers*. Further right it is undercut by a band of shaly rock below a steep wall of good dolerite. This section is climbed by *Raven's Nest Wall, W.O.B.* and, at the extreme right-hand end, *Hogmanay Hangover*.

# Access

The land at Craig Pant Ifan and Craig y Dre is within a National Nature Reserve (NNR) and a Site of Special Scientific Interest (SSSI), which shares many common features with Bwlch y Moch. It is managed by the Countryside Council for Wales (CCW) to safeguard its nature conservation interests. There are access problems within the NNR however, due to concerns over safety and occupiers' liability and, because of this, CCW have withdrawn permission for climbing. The problems arose due to the serious rockfall which occurred in 1977 in the area between Pant Ifan and Bwlch y Moch and caused extensive damage. This highlighted the general instability of the crag and consultant engineers and geologists were contracted to produce detailed surveys. Their conclusions indicated that further rockfalls were inevitable and that climbing activity may even bring forward the time of such falls. The predecessors of CCW (NCC) took steps to minimise the damaging effects of possible falls, including the erection of a barrier wall to prevent falling rock from reaching the road. Treasury Solicitor advice about liability in the light of the consultants' report indicated that NCC as legal occupier of the land had an obligation to prohibit access to the Reserve by members of the public and to take reasonable steps to enforce this prohibition. This has been implemented by the erection of a fence and no entry notices at all obvious access points and through the presence of a warden. CCW have no underlying wish to deter climbers but, having taken legal advice from the Treasury Solicitor, are obliged to act upon it. This is unfortunate as, previous to these problems, there was a perceived need to integrate nature conservation and rock-climbing on the reserve. The situation is a difficult one and steps are being taken to find a solution. The BMC are lobbying government for a change to the occupiers' liability legislation (for this and for many other access problems) and discussions are continuing between BMC and CCW.

## Approaches

### Peuterey Buttress, Avalanche Buttress, Strangeways Buttress, Hogmanay Buttress

For these, the main climbing sections of Pant Ifan, access to the crag is by a stile about 200 yards from the cafe along the road towards Tremadog. A boulder field leads to scree and the base of the cliff; once there, one can find a path under the whole length of the crag and this gives access to all the climbs.

### Upper Tier, Two Face Buttress

Perhaps the best way to approach the Upper Tier and Two Face Buttress is from the village of Tremadog itself. Starting near the garage, and parking somewhere close to the site of the demolished laundry, follow the minor road behind the site of the laundry (strictly no parking on this road) to a school and a bend in the road. Just past the elbow of the bend, a path leads up through fields and woods; the path levels out at a gate. A little after the gate the path reaches a compact little crag, this is the Upper Tier. Two Face Buttress is to be found directly below. Helsinki Gully is located on the left where a path and steps leads over a stone wall, this is also the descent path for the routes on this buttress.

Another approach to Two Face Buttress can be made by leaving the track leading to the Waldorf School, about 30 yards up from Tanrallt Lodge. A woodland path has been constructed by the school, however, after only 10 yards on this path take a faint track on the right, which leads to a fence and stile. This faint path then goes steeply through the woods to the base of Two Face Buttress. The Upper Tier can also be reached by going up Helsinki Gully on the left.

**Fear Buttress, Eifionydd Buttress, Pen y Ci Buttress**
These buttresses occupy the seeming no man's land of escarpment
between Two Face Buttress and Peuterey Buttress. From the very left
edge of Peuterey Buttress a faint path leads through trees to a large
boulder field. Continue across the boulders, rising slightly, until some
towers of rock poke out of the trees. Pen y Ci Buttress is denoted by
the prominent arête of *Curved Air* while Eifionydd Buttress is a little
further to the left. Fear Buttress is further left again and best located
by finding the huge square cut overhang tackled by the route *Fear*.
An alternative approach which may be found easier in summer,
when the brambles are high, is to approach underneath Two Face
Buttress via a fairly worn path which eventually climbs the gully left
of Fear Buttress.

## Craig y Tarw (The Bull Crag)
This is the prominent outcrop facing the valley on the bluff called Y
Glog on the further, northwestern, side of the outlet from Llyn Cwm-
Bach. The crag carries on the line of Craig Pant Ifan to the north-
west. One climb has been recorded.

**Forest View's Shattered Cracks**  Severe        (22.5.64)
Start 30 feet left of the stone wall. Climb the long sweep of clean
rock to a grass ledge to a move right around the corner. Return to
the left and follow the arête to finish.

## Upper Tier
A compact cliff, set back from the top of the main scarp system of
the Pant Ifan Crags provides some excellent rock and superb views
across the former estuary of the Glaslyn. Its only detraction is its use
as a 'Centre' crag. On certain days there may well be a great
number of others around you, noisily extolling the pleasures (or not)
of rock-climbing. Unfortunately, the base of the cliff and some of the
trees have suffered in the past. It is hoped that the cliff's inclusion in
the guide will highlight the need for care.

**K.M.A.**  75 feet   Hard Severe 4a          (18.11.56)
A tricky little offering. Start on the left-hand side of the crag at an
obvious open chimney-line. Squirm up this to gain a continuation
crack, tackle the crack, and make a step right to finish up the
rounded arête above.

**Madog**  80 feet   Very Severe 4c           (1960s)
A pithy exercise in jamming. This well-protected route starts just
down and left of the large triangular overhang. Ascend the
stepped wall to the base of the parallel cracks. These eventually
lead to an awkward little bulge; surmount this to finish direct.

**Myomancy**   80 feet   Hard Very Severe 5b        (1970s)
Surprisingly good climbing which starts directly below the
triangular overhang at 10 feet. Bridge up the groove and turn the
overhang on the right. Step left onto the wall and move up to the
small overlap. Climb straight up on finger jams to finish up rather
easier rock.

**Falling Block Crack**   80 feet   Severe        (18.8.54)
A good route starting just to the right of a vague arête. Climb to
a prominent niche up to the right of the triangular overhang.
Climb the crack and groove above and finish direct. A direct
start can be made by climbing the left side of the vague arête to
gain the niche.

**Mistook**   80 feet   Very Severe 4c        (Summer 1961)
Another good route which starts below some bubbly rock. Climb
the bubbly wall to reach a ledge beneath the crack trending up
rightwards; follow the crack to the top.

**Gwynedd**   75 feet   Very Severe 4b        (1950s)
Rather artificial. Start just down and right of a small sentry box at
10 feet. Climb up to the sentry-box and gain a ledge below the
diagonal crack of *Mistook*. Move 5 feet to the right and climb
straight up to a ledge and a scrambly finish.

**Rammer's Route**   75 feet   Very Severe 5a        (24.9.55)
A fairly delicate route where technique pays dividends; low in the
grade. A couple of large cams help to lessen a sense of boldness
on the upper section. Start at the base of the obvious, striated
groove curving its way up the slab. The crux is to be found going
straight up the wall above.

**Marath**   70 feet   Hard Very Difficult        (13.8.55)
Start below the obvious weakness on the right of the slab. Tackle
the crack to the right of the groove, stepping out right to a ledge
and finishing up a little wall with a thin crack.

**MTN**   75 feet   Severe        (1950s)
Climb direct to the ledge 6 feet up the initial section of *Marath*.
Continue to twin cracks which lead steeply to a wall above and
the finish.

**Central Arête**   80 feet   Severe        (8.8.54)
Rather poorly protected; start at a shallow open corner, down
and left of an oak tree. Ascend the corner and step left to a
vague rib. Go up to a ledge below the obvious wedge-shaped
arête. Climb this boldly and airily to the top.

**Central Staircase**   80 feet   Very Difficult                    (1950s)
A filler-in; start behind a small hawthorn. Follow steps and blocks, trending up left towards a small oak tree. Climb the open slabby corner above to finish.

The next section of cliff is obscured by a small clump of trees; the starts are steep, all focused on one short wall.

**Bulging Wall**   80 feet   Hard Severe 4a                    (8.8.54)
Start on the left side of a compact wall where a small block leans against the crag. Ascend the left edge of the wall via a series of steps and trend leftwards to reach the base of an awkward groove; climb this and a rib above.

**Quatre Fois Direct**   80 feet   Very Severe 4c                    (25.8.54)
A fine initial section makes for a better route than the original. Start at the base of the crack near a couple of embedded blocks. Jam up the slanting crack to the edge of a ledge. Either step left and up to gain the base of the left-hand crack and follow this, or ascend the slabby wall between the two cracks in the upper section of the cliff. The original route started about 20 feet to the right and traversed across to gain the upper wall.

**Meirionydd**   80 feet   E1 6a                    (1960s)
A well-protected testpiece; a tad easier for the tall. Start below the obvious thin crack. A fingertip sprint gains the prominent jug; heave on up to gain the ledge. The right-hand crack in the upper slab comes as a pleasant contrast to the ferocity below.

There is very little of worth further to the right, apart from the original start of *Quatre Fois* and a short pitch starting just left of a chimney, both about Severe.

A girdle traverse of the Upper Tier has been made at about Very Difficult. The exact line is of little consequence as one can traverse almost anywhere.

On a short cliff behind the Upper Tier may be found:

**Goop**   35 feet   6b                    (1999)
Ascends the 'old' peg crack.

## Badger's Buttress

The initial section of rock on the Pant Ifan scarp just about manages to poke up out of the trees about 100 yards to the west of Two Face Buttress. A number of poor lines have been claimed there in the past, the following route is perhaps the best offering available to those with a bushwhacking bent.

**Badger's Buttress**   130 feet   Very Difficult   ‡        (3.1.54)
A thick skin is far more useful than any particular technique. Start at the lowest point of the Buttress.
**1** 90 feet. Go up the edge to an alcove and a tree belay on the right.
**2** 40 feet. From the tree enter a niche, follow a steep cracked wall to a prickly finish or go out to the right and climb a slab.

## Two Face Buttress

The first 'real' climbing area on this extensive rock scarp. The lower portion of the cliff has a band of shale which can be very slippery in the wet. In contrast, the rock of the upper section displays some of the finest qualities associated with Tremadog dolerite and provides a collection of fine pitches.

The first two routes climb the same general area of rock but in a slightly differing manner.

**Drug Test**   120 feet   E1        (1.10.88)
Initially this route takes in pretty much the same area of rock as *Next of Kin*, the top tackles the left face. Start left of the corner taken by *Next of Kin*.
**1** 40 feet. 4c. Ascend the slabby wall until a move left gains a small ledge and a stance at the left end of the overhangs, below a groove.
**2** 80 feet. 5b. Climb the groove, past a peg just to the left, then make some difficult moves leftwards to gain a ledge. Step back right and climb the weakness in the wall above.

**Next of Kin**   135 feet   Hard Very Severe        (10.11.56)
A rather wandering route that is now harder after the removal of some dubious blocks. Start below a small right-angled corner.
**1** 80 feet. 5b. Ascend the corner until it becomes a V-chimney. Step left and up steeply until a move back right gains a shallow groove. A hand-traverse along a narrow horizontal ledge leads to the stance below the final pitch of *Helsinki Wall*.
**2** 55 feet. 5a. Climb the wall and groove behind the stance to the overhang. Move left and climb the crack to a step right and so to the top.

**Ringwraith**   130 feet   E3        (4.81)
Difficulties are heightened because of the rather suspect nature of the rock; a reasonably good route nevertheless. Start 15 feet left of *Helsinki Wall*.
**1** 60 feet. 6a. Climb diagonally rightwards across the slab to the obvious break in the roofs. Surmount the roof direct by a demanding sequence of moves in order to gain the second stance of *Helsinki Wall*.

# Two Face Buttress

1. Olympic Slab VS
2. Plastic Nerve E2
3. Stromboli HVS
4. Sexual Salami E4
5. Cardiac Arête E4

**2** 70 feet. 5b. Follow *Helsinki Wall*, by climbing the wall and the groove to its top. Traverse right under the roof to the arête and climb an easy crack to finish.

**Helsinki Wall** 140 feet E1 (27.9.55)
A very good route with enjoyable and interesting climbing. Start at the steepening of Helsinki Gully, where an obvious traverse leads onto a yellow-coloured slab.
**1** 60 feet. 5a. Traverse right across the slab to a ledge, step back left and climb up to a niche. Move out right into a diagonal crack and follow it to a stance.
**2** 25 feet. Traverse back left below a small overhang. Climb up through the obvious break and then move left to reach a stance below the upper wall.
**3** 55 feet. 5b. Climb the wall and groove behind the stance to the overhang. Make a difficult move left and continue up to climb the steep crack which finishes with a step to the right.
Variation
**3a** 25 feet. 5b. Instead of stepping left it is possible to climb directly up the groove to an exit right below the overhang.

**Olympic Slab** 155 feet Very Severe (4.1.54)
A diverting climb with a difficult and delicate top pitch. Start at the bottom left-hand corner of the Buttress, beneath an obvious groove capped by a roof.
**1** 90 feet. 4b. Traverse into the groove; climb it and step round the rib on the right. Traverse right until it is possible to climb up to a tree belay.
**2** 65 feet. 4c. Trend easily left to a small ledge at the foot of the final slab. Climb the thin crack with difficulty to reach a good crack, step left into a short groove which leads to the top.

The next three climbs all start as for pitch 2 of *Olympic Slab*.

**Blade Runner** 60 feet E4 5c (13.11.82)
The left arête of *Olympic Slab* is a short but good test of adherence. Originally done with a first pitch which was a direct variant upon *Helsinki Wall*. Step left onto the very edge, take a deep breath and layback up the arête, which eases off a bit towards the wide crack at the top. Gaining the blade-peg is both precarious and bold.

**The Olympiad** 70 feet E2 5c (2.10.77)
A route for those who fail to throw themselves upon the Blade; low in the grade. Follow *Olympic Slab* onto the final slab. Traverse left, as low down as possible, to the arête; traversing at a higher level reduces the difficulty by a full grade. The wide crack above leads to an easy finish.

**Orodruin**   65 feet   E2 6a                              (1956)
A rather problematic pitch and quite high in the grade; entering
the groove 'free' provides much entertainment. Climb up to a
large flake and then move right into a groove. Follow this to a
ledge and step left delicately onto a slab and so to the overhang
just to the left of a huge roof. Climb through the overhang and
into a groove, which leads to another slab to finish.

A little further to the right, attacking the area of rock above the huge
jutting roof, are three bold and technical pitches all gained by ascending the first half of *Plastic Nerve*. Placing a crucial *Friend* blindly
in a slot up and behind one's left ear, whilst maintaining adherence
to the rock, proves to be the most testing part of the climbing.

**Surreal**   100 feet   E6 6b                            (4.82)
A poorly protected and strenuous route. Follow *Plastic Nerve* to
the large corner. Step out onto the arête, just above the lip of the
overhang, move left again into a shallow corner (small and poor
wire). Launch out onto the lip of the huge roof and attempt to
place a *Friend* 'over the shoulder' blindly into a slot. Pull round
the roof to gain a small ledge on the slab above. Escape easily
up leftwards
Variations
**The Unreal Finish**   100 feet   E6 6b                    (12.5.82)
An excellent and technically sustained finish. Start as for *Surreal*.
Follow *Surreal* to the difficult *Friend* placement in the second roof;
pull over this and step back right into the bottomless corner and
surmount the roof in this to finish up another corner and over a
further roof.

**Surreal McCoy**   90 feet   E6 6b                        (28.5.84)
A good finish, giving a bold outing in an impressive situation.
Climb *The Unreal Finish* to the bottomless corner, then go right
onto the arête and follow this to the top.

**Plastic Nerve**   65 feet   E2 5c                        (4.80)
A gratifying and varied route that is harder for the short. Start just
left of pitch 2 of *Stromboli*. Climb diagonally left across the slab
to reach ledges below a thin crack leading up to the right-hand
end of a large roof. A precarious move past a peg, with a very
long reach for a crack, gains the base of the large corner. Follow
the corner and layback round the next overhang. The final wide
off width is overcome by strenuous chimneying or, bypassed by
elegant bridging.

**Stromboli**   190 feet   Hard Very Severe                (7.8.56)
A good climb with exciting positions; the final pitch is really quite
a reasonable proposition, despite its forbidding appearance.

Start as for *Olympic Slab*.
**1** 120 feet. 4c. Traverse right, along ledges, until it is possible to climb up over two small overhangs, these lead to vegetation. Scramble right and up to a tree belay below the central breach in the overhangs.
**2** 70 feet. 5a. Climb towards the wide, capped chimney for 15 feet. Traverse left under the overhang and pull onto the slab. Climb up to and over another overhang and move up into a V-chimney. Pull over onto the next slab and move right with difficulty to finish, or, climb the final overhang direct with a very long reach through.
Variation
**The Creature Variation**   70 feet   E1 5b          (18.3.81)
**2a** Move diagonally left as for *Plastic Nerve* for a few feet but go up and make a hard move to reach the left-hand side of the overhang on the normal route, finish as for that route.

Just to the right of the top pitch of *Stromboli's* top pitch is another area of very good rock. This part of the buttress is distinguished by a number of overlaps, bounded by an arête, helping to make up one of the two 'Easter Island' faces that characterise this section of cliff. Three very good routes, all starting at the foot of pitch 2 of *Stromboli*, ascend this face.

**Hitler's Buttock**   60 feet   E5 6b          (29.3.81)
A very impressive line through the overlaps on the left side of the buttress; small wires protect. Start just to the right of *Stromboli* pitch 2, about 10 feet left of the belay. Climb into a short groove through an overhang and exit onto a slab. Move up right to a large roof and make a difficult move back left to gain tiny holds above it. A searing finger-traverse leads delicately left on tiny crystals, with only smears on the slab below. At the end of the traverse pull over onto the slab above. Go up to the final bulge and finish with a very long reach for some small holds.

**Sexual Salami**   60 feet   E4 6b          (15.3.80)
An excellent pitch which is both strenuous and delicate. Start at the tree belay below a small groove. Follow the open groove until it is possible to step left and climb up to the first overlap. Hard moves leftwards over this lead to a slab and a second overlap. A difficult sequence leads straight over this to and easy finish up a faint groove.

**Cardiac Arête**   60 feet   E4 6a          (7.12.80)
A good technical pitch on superb rock; quite safe if all the pegs are in place. Start as for *Sexual Salami* at the tree. Follow *Sexual Salami* up the open groove to step left and climb up to the first overlap. From there make a step right to reach a ledge on the

arête. Climb over the overhang and swing left onto the arête. Follow the arête in a fine position to the top.

**The Agony and the Ecstasy**   140 feet   E5          (1987)
A bold girdle of the upper section of Two Face Buttress on superb rock and in a great situation.
**1** 60 feet. 6b. Follow *Sexual Salami* to the second overlap and make some very difficult and bold moves leftwards into *Hitler's Buttock*. Swing left again to gain *Stromboli* and a belay.
**2** 80 feet. 6b. Traverse down and left into the corner of *Plastic Nerve* and finish as for *Surreal*.

## Fear Buttress

To the right of Two Face Buttress is a tree-filled gully, then comes a scrappy section of rock and vegetation. The next area of interest to rock-climbers is further right, this is denoted by an obvious and very large roof which is tackled by the route *Fear*.

**Rhywbeth Bach**   50 feet   Very Severe 4b          (14.3.98)
Just left of the main buttress a large pinnacle leans against a buttress featuring an obvious rectangular overhang. Climb a short rib and the left corner formed by the pinnacle. From its top pull directly over the overhang.

**Mab y Bwthyn**   100 feet   E1 5b          (14.6.97)
Takes the area of rock just left of the *Saffron Sunset* groove. Start below the huge roof of *Fear*. Climb up to a recess just left of the pointed overhangs and gain the rib on the right. Go straight up to a horizontal break, move left, and climb straight up the wall to a large heathery ledge. Ascend the centre of the wall above the ledge.

**Saffron Sunset**   60 feet   Hard Very Severe 5b          (12.1.85)
Takes the bottomless groove to the left of the overhang of *Fear*. Start below the huge roof. Climb up to the bottomless groove, follow this until it is possible to move right onto an arête and follow this to the top.

**Fear**   110 feet   E3          (1979)
Tackles the obvious roof direct. Start below the huge roof.
**1** 60 feet. 6a. Gain the ledge below the right-hand side of the overhang. Pull over the right-hand side, very awkward, and climb the edge to a ledge.
**2** 50 feet. 4c. Traverse left and climb the obvious short corner crack left of the arête to finish.

**Mab y Mynydd**   80 feet   E2 5c          (6.6.97)
A fairly bold route tackling the fine crackline in the wall right of

the *Fear* overhang. Start at the base of the crack. Climb the crack to a good block hold, move left to gain a wider crack which leads to the upper slabs. Follow the arête to the top.

Right again is another area of rock poking out of the trees.

## Eifionydd Buttress
This can be reached either via the Peuterey Buttress or the Two face Buttress approaches. The left edge of the buttress is taken by *Tam Lin*; the right arête of the initial stretch of rock ascended by *Electric Edge*. For routes in the gully right of *Electric Edge* it may be best to abseil in. A small stream runs down from Pant Ifan farmhouse, cross the fence about 20 yards right of where the stream reaches the fence. Skirt round leftwards underneath a small rock bluff to reach a large platform at the top of the gully. An easy abseil reaches *Eifionydd Wall* etc.

**Tam Lin**   85 feet   E2                                      (11.1.85)
A somewhat painful approach. Start below the obvious left arête.
**1** 20 feet. 4b. Go up right to a short crack and climb it to a tree.
**2** 65 feet. 5c. Ascend the arête direct to the top; small wires are needed to protect the crux section.

**Electric Edge**   90 feet   E2 5c                             (3.78)
A bushwhacking approach gains a clean arête, well worth hunting out. Start at the right-hand side of the arête, about 50 feet above the path. Climb up the right-hand side of the arête for 10 feet and then move round onto the front face. A hard move enables the arête proper to be gained. Follow this to a recess below an overhang. Move left beneath the overhang and then straight up to finish.

A little up and to the right of *Electric Edge* is a tree-filled gully rising above a large scree fan. The wall on the left of this gully has three obvious groove-lines, which are reached by climbing over vegetated rock from the largest tree in the gully. Despite the almost Matto Grosso approaches the climbs are quite good.

**Mons Meg**   120 feet   Hard Very Severe                      (8.9.67)
An entertaining little route. Start from the largest tree in the gully.
**1** 30 feet. Climb the short corner and traverse left over ledges to belay below a V-groove.
**2** 90 feet. 5a. Step left and follow the corner-groove easily until it narrows to a crack and steepens. Strenuous moves past an overhang lead to a ledge and a bit of a breather; finish up the deep crack above.

**Huntley**   120 feet   Very Severe                    (7.9.67)
Much better than it looks. Start from the largest tree in the gully,
as for *Mons Meg*.
**1** 30 feet. Climb the short corner then traverse left over ledges to
belay below a V-groove.
**2** 90 feet. 4c. Ascend the groove above to two small roofs at 45
feet. Step right and go up to a deep V-shaped chimney which is
followed to the top.

**Millipede**   130 feet   Hard Very Severe              (1967)
Interesting and varied climbing. Start as for the previous routes at
the largest tree in the gully.
**1** 30 feet. Climb the short corner then traverse left over ledges to
belay below a V-groove.
**2** 100 feet. 4c. Climb the crack and slab about 5 feet to the right
of the groove of *Huntley* until the crack peters out. Go up the left
arête until a move back right gains a groove. Follow the groove
for 40 feet until difficult moves gain a niche in the slab, step left
to a thin flake and go up to a roof. Step left into the chimney of
*Huntley* but step back right almost immediately to another
chimney and so to the top.

To the right of these routes the gully wall gives another interesting
couple of climbs; they are probably the best in this section of cliff.
Approach can be made by bushwhacking up the gully or, better, by
abseiling in from the top of the crag.

**Eifionydd Wall**   110 feet   Hard Very Severe      (24.12.56)
A good little route, well worth the effort of finding. The final pitch
is quite strenuous and has one awkward move near the top. Start
about 30 feet up from the largest tree in the gully.
**1** 50 feet. Climb up the left wall of the gully to a large blocky
ledge overlooking the tree-filled and bramble-covered ravine.
**2** 60 feet. 5b. At the right end of the ledge are two V-grooves.
Climb the right-hand one for a few feet and then move right and
up to a small ledge. Climb diagonally left for 15 feet over a little
bulge to another ledge. A tricky move up allows one to finish up
a blocky chimney, a large *Friend* is useful.

**Strempan**   70 feet   E2 5b                       (25.1.98)
A companion route to *Eifionydd Wall*. Start in the gully bed just
below and to the right of the ledge stance at the top of pitch 1 of
*Eifionydd Wall*. Climb leftwards to the belay ledge but immediately swing right to enter a groove. An awkward bulge leads to a
ledge. A bold move up the left arête leads onto another ledge.
Take the diagonal crack, moving out left at the top.

To the right of these buttresses and the gully are the remains of Hound's Head Buttress and the obvious arête of *Curved Air*.

## Pen y Ci Buttress

This is the area which was once dominated by an obvious pinnacle, quite well-known in the area due to its use on picture postcards. The Welsh name for this was Pen y Ci or, in English, Hound's Head. This prominent feature of the Tremadog cliffs was sadly blown up in 1963. The first route starts up a crack in the front of the buttress and then continues up the vegetated groove above.

**R.I.P.** 140 feet  Very Severe  ‡ (9.63)
A poor and vegetated route ascending what is left of Hound's Head Buttress. Start at the lowest point of the buttress, below a crack.
**1** 60 feet. 4c. Tackle the thin crack, not without difficulty, to reach a slab and a ledge above.
**2** 80 feet. 4a. Ascend the prominent V-groove and the slab above to a ledge about halfway up, then traverse into a chimney. Follow this and the blocks above to finish.

A much better route takes the obvious sharp arête to the right.

**Curved Air** 120 feet  E4 (12.2.78)
Excellent climbing; the main pitch is both precarious and intimidating although it is much easier the second time around. Start below the first crack on the right side of the buttress.
**1** 50 feet. 5a. Ascend the crack and follow easier ground to belay at the foot of the vegetated groove.
**2** 70 feet. 5c. Climb up to the overhang and step right underneath it to the arête. Step up right again and then move back left to climb the arête direct to the top.

**Pengo's Eliminate** 70 feet  E4 5c (30.1.81)
A rather pointless exercise; after having done the crux of *Curved Air* this route takes the groove in the right wall of the arête. Start at the top of *Curved Air's* first pitch. Climb as for *Curved Air* to the base of an obvious groove and follow this to the top.

**Cerberus** 120 feet  E1 (21.12.84)
Takes the area of rock immediately to the right of *Curved Air*. Unpleasant scrambling or an abseil is required to reach the base of the route.
**1** 50 feet. 4b. Ascend a slab and traverse left below a large perched block to continue up its left-hand side to reach a small stance.
**2** 70 feet. 5b. Swing left and traverse to a groove. Follow this to finish up the cracked wall above.

Further right two small wedge-shaped buttresses rise just above the trees. A number of routes have been climbed in this area.

### Rock 'n' Roll   90 feet   Hard Severe   ‡   (8.12.56)

A once popular route scaling the left-hand of the two wedge-shaped buttresses. Start at the base of the buttress. Climb diagonally up right to a tree. Step off the tree onto the wall above and move left to a small ledge. Move left round the corner to a chimney and go up this until it is possible to step back right to a block-filled crack, finish up this; somewhat worrying.

### Basin Street   90 feet   E3 6a   (9.4.95)

An old and obscure peg route, recently freed and providing tremendous interest in its upper half; high in the grade. Follow *Rock 'n' Roll* to a ledge below a small overhang with a curved headwall above. Technical moves up and over the overhang allow one to gain the final wall. A strenuous and sustained section.

### Oak Tree Wall   140 feet   Very Severe   ‡   (10.57)

A scrappy route ascending the wedge-shaped buttress immediately right of *Rock 'n' Roll*. Start at the base of the buttress.
**1** 70 feet. Take the slabby wall left of the corner to a flake, move right across the top of the corner onto a sloping ledge. From the right-hand side of the ledge climb a groove for a few feet followed by a move left and up to a grass ledge and belay.
**2** 70 feet. From the left end of the ledge climb the arête just left of the crack to a further ledge. Take the steep shallow groove above making an awkward move right at the top. Trend easily leftwards then up to finish.

To the right of this broken area of rock is the descent route of Porker's Gully. The path in this gully has recently been improved. To the right of the gully is the main section of Pant Ifan.

## Peuterey Buttress

The next section of crag is the pride of Pant Ifan with a large selection of high quality routes. A series of steep slabs overlap to form prominent corners and arêtes which combine to produce strong lines on magnificent rock. *Poor Man's Peuterey*, *Scratch Arête* and *Silly Arête* are just three routes offering particularly fine climbing at their respective grades. Descent is to the left of the crag, down Porker's Gully.

### Tea Time Arête   220 feet   Very Severe   (1979)

A clean line amongst the most vegetated part of the buttress. Start a little way up Porker's Gully at what appears to be an easy-angled arête snaking up into the trees. This is directly above the

Ger Davies seconding the first ascent of *Blas y Cynfyd* HVS, Craig Cra'r Neidr.
Photo: Mike Lewis

cave start of *Krakatoa*.

**1** 90 feet. 5a. A technical little move to start leads to a short crack and a pull onto the arête. Follow the arête, keeping to the edge until a step right leads to a tree belay.

**2** 50 feet. 4c. Move left onto a slab and make a steep move up to a good hold. Follow the line of the arête to a grassy ledge and tree belay.

**3** 80 feet. 4c. Move up to the line of the arête. Climb the groove on the right for 15 feet and swing left onto the arête. Follow the rib above to finish up a groove.

**Ave atque Vale**  200 feet  Severe  (4.4.54)

A new start has improved an old route, low in the grade. Start as for *Tea Time Arête*, level with the top of the cave of *Krakatoa*.

**1** 60 feet. Climb diagonally right to mossy ground then go up to the apex of the flying buttress. Scramble over pinnacles and flakes to reach a treee embedded in a chimney.

**2** 40 feet. Tackle the chimney to reach the base of some slabs.

**3** 100 feet. Climb the slabs to trees and then follow the easiest line to the top.

**Krakatoa**  270 feet  Severe  ‡  (7.10.56)

A devious climb with some pleasant moves and a little vegetation. Start in Porker's Gully, below a cave.

**1** 80 feet. Climb up to the cave and turn the roof on the left to reach a grass ledge. Traverse diagonally right across a slab to join a crack, which is climbed to the crest of the rib.

**2** 80 feet. Traverse horizontally right across the slab to a short rib. Move round the rib and traverse right across another slab and climb up to an oak tree belay.

**3** 30 feet. Climb straight up to another tree.

**4** 80 feet. Traverse horizontally left for 30 feet on good holds under the overhang. Climb up into a short groove and then continue up a rib to a tree belay. Scramble through vegetation to the top.

At the very base of Porker's Gully is a rib which is isolated from the main cliff, forming a low-level flying buttress. Two routes have been climbed up this section of rock and these provide testing little problems at their respective grades.

**Gwrywgydiwr**  70 feet  E1 5c  (24.1.98)

A technical move low down is followed by pleasant crack climbing. Start directly below a very shallow chimney at the lowest point of the buttress. Climb up to a bulge and make a thin move over this to get established in the shallow chimney. Follow this to a pull out left onto good holds. Follow the easier jamming crack over a small bulge to the crest of the rib.

**Terraqua**   60 feet   E2 6a                                    (5.76)
A difficult start leads to a perplexing crux; small wires protect.
Start at the base of the broad rib abutting the main part of the
cliff. Climb straight up and then trend right to a blunt pillar below
the bulging wall; it is difficult to clip the peg above. As one
moves left below it a cunning lassoo is possible but is not really
required. A long reach left gains tiny sidepulls which may allow
access onto the slab. Move up and then trend rightwards to the
arête and follow this to the top.

**Strumpet Blower**   80 feet   E1 5c                             (3.5.98)
Start at the bridge joining the flying buttress of Terraqua to the
main cliff. Scramble up to reach slabs and follow a crack to an
arête leading up to a large overhang. Traverse left to pull through
the overhang at its left end. Finish up easy slabs.

A number of routes have been climbed in the area of foliage and
rock to the right of the flying buttress of *Terraqua*. Due to the general
profusion of vegetation, and the lack of distinctive features, they
have been allowed to remain in obscurity. The following route is,
however, worth doing.

**Etna**   210 feet   Severe
A direct line up the vegetated slabs to the left of *Pear Tree
Variation* gives an enjoyable climb. Start at the foot of the
vegetated groove, to the right of the prominent rib of *Terraqua*, at
the base of the buttress.
**1** 40 feet. Climb up the rock on the right of the groove to a tree
belay at the foot of the slab.
**2** 60 feet. Climb diagonally up to the right to a small niche. An
obvious traverse leads back left to below a large tree. Climb
straight up to this.
**3** 60 feet. Climb up and slightly left to another tree. Pull over
some blocks to reach the tree belay below the final pitch of
*Krakatoa*.
**4** 50 feet. Move into the niche at the foot of a groove (*Pear Tree
Variation*). Make an awkward stride across the foot of the slab on
the left to below a steep wall. Climb up this boldly on apparently
loose holds and pull round left to easier ground and a tree belay.
Alternatively, finish up the last pitch of *Krakatoa*. Scramble to the
top.

**Pear Tree Variation**   170 feet   Very Severe      (25.12.55)
This route takes the left-hand side of Peuterey Buttress and has a
good final pitch. Start at a groove on the left of the break in the
lower slabs directly below the obvious deep chimney of
*Strapiombo*. A variation start exists a little further left of the
groove; this is also 4c.

**1** 70 feet. 4c. Climb the groove for a few feet and move left into a prominent crack. Thrutch up this and climb over a large block to a tree belay.
**2** 30 feet. 4b. Climb vegetated slabs on the left followed by a short steep corner to another tree belay in a fine position.
**3** 70 feet. 4c. Climb left into a recess at the foot of a groove, which leads to a short crack. Climb this, step right and back left into another groove to finish; a fine pitch.

### Silver Crow   70 feet   Hard Very Severe 5b   (19.4.81)

A worthwhile and exposed outing up the arête to left of *The Struggler*. Start from the final stance of *Pear Tree Variation*. Climb up into the recess above the tree and swing out right. Move up and go back left to gain the arête. Climb up and do the crux of *Pear Tree Variation* to reach a large block. Step off this and climb the short wall and groove above to finish.

### The Struggler   70 feet   E2 5c   (5.4.64)

This well-positioned climb takes the groove in the upper part of the towering buttress just to the right of *Silver Crow* and is high in the grade. Start at the top of pitch 2 of *Pear Tree Variation*. Make a very hard move over the bulge to gain the groove. Climb this, and a roof, to finish. This pitch can also be reached from the final stance of *Strapiombo*.

### Borchgrevinck   220 feet   Severe   (22.4.57)

A damp but interesting start and an enjoyable finish. Start just to the left of the obvious break which leads directly up to the deep chimney that is *Strapiombo*.
**1** 50 feet. Climb the groove for a few feet and move right onto the rib and climb it to a tree belay.
**2** 40 feet. Climb the damp cracks to another tree.
**3** 30 feet. Traverse horizontally right to a ledge below a wide crack in the slab.
**4** 50 feet. Climb the crack and continue up the corner above to a ledge.
**5** 50 feet. Traverse left over some blocks to reach a wide ledge. Traverse left and climb up the front of the buttress to finish.

### Groove of Horror   160 feet   E5   (14.1.78)

An extremely strenuous line, few ascents are made without a 'rest'. It takes the obvious line left of the chimney of *Strapiombo*.
**1** 80 feet. As for *Strapiombo* pitch 1.
**2** 80 feet. 6a. Traverse left across the slab to a niche below an overhanging crack. Climb the overhang up and left to gain the crack and go up it with increasing difficulty to a short groove. Exit left from the groove onto a slabby wall, then move back right to finish up *Strapiombo*.

# Craig Pant Ifan
## Peuterey Buttress

1. The Struggler E2
2. No Holds Barred E6
3. Tall Dwarfs E3
4. Poor Man's Peuterey S
5. Pincushion E2

6. Silly Arête E3
7. Barbarian E1
8. Scratch VS
9. Itch E2
10. Scratch Arête HVS

11. Laser Crack E1
12. Integral E2
13. The Toit E4
14. The Sandbagger E5
15. Clown of Thorns E1

**Strapiombo**  140 feet  Hard Very Severe  (21.5.55)
To many this route is totally ungradeable and, as such, is a
classic of its kind. The climb takes the obvious deep chimney
and provides an awkward and strenuous struggle.
**1** 80 feet. Climb straight up to the tree at the foot of the
chimney.
**2** 60 feet. 5a. Climb the flared chimney to the top with a lot of
effort and little in the way of protection. It is possible to rest
almost anywhere but making upward progress constitutes the
main difficulty and is a guaranteed full body pump.

The impressive buttress to the right of *Strapiombo* gives three
steep and technical pitches.

**Erebus**  160 feet  E3  (9.4.66)
A fine and varied climb in a very exposed position which
gives quite a committing lead.
**1** 80 feet. As for *Strapiombo* pitch 1.
**2** 80 feet. 6a. Finger-traverse right across the wall to the
arête. Move round the arête and climb up to a roof. Move out
right onto a slab and climb it, trending left at first.

**No Holds Barred**  110 feet  E6 6c  (5.5.91)
A stunning route attacking the two huge roofs to the right of
*Erebus*. A number of longish quickdraws are required on some
of the pegs. Start as the for the first pitch of *Strapiombo*.
Ascend the slabby wall to the right of the chimney until a
swing left allows one to gain the wall beneath the first roof.
Go up to the roof, a desperate sequence of moves now lead
over this obstacle, via a crucial hold. Once one is established
in a standing position in an easy groove, a bit of a breather
allows one to view the second roof. This massive overhang is
surmounted by going from right to left, undertaking some
impressive 'upside down' manoeuvres. A final wall section is
then followed to the top.

**Tall Dwarfs**  110 feet  E3 6a  (1977)
The undercut groove on the right-hand side of *Erebus* buttress.
The difficulties are short but fierce; long arms and short legs
help. Start from the big ledge below the last pitch of *Poor
Man's Peuterey*. Climb the slab 5 feet left of the *Borchgrevinck*
crack, making for an obvious groove. Entering the groove from
the right proves to be the crux, follow it to a large ledge.
Continue up the easier groove above and move left to the top.

**Poor Man's Peuterey**  200 feet  Severe  (20.12.53)
A good, varied climb with a superb main pitch; one of the best of
its standard in this guide. Start at an earthy ledge at the lower

left-hand end of the massive overlapping slabs and about 50 feet to the right of the chimney line. The first two pitches of *Borchgrevinck* can be climbed to give an alternative start.

**1** 40 feet. Climb the wall on the left to a sloping ledge below a triangular overhang.

**2** 40 feet. Turn the overhang on the right to reach a cracked groove, at the top of this exit left and climb up to a tree.

**3** 100 feet. Climb up to the right, then make an exposed move right onto the nose and climb this to a small ledge. Climb up exposed cracks in the slab to a long step right and continue up to a good ledge.

**4** 20 feet. Step over a block and climb a short chimney.

**Great Western**   220 feet   Very Severe                    (19.1.57)
The large slab to the right of *Poor Man's Peuterey* has an obvious square-cut overhang and a shallow groove on the left. This route climbs the lower part of the slab, crosses the groove and takes the slab between the finishes of *Poor Man's Peuterey* and *Borchgrevinck*. Start at the left-hand corner of the slab below the shallow groove.

**1** 50 feet. 4b. Go across right into another shallow groove and climb it for a few feet. Step left and climb a bulge to a ledge and large tree. Traverse right and go up to a tree at the foot of a big chimney.

**2** 40 feet. 4b. Step left and climb the obvious diagonal crack in the slab to a tree in the groove.

**3** 20 feet. 4c. Climb up to the overhang and into the short awkward corner on the left.

**4** 60 feet. Climb the crack, trending left to a good ledge below the corner of *Borchgrevinck*. Climb this to a tree at the foot of the final corner.

**5** 50 feet. 4b. Climb up to the right into a wide chimney. Climb this to a small ledge and then take the narrow chimney to finish.

**Monkey Puzzle**   150 feet   Hard Very Severe
A devious climb which becomes more exposed the higher one gets, good value. Large cams are particularly useful for the top pitch. Start from the stance after pitch 2 of *Great Western*.

**1** 100 feet. 5a. Climb the awkward corner above the belay until it is possible to move onto the slab above the overhang. Climb this to the roof and move right into the bottomless groove, which is climbed to another roof. Move left to the small ledge below the final slab of *Poor Man's Peuterey*.

**2** 50 feet. 5a. Make a thin traverse right, just above the over-hang, to an obvious wide crack. Climb this to the top.

**The Quakermen**   170 feet   E2                                    (8.79)
Takes in some interesting climbing; the top arête is similar to, but
a little bolder than, *Silly Arete* and, thus, high in the grade. Start
just left of the base of the diagonal crack on pitch 2 of *Great
Western* at some thin cracks leading up to join the main diagonal
feature.
**1** 40 feet. 5a. Ascend the cracks to the main diagonal break and
follow this into the corner.
**2** 60 feet. 5b. Tackle the awkward corner above the belay until it
is possible to move right into a bottomless groove (*Monkey
Puzzle* ascends this groove). Traverse right across the slab above
the overhang to gain *Pincushion*. Climb this to the roof and
ascend the wall on the left to gain the upper slab. Move up and
right to belay at a tree on the arête.
**3** 70 feet. 5c. Move up to a wide crack and arrange protection;
large *Friends* useful. Step right again to the base of a sharply
defined arête, sprint for the top.
Variation
**Harvey Proctor's Spanking Slap**   E2                       (1986)
A good variation on *The Quakermen*.
**2a** 110 feet. 5c. Climb the awkward corner above the belay to a
downward-pointing fin of rock on the right, pinch this, and
layback round into a groove. Ascend the groove to the large
capping overhang and traverse delicately rightwards to its right-
hand end. Step up into a short corner and move left onto the
slab. Continue directly up the slab on tiny crimps, to the top, or a
possible extension can be made by taking another horizontal
break and a wide slanting crack.

**Pincushion**   150 feet   E2 5c                             (6.10.56)
High in the grade. The smooth chimney and overhang give
access to a superb and exposed final slab. Start from the tree
stance at the foot of the big chimney. Climb the chimney to the
roof and move left awkwardly to make a difficult pull over the
roof onto the slab. Climb the slab, via a thin crack, until about 10
feet below the next overhang. Traverse right into another crack
and follow this to the third overhang. Traverse horizontally right
and climb a crack to finish.

**Silly Billy**   140 feet   E2 5c                              (1979)
Although an eliminate this route still has some good moves,
particularly in the upper section and is worth doing for its own
sake. Start as for *Pincushion*. Climb the chimney and pull over the
overhang as for *Silly Arête*. Follow cracks up the slab between
*Pincushion* and the arête to finish up a tricky groove.

**Silly Arête**   130 feet   E3 5c                            (18.4.71)
Superb climbing up the right edge of the *Pincushion* slab; an

impressive pitch with good but sparse protection if done properly. Start at the tree below the chimney; stepping off this tree is now harder for the short. Step onto the slab and move right to the arête, ascend it to the overhang; serious. Climb the overhang directly above the chimney, move up a few feet and traverse immediately right to gain the arête once again and follow it to the top.

A prominent landmark, the huge corner right of *Pincushion* slab, is climbed by *Barbarian*. The foot of this corner is also the starting point of *Fingerlicker* and *Scratch*.

### Fingerlicker   170 feet   E4                                (11.5.75)
The first pitch of this climb takes the thin crack in the left wall of *Barbarian*. Steep and very strenuous; a fine testpiece. Start by scrambling up vegetated ground to the foot of the large corner.
**1** 65 feet. 5c. Climb the pod in the left wall to gain the finger crack. Follow this to the roof and climb the corner above to a ledge; go right to a stance on *Barbarian*.
**2** 105 feet. 6a. Climb *Barbarian* for 10 feet and then go diagonally left across the wall (peg runner) to join *Silly Arête* and finish up this.
Variation
### Direct Finish   90 feet   E6 6b                             (29.5.82)
A very strenuous and technical pitch taking the obvious scar up the left wall of *Barbarian*.
**2a** Follow pitch 2 to the peg runner, then pull up to the right to a second peg runner. Desperate moves then lead up to a good jug and another peg runner. A final hard pull leads to the crack at the top of *Silly Arête* which is followed to the top.

### Barbarian   160 feet   E1                                   (16.8.58)
The huge corner gives a classic climb with some hard moves over the roof. Start by scrambling up vegetated ground to the foot of the huge corner.
**1** 50 feet. 4a. Climb the wall just right of the corner moving into the corner for the last few feet.
**2** 90 feet. 5b. Make a difficult move to surmount the overhang, and continue in the corner until it is possible to step right into some cracks. Climb these to a niche under the main overhangs. A strenuous pull out is made to a step left and a stance.
**3** 20 feet. 4c. Step right into a shallow groove to finish.

### Scratch   170 feet   Very Severe                            (19.12.53)
The main feature of this climb is the fine corner-crack which is reached by traversing right from the foot of *Barbarian*. Start as for that route; justifiably popular.
**1** 70 feet. 4b. Climb the slabby wall on the right for a few feet

and then make a slightly rising traverse right to a good tree belay at the foot of the corner.
**2** 100 feet. 4b. Climb the corner until it is possible to make a rising traverse rightwards to a crack, climb this, or the wall to its left, to finish.

**Mangoletsi**  180 feet  E3                          (1.64/Spring 77)
This route climbs directly up to the stance on *Scratch* and then takes the slab on the left and crosses the roof right of *Barbarian*. Well-protected climbing with a strenuous roof. Start by the step in the path to the right of the start of *Barbarian*.
**1** 90 feet. 5b. Climb the left-hand side of a pinnacle and step left to a grass ledge. Move right and go up a short groove to a small oak tree. Step right and go up another groove, move left at the top and then climb straight up to a good tree belay and junction with *Scratch*.
**2** 90 feet. 6a. Move left onto the slab and climb a thin crack to the overhang. Traverse left under this to a roof-crack just right of the *Barbarian* niche. Pull over the roof and climb the groove above to finish.
Variations
**Pitch One Direct**  E2 5c                          (Spring 77)
**1a** 80 feet. 5c. As for *Mangoletsi* to the small oak tree but instead of stepping right go straight up to make a long and difficult reach to regain the original line; continue to the tree belay.
**The Original Way**  130 feet  E1                          (1.64)
**2a** 90 feet. 5b. Follow the route up to the roof-crack and then climb into the niche of *Barbarian*. Climb this to the stance.
**3** 40 feet. 5b. Make a hard traverse left to the arête and finish up this.

**Spare Rib**  170 feet  E4                          (1977/23.6.79)
Two bold and contrastingly technical pitches give a good excursion up this part of the cliff. Start as for *Mangoletsi*.
**1** 90 feet. 6a. Climb *Mangoletsi* until about 5 feet right of the groove, where a line of holds leads right underneath the clean-cut overhang, with strenuous moves onto the rib on the right. Step up and move left and upwards to join *Mangoletsi*.
**2** 80 feet. 6a. Step left onto the arête, as for *Mangoletsi*, and climb it direct to the overhang. Move right onto the wall and step back left immediately above the roof. Climb just right of the arête to finish.

**Itch**  200 feet  E2                          (31.7.66)
An entertaining climb with one very intense move on the first pitch. Start just to the right of *Mangoletsi* above a rock step by a large oak.

**1** 90 feet. 6a. Climb straight up slabby rock to a right-facing corner and follow this, or take the slabs to the right, to gain a bulge. Pull through and over the bulge with difficulty to vegetated ledges. Follow these up right to a final greasy sequence to gain the big ledge.

**2** 110 feet. 5b. Start 10 feet right of the corner just to the left of the obvious crack. Climb the slab to a thread and trend up right to reach the corner formed by the left end of the overhang. Go up the corner to meet *Scratch*. Move left and go straight over a bulge to finish by a small overlap high on the steep part of the wall.

Variation

**2a** 100 feet. 5b. Climb the slab past the thread, or the obvious crack on the right, to the overhang. Move right and make a long reach through the overhang to gain the upper slab; finish up *Scratch*.

**Rhych dy Din**   100 feet   E2 5b                    (7.9.84)
Somewhat of an eliminate but still worth doing. Start about 10 feet right of the final pitch of *Itch*, below an obvious crackline. Ascend the obvious layaway crack leading up to the overhang, step down and right to gain some thin cracks leading up through the overhang. Pull up onto the slab and climb directly up to join *Scratch* near the top.

**Scratch Arête**   200 feet   Hard Very Severe         (24.3.62)
A very diverting piece of climbing in a fine position on the edge of the buttress, the overhang still manages to confound the unwary. Low in the grade. Start at the foot of a rib about 20 feet right of *Mangoletsi* where the path first reaches the rock.

**1** 100 feet. 4c. Climb the rib and a shallow groove to a ledge at the foot of the crack. Climb the crack, move right at the top and make a hard move over the bulge to a tree belay. There is a good variation to this pitch up the obvious T-shaped crack, moving left to join the groove.

**2** 100 feet. 5a. Climb the slab, first slightly left then back right, to reach the arête just under the overhang, peg runner round to the right. Climb the overhang direct and continue up the edge of the upper slab to join the finish of *Scratch*.

**Ivy Crack**   80 feet   E1 5b                         (7.73)
From the tree belay of *Scratch Arête* scramble across right to a ledge beneath a crack in the right wall of the arête, belay. Climb the crack strenuously to a large ledge; pull over a bulge and continue up loose flakes to finish.

**Slabby Flues**   120 feet   Severe                    (26.5.73)
The steep wall defining the eastern end of Peuterey Buttress gives

a short climb. Start by an unpleasant scramble to a ledge 35 feet to the right of the first stance of *Scratch Arête*, at a slabby, rightward-slanting chimney.

**1** 120 feet. Climb the chimney to an overhang and step right onto a loose flake in a niche. Move back into the chimney and continue to an oak branch, where it is possible to step left into a cave. Climb an easier chimney to join *Scratch Arête*; finish up this.

### Girdle Traverse of Peuterey Buttress    400 feet   E1
(4.75)

A fine excursion across some very interesting territory. Start as for *Scratch Arête*

**1** 100 feet. 4c. As for pitch 1 of *Scratch Arête*.
**2** 150 feet. 5b. Climb the slab, trending left, to reach the left-hand end of the overhang. Continue up and left to reach the top of the obvious rightward-facing corner (*Scratch* — possible stance). Move left onto the slab and traverse left under the roof to a niche. Climb the roof as for *Barbarian* and step left to a stance.
**3** 80 feet. 5b. Traverse strenuously left to the arête to join *Pincushion* and descend to a stance by a tree under the roof. Swing left and continue to a stance on *Poor Man's Peuterey*.
**4** 70 feet. Climb the pleasant slabs and a chimney to finish (as for *Poor Man's Peuterey*).

The buttress to the right of *Scratch Arête* provides a number of good routes, and is characterised by large overhangs high up on the right-hand side. It is approached by climbing up a dirty vegetated gully below the steep part of the buttress.

### Laser Crack    150 feet   E1
(7.79)

A good little climb. Start just left of the second pitch of *Integral*.
**1** 70 feet. 5b. Climb the small roof and cracks to a tree belay.
**2** 80 feet. 5b. Climb the bulging crack above to finish up a short chimney.
Variation
### Blobby Goes Ballistic    90 feet   E1 5b
(22.11.94)

An exposed variation to pitch 2.
**2a** From the tree belay step right into the groove and go up to a small overhang. Step right again round to a sloping ledge in an exposed position. Take the short wall at the right-hand end of the grassy ledge and climb the steep crack to the top.

### Integral    240 feet   E2
(10.4.65)

The left-hand side of the buttress forms a steep clean rib. Bold and technically interesting. Start at the vegetated gully below the rib.
**1** 30 feet. Climb the gully to a detached block below the steep

part of the wall.
**2** 60 feet. 5b. Step left off the block and climb the wall, trending rightwards to the arête. Climb this with difficulty for 15 feet until it is possible to traverse across the steep right wall to a belay beneath some overhangs.
**3** 80 feet. 5c. Climb the wall to a good hold and move back left onto the arête. Follow this, trending left to a short crack. This leads to a swing right, another crack and a tree belay.
**4** 70 feet. Step left and climb the grooved slab to the top.

**Integral Direct**   190 feet   E3                    (16.4.79)
This bold and technical climb straightens out the original line. Start at the detached block below the second pitch of *Integral*.
**1** 120 feet. 5c. Step off the block and climb the wall, trending rightwards to the arête. Climb straight up this until beneath the overhang. Traverse left for 12 feet, move up, and then traverse back right above the lip of the overhang to make a mantelshelf move onto a ledge. Gain a crack system leading up to a tree belay.
**2** 70 feet. As for *Integral* pitch 4.

**Limited Edition**   120 feet   E5 6b                 (6.9.84)
A bold and technical offering. Start as for *Integral Direct*. Ascend the arête of *Integral Direct* to a large spike runner, step onto the right wall and, with continuing difficulty, follow a line of thin cracks. The protection is very awkward to place.

**The Toit**   140 feet   E4 6b                        (16.9.61)
This provides an extremely hard roof pitch. Start from the top of pitch 2 of *Integral*. Climb the wall on the right of the corner to the roof. Move over this with extreme difficulty and into the bottomless groove. Climb the crack on the right to a tree belay.

The next two routes are best approached by abseiling into the tree in the gully.

**The Sandbagger**   120 feet   E5 6b                  (8.9.84)
Another bold offering. Start 30 feet right of *The Toit*, at a large tree. Scale the steep groove behind the tree for 30 feet until it is possible to move left across the steep wall into the cracks of *The Dune Child*. Climb the cracks to the roof and pull straight over and continue up the wall for about 35 feet, trending right and with no protection. Follow a flake crack to finish at a dirty ledge.

**The Dune Child**   150 feet   E4                     (2.10.80)
This very hard climb takes the area of rock through the roofs to the right of *The Toit*. Start 30 feet right of *The Toit*, at a large tree.
**1** 65 feet. 6b. Climb up the overhanging groove to the large

roofs. Traverse right to reach the thin crack in the wall overlooking the gully. Climb the crack to another roof. Move left to reach a ledge and belay.

**2** 85 feet. 5c. Make a short layaway move up the arête and then swing out onto the wall. Climb the wall and thin crack to the top. To the right of the huge overhang of *The Toit* there is a large area of vegetated rock; this is Avalanche Buttress.

## Avalanche Buttress

Most of the routes were considered to be substandard, however, in the interest of completeness — and to stop people from bothering to claim them as new — here they are once again.

**Lucretia**   285 feet   Very Severe   ‡               (6.2.55)
Not a particularly good route. Start at vegetated ledges diagonally down and left of the rock scar left by the fall of the huge flake of *Fandango*. This is gained by scrambling up from the path.

**1** 110 feet. Climb the slabs and grooves trending first right then left. Move left and then up to a ledge below a long heather-filled corner left of the nose of the buttress.

**2** 45 feet. Traverse into the corner and climb it until it is possible to pull up and out of it.

**3** 130 feet. Ascend short walls and an ivy-covered arête.

**Lakeland Gem**   290 feet   Very Severe   ‡          (25.5.58)
In general a poor climb, although the final slab gives it some merit. Start as for *Lucretia*.

**1** 110 feet. Climb pitch 1 of *Lucretia* followed by the heather-filled corner left of the nose of the buttress.

**2** 40 feet. Go round the corner on the left and up to a good stance.

**3** 90 feet. Ascend the wet slab to the black corner on the left and follow this up to a tree. Go up vegetation to a good ledge round the corner on the right.

**4** 50 feet. Climb the slabs ahead from left-to-right.

**Whistling Rufus**   290 feet   Hard Very Severe (1pt)   ‡
                                                      (31.7.66)
A fairly poor route. Start as for *Lucretia*.

**1** 110 feet. Climb pitch 1 of *Lucretia*.

**2** 60 feet. Ascend the obvious groove on the right for 25 feet. Step left onto the steep slab and make a long stride down left (with the aid of a peg) to a sloping foothold, then continue along a very thin traverse line leading to the arête. Climb the arête via another groove to reach a large flake belay.

**3** 120 feet. Go straight up above the flake to the slab above and climb this by its right-hand side.

**Clown of Thorns**   300 feet   E1                    (31.8.97)
Takes the area of rock left of *Technical Master* to join the upper
section of the old route *Fandango*.
**1** 120 feet. 4b. As for *Technical Master* to the base of a thin
crack. Swing round the nose on the left and scramble up to belay
below a crack in the nose of rock in the left-hand side of the slab.
**2** 80 feet. 5b. Climb the crack in the arête direct and continue to
a large spike. (*Fandango* came in from the right about 25 feet
up). Go up and across right to belay at an oak tree.
**3** 100 feet. 4c. Climb directly up the clean slab above. Go up to
the right lip of the huge overhang and move back right onto the
slab; finish direct.

**Technical Master**   140 feet   E3                    (5.79)
A hard climb which takes the thin crack just left of the rock scar
which is reached by scrambling up from the path. Start below the
thin crack in the slab.
**1** 80 feet. 6a. Climb up for about 50 feet to reach the crack.
Make some progressively harder moves up this until a step right
can be made into a short corner; a difficult move up and left
allows one to reach a jug. Moving left before stepping right into
the corner brings the grade down to 5c.
**2** 60 feet. 5c. Move right across ledges to an arête. A bold move
in a fine position leads up past an overlap/flake and then to a
crack to finish.

**Wanda**   180 feet   Very Severe   ‡                    (1.1.77)
The prominent cracked tower high up on Avalanche Buttress is
climbed after a vegetated approach. Start directly beneath the
rock scar.
**1** 80 feet. Climb vegetated rock, trending a little right, to a good
tree belay.
**2** 100 feet. 4b. Climb straight up behind the stance to another
tree. Move up to the bottom of a groove and traverse round the
arête to reach a tree below a wide crack. Climb this to a ledge
just below the top.

To the right of Avalanche Buttress the rock improves to give the
steep Strangeways Buttress.

## Strangeways Buttress
This buttress can be reached by traversing through vegetation from
the foot of *Technical Master*. Alternatively, the first pitch of *Holloway*
can be used to reach any of the climbs. A large flake, Strangeways
Pinnacle, situated in the centre of the Buttress, is an obvious feature.

**Rapunzel**   80 feet   Very Severe 5a                    (9.10.84)
On the small buttress almost immediately left of the tree-filled gully
bordering *Alcatraz*. Start beneath the arête and take a short wall
to the foot of the arête; climb this on its left-hand side.

**Bucket Rider**   80 feet   E1 5b                         (5.79)
Quite an entertaining climb which starts just to the left of
*Alcatraz*. Ascend the corner-groove until it is possible to move left
to reach a leaning flake/pillar. From the top of this step right onto
the face and go up to a crack, which is followed to the belay.

**Alcatraz**   100 feet   Very Severe 4c                   (12.61)
The prominent crack on the left of Strangeways Buttress gives a
fine sustained pitch. Start below the crack. Move up to the crack
and climb it to a bulge. Pull over into a niche and climb the wall
on the left to a tree just below the top.

**Hey!**   100 feet   E1 5b                                (24.6.79)
An eliminate, but giving good bold climbing. It ascends the wall
15 feet right of *Alcatraz* via some quartzy slots finishing up the
wall between *Alcatraz* and *Holloway*.

**Holloway**   210 feet   Hard Very Severe                 (12.61)
The final pitch is technically interesting and in a good position.
Start from the path running under the vegetated lower section of
the buttress. A rib leads through the vegetation to Strangeways
Pinnacle.
**1** 60 feet. 4c. Climb the rib to below the steep face of the
Pinnacle.
**2** 40 feet. 4c. Traverse right to the foot of a steep chimney and
follow this to a belay on the Pinnacle.
**3** 110 feet. 5a. Climb up into the niche above, pull out left onto
the wall and move up to another niche, below a steep crack.
Climb diagonally across the wall to a good resting place and go
straight up to a tree and continue past another tree just below the
top.

**Back to Nature**   110 feet   E3 6a                      (1.7.79)
This takes the wall left of *Holloway*, crosses that route and finishes
up a thin crack; high in the grade. Start just left of the foot of the
top pitch of *Holloway*. Climb diagonally up the flakes on the wall
to the diagonal traverse of *Holloway*. Cross this and finish up the
thin crack between *Holloway* and *Crocadillo*.

**Crocadillo**   200 feet   E2                             (26.2.74)
A good climb which starts as for *Holloway*.
**1** 100 feet. 5b. Climb the rib to below the steep face of the
Pinnacle. Climb the face to a good hold on the left edge.

Continue up until it is possible to traverse to the right edge, just below the top of the Pinnacle.

**2** 100 feet. 5b. Traverse right into the bottom of an obvious reddish-coloured groove. Climb this precariously until it is possible to step left to join *Holloway* at the second niche. Climb the crack, steep and fingery, to a difficult finish on a grass ledge just below the top.

Variation

A very good alternative route.

**2a** 90 feet. 5b. Start up *Holloway* and continue up the crack.

**Strangeways**   130 feet   Very Severe                    (28.12.55)
A poor route which crosses the foot of the steep section of the Buttress, past Strangeways Pinnacle, to climb the right edge of the Buttress. Start from below the steep crack of *Alcatraz*.

**1** 40 feet. 4a. Traverse diagonally right to Strangeways Pinnacle. Move across the top of the groove on the right to a small stance.

**2** 60 feet. 4b. Climb the slab, continuing through the overhangs on the right to a large perched block in a groove. Follow this to the foot of a vegetated gully.

**3** 30 feet. Climb the gully to the top.

**Agoraphobia**   120 feet   Hard Very Severe 5a       (29.5.67)
A bit of a non route starting up *Strangeways* and wandering across into *Holloway*. Start above pitch 1 of *Strangeways*. Climb the slab to the small overlap and step left into a groove. Move left onto the front face of the buttress and traverse delicately left for 20 feet until it is possible to climb up to an oak tree. Traverse left to another oak tree, step right and climb a short crack to the top.

## Hogmanay Buttress

Much of this part of the cliff is characterised by a band of rather shaly and friable rock low down, but topped by a fine crest of good dolerite seamed with cracks and grooves.

**Life in a Day**   90 feet   E3 5c   ‡                (18.4.81)
Quite bold in parts; the start is gained by abseil. Move right and layback a large flake, move up and step left onto a ramp. Traverse the ramp until a hard move leads to easy ground then follow obvious flakes, trending right to the top.

**Broadmoor**   100 feet   E1 5b   ‡                    (1972)
Best reached by abseil; the ramp is becoming increasingly vegetated. Start at the large tree, at the top of pitch 3 of *Hogmanay Girdle*. Climb up to gain the obvious ramp line, this leads up rightwards towards the top of the corner of *Vulcan*.

# Craig Pant Ifan
**Hogmany Buttress**

1. Psyche 'n' Burn E6
2. Vulcan E3
3. Falcon E1
4. Scarecrow E3
5. Steelfingers E2
6. Raven's Nest Wall E2
7. Gothic Grooves E1
8. Hogmanay Hangover HS

The next few climbs take the impressive left wall of Hogmanay Buttress, which is split by the superb corner of *Vulcan*, giving perhaps the best line at Tremadog. However, the smooth-looking wall to the left of the corner has also been climbed to give an unrelenting, bold and technical pitch.

**Psyche 'n' Burn**   140 feet   E6 6b                                    (7.81)
A desperate piece of climbing. Most aspirants check the peg by abseil. Start at a small stance below a thin crack in the wall left of *Vulcan*. To reach the peg either climb boldly up the wall on the left, or, tackle the thin crack. The crack is technically harder at about 6c, but safer. Difficult moves past the peg gain good holds which lead past a further peg to a ledge. Take the thin crack on the left to a ramp-line leading up leftwards, follow this but move back right to finish.

**Vulcan**   180 feet   E3                               (20.4.62/Spring 77)
Magnificent climbing up a superb and uncompromising line. One of the best routes at Tremadog. Start by scrambling up to the foot of a slab in the vegetation below and to the right of the corner.
**1** 60 feet. Climb the slab, step right, and climb a short groove to a tree, head up left to belay below the overhangs.
**2** 120 feet. 6a. Ascend a steep crack, past a bulge, to a short smooth groove capped by an overhang. Bridge up the groove until a step left can be made into the corner proper. Steep and technical moves now lead up to an overhang; negotiating this hurdle proves to be the crux. Continue up the corner, still steep and quite sustained, to the top.

**Falcon**   120 feet   E1 5b                                    (10.62)
Steep and enjoyable climbing up the crack to the right of *Vulcan*; one of the best of its grade at Pant Ifan. Start at the top of pitch 1 of *Vulcan*. Climb a steep crack, past a bulge, to a short smooth groove capped by an overhang, as for *Vulcan*. Step up and right to a small ledge below the overhang, where a swing right leads out onto the face below a steep crack. Follow the crack in a fine position to the top.

**Pippikin**   120 feet   E4 6a                                    (5.6.77)
A good, steep and difficult climb which crosses *Falcon* to a series of intimidating flakes and then climbs a slim groove between the upper crack of that route and the groove of *Vulcan*. Start from the tree gained via pitch 1 of *Vulcan*. Climb the overhanging crack directly above the tree to a junction with *Falcon* below the upper crack. Step up and left to reach some undercut flakes and follow these to a small ledge. Enter the slim groove above with difficulty and follow it to the top. Or, once *Falcon* is reached, follow this

route until a traverse left can be made to gain the base of the slim groove thus missing out the 'Damoclean' flakes.

**Sonic Sinbin**  120 feet  E4 6a                    (22.8.80)
A hard and poorly protected pitch. Start from the tree gained via pitch1 of *Vulcan*. Follow *Falcon* to the traverse right, but continue traversing to gain the bottom of a groove via a long reach. Climb the groove until beneath an overhang and move over this rightwards, crux, to reach another overhang. Climb up the wall above and finish up a groove on the left.

**Scarecrow**  170 feet  E3                         (26.2.77)
There is a prominent roof right of the start of *Vulcan*. This route traverses boldly left from under the roof to climb a steep groove and then a crack right of the upper crack of *Falcon*. Start from the tree gained via pitch1 of *Vulcan*.
**1** 30 feet. Walk along the grass ledge and climb up to a tree belay under the roof.
**2** 60 feet. 5c. Traverse awkwardly left to an overhanging groove and climb it to a stance and belay on the *Girdle*.
**3** 80 feet. 5b. Climb the steep crack above the belay, difficult at first and then easing.
Variation
**Direct Start**  50 feet  E4
**1a** 50 feet. 6a. Climb straight up into the overhanging groove and follow it to the stance of the *Girdle*.

**The Steal**  80 feet  E4 6b                       (18.7.84)
An interesting and technical pitch; start as for *Steelfingers*. Ascend to the left-hand side of the roof, to the left of *Steelfingers*, the pull-round to gain the shallow groove is the crux. Follow the groove to a junction with *Steelfingers* at the thin crack; finish as for that route.

**Steelfingers**  170 feet  E2                      (29.4.77)
An intricate route at the top end of its grade with a good main pitch. Start from the tree gained via pitch1 of *Vulcan*.
**1** 30 feet. Walk along the ledge and climb up to a tree belay under the roof, as for *Scarecrow*.
**2** 140 feet. 5c. Move out right and climb the short wall to a steep groove. Climb the groove with difficulty to a peg runner and make a hard move out right to a hold on the rib. Climb the rib to a traverse-line left, junction with the *Girdle*, which leads to a peg right of the stance of *Scarecrow*. Take the thin crack above, then go up the groove to the right of the obvious pillar.

The path meets the foot of the right-hand part of Hogmanay Buttress beneath an overhanging band of shaly rock. An overhung bay on the left with a prominent tree above gives one a landmark, and a slatey pillar on the extreme right gives another.

**Raven's Nest Wall**   170 feet   E2                              (6.10.56)
This route climbs up to the prominent tree and then follows a line of cracks and grooves to finish. Start by scrambling through vegetation to a ledge in the overhung bay.
**1** 50 feet. 5b. Climb the bulging wall left of a narrow slatey slab and then make a hard stride to the right. Continue up the steep rib to a ledge and traverse left to the prominent tree.
**2** 60 feet. 4c. Move up behind the tree and move round the corner on the left. Move up into the groove above and climb it to a fine stance.
**3** 60 feet. 4c. Scale the groove behind the stance to the top.

**Dead Rooks Don't Speak**   60 feet   E3 5b            (16.8.86)
Start just left of *Gothic Grooves*. Gain the overhanging chimney left of *Gothic Grooves* by a slab and a wall on the right. Ascend the chimney direct to reach a tree belay. Finish up *Rookery Nook*.

**Gothic Grooves**   180 feet   E1                         (19.3.67)
A devious line, with some hard climbing, crossing *Raven's Nest Wall* at the tree and finishing to the right. Start as for *Raven's Nest Wall*.
**1** 60 feet. 5b. Climb the wall on the left for 10 feet to a small well-defined rib and traverse horizontally left to a black recess. Climb up trending right, then step right onto the lip of the overhang and climb up to the tree on *Raven's Nest Wall*.
**2** 70 feet. 5b. Traverse right from the tree to a V-groove, which is climbed with a move left at the top to a ledge; awkward.
**3** 50 feet. 4c. Climb the groove above to finish.
Variation
**Rookery Nook**   100 feet   Hard Very Severe          (10.77)
**2a** 100 feet. 5a. Step right from the tree and climb over the overhang above, moving left to an old peg runner. Move back right and climb a steep wall to finish up a thin crack.

**W.O.B.**   160 feet   Hard Very Severe               (8.7.56)
The airy finish contrasts nicely with the gloomy start. Start 20 feet left of the edge of the buttress.
**1** 90 feet. 4c. Step up and right round the rib and make a strenuous pull onto a small sandwich slab. Traverse right and move up into a niche under the overhangs; this niche is on the left wall of another overhung bay. Move left over doubtful rock to a good ledge. Step left again to a hanging flake on better rock. Climb up over the flake to the wall above and follow a shallow groove to a small stance.
**2** 70 feet. 4b. Climb diagonally left to reach the foot of a

groove. Climb the right wall of this to a niche and move right to finish. Alternatively, climb the groove direct.

**Stormy Weather**   130 feet   E3 6a                    (3.8.84)
An eliminate but with some good climbing. Start as for *Hogmanay Hangover* and climb this for 30 feet, then move left across a small slab into a wide groove. Follow this to the overhang, as for *W.O.B.* Step right and move up leftwards to the stance on *W.O.B.*; possible belay. Step right and climb the rib and wall above via twin cracks to the top.

**Hogmanay Hangover**   160 feet   Hard Severe       (2.1.54)
A pleasant route on the right edge of the buttress. Start at a slatey overhang on the right-hand side of a recess just above the path.
**1** 70 feet. Climb up left to a corner in the right-hand side of the recess, struggle over an awkward bulge and up to a ledge on the rib. Ascend the left-hand side of the bulge above and step right almost to the edge. Move back left to the foot of a tree-filled groove.
**2** 30 feet. Climb the tree-filled groove which slants left to the tree at the foot of the final corner.
**3** 60 feet. Climb the corner until it is possible to traverse delicately right along a sloping slab to the arête. This is followed to the top.
Variation
**Direct Finish**   50 feet   Hard Very Severe
**3a** 50 feet. 5b. Clamber up the corner direct to the top.

**Eleventh Hour**   160 feet   E4                     (1991)
A hard eliminate in a good position.
**1** 70 feet. As for *Hogmanay Hangover*.
**2** 90 feet. 6a. From the tree-filled groove move up to a ledge and a spike. Climb up right passing a bulge, peg runner. Move right again onto the arête and finish in a fine exposed position.

**Omerta Crack**   60 feet   E3 6a                   (28.6.85)
Quite a stiff proposition on sight. Start below the obvious crack splitting the overhanging wall overlooking the descent gully. Climb the crack with difficulty, or ease, depending on your jamming technique.

**Hogmanay Girdle**   570 feet   E3                    (7.5.73)
An interesting, though not popular, route. Start from below the crack of *Alcatraz*.
**1** 40 feet. 4a. Traverse diagonally right to Strangeways Pinnacle. Move across the top of the groove on the right to a small stance; pitch 1 of *Strangeways*.
**2** 60 feet. 4b. Climb the slab, continuing through the overhangs

on the right to a large perched block in a groove. Follow the groove to the foot of a vegetated gully; pitch 2 of *Strangeways*.
**3** 40 feet. Scramble across right to an oak tree belay.
**4** 80 feet. 6a. Ascend to a small tree and holly roots above. Climb up with difficulty to a bold and precarious traverse rightwards on creaking holds into the smooth corner of *Vulcan*.
**5** 60 feet. 5c. Move round the rib and across into *Falcon*. Descend a few feet and traverse right to below the final crack of *Scarecrow*.
**6** 50 feet. 5b. Traverse right, go under a bulge and move round the corner to an obvious nose. Continue rightwards to a ledge.
**7** 50 feet. 4c. Descend the obvious groove and move right under the overhang to belay on the large tree, pitch 2 *Raven's Nest Wall* reversed.
**8** 100 feet. 4c. Traverse right on the obvious line to below the tree-filled groove of *Hogmanay Hangover*. Continue to the sloping stance and peg belay on the edge.
**9** 90 feet. 5a. Climb the left-slanting groove to a hard move at 20 feet. Move up into a shallow groove and climb this to the finishing rib.

**Valerian**   220 feet   E1                               (27.12.65)
A short counter girdle of the *Hogmanay* area provides some diverting climbing. Start as for *Hogmanay Hangover* at a slatey overhang on the right-hand side of a recess, just above the path.
**1** 70 feet. Climb up and left to a corner in the right-hand side of the recess, struggle over an awkward bulge and up to a ledge on the rib. Ascend the left-hand side of the bulge above and step right almost to the edge. Move back left to the foot of a tree-filled groove.
**2** 40 feet. Traverse 20 feet left to a ledge and then traverse another 20 feet to an obvious nose.
**3** 110 feet. Traverse 15 feet left to an obvious ledge at the foot of the final crack. Ascend the crack to finish as for *Falcon*.

# Craig Bwlch y Moch (Crag of the Pass of the Pigs)

OS Ref 577 406

### Craig Bwlch y Moch — ownership and access
Craig Bwlch y Moch has been owned and managed by the BMC for the benefit of climbers since 1979. The crag forms the eastern extension of the Tremadog cliffs, the upper boundary of the BMC's land being the cliff-top itself and the lower boundary the ditch on the crag side of the A498. Snowdonia National Park Authority has an access agreement with the owner of the cliff-top land to safeguard climbers' access along the top of the cliff.

**BMC management aims for Bwlch y Moch**

The BMC manages Bwlch y Moch with advice from the North Wales Mountaineering Liaison Group which comprises representatives of the Countryside Council for Wales (CCW), Snowdonia National Park Authority, National Trust, BMC and local climbers. The BMC's main aims in managing the area are:

• to maintain access for climbers and to promote good practice

• to safeguard important nature conservation interests

• to meet all legal obligations and

• to promote good relationships with neighbouring landowners.

**Practical considerations for climbers**

• Parking: the main parking area is at Eric Jones's cafe where a small charge is payable. Except for the parking bay beneath *Vector*, climbers should avoid parking on the roadside as this may cause a road safety hazard on busy days.

• Toilets: climbers visiting the cafe may use its private toilet facilities but please note — this is not a public toilet. If you get caught short at the crag, please be discreet and do not leave piles of used toilet paper lying in the open or under boulders near the bottom of the crag.

• Cliff-top descents: the BMC recommends climbers to descend by walking down the paths and gullies marked on the noticeboard in the parking bay beneath *Vector*. The cliff-top path is cleared of vegetation annually by Snowdonia NPA wardens to ensure that it remains passable. If you need to abseil off the crag (say if it is raining or getting dark), take care not to abseil or throw ropes onto people below you as this is both dangerous and very unsociable for other climbers — don't forget, you could be on the receiving end one day.

• Trees: all individual climbers and instructors can help to reduce damage to trees and tree roots by using rock belays whenever possible and not running abseil ropes directly around trees.

• Fences: the field at the top of the cliff is private land used for grazing livestock. Climbers are asked to stick to the cliff-top path and not to cross the fence into the field.

• Rockfalls: there have been a number of rockfalls at Tremadog in recent years. Please treat areas of newly exposed or unstable rock with caution and be watchful for climbers below.

The BMC would like to hear if you have any concerns about the management of Bwlch y Moch. Contact the BMC Access & Conservation Officer to raise any issues and check out the BMC web site www.thebmc.co.uk for the latest access information.

These crags are arguably the pride of Tremadog, even though the cliffs of Bwlch y Moch seem to have lost their reputation as being at the forefront of rock-climbing in Wales, this small area of rock is still a major venue. Here, one can find a tremendous variety in styles of climbing, a broad range of difficulty and a concentration of very high quality routes.

The cliffs of Bwlch y Moch lie parallel to the A498 between Bwlch y Moch Cafe and the sharp bend in the road at Portreuddyn Castle. This is certainly the most accessible climbing at Tremadog. Apart from the added attraction of the now famous Cafe, the associated facilities of camp site, bunkhouse and climbing make this a convenient stop-off on anyone's travels.

The towering Grasper Buttress is the first feature seen when approaching the crag from the car-park, the elegant *Valerie's Rib* soars up on the left while the open corner of *Clapton's Crack* bounds it on the right. Beyond this is a huge roof split by a fine crack, this locates the top of Neb Buttress. Further to the right of *The Neb* is the area of slabs climbed by *Grotto* and *Christmas Curry*, with *The Plum* superbly situated on the right-hand arête.

Right again is a small buttress emerging from the trees with a fine undercut slab on its right. This slim slab is further identified by the inverted rock spike 'The Fang' and the prominent gully of *Striptease* on the right. Beyond this is a rather indefinite and vegetated section of rock eventually gives way to the magnificent overhanging Vector Buttress and its stupendous headwall, the showpiece of Bwlch y Moch.

The clean slabs and walls of Shadrach Buttress follow; these are gained by a path leading round below Vector Buttress to a rock step and arboreal ledge system at the start of the routes. The two grooves of *Leg Slip* and *First Slip* denote the right-hand edge of this section of cliff; their starting area is much lower down and gained by a separate path.

A large area of vegetation now hides one or two small buttresses quite high up; it is easiest to abseil into these. At a lower level an area of rockfall marks the remains of Ivy Buttress. High up to the right of the rockfall, and usually hidden by trees, is Oakover Slab; to the right of this is the descent for the routes in this area, namely Belshazzar Gully.

To the right is the next area of rock; Merlin Buttress. The first significant route is *Belshazzar* and then, to the right of a large area of rockfall, is *Merlin* itself. Round the arête on the right is the diamond-shaped *Geireagle* wall with the slab of *Oberon* below; this buttress is very close to the road.

Beyond Merlin Buttress the crags become much smaller and much more indefinite, the vegetated Far East Slabs containing *Boo-Boo* being the next feature, with the steep *Hot Rats* wall to its right. This area is followed by the slabs and arêtes of *Yogi*, just right of some huge blocks by the old road. The remainder of the cliff then gradually degenerates shortly before Plas Portreuddyn.

The trees and dense vegetation make location of the starts of many climbs rather difficult, especially in summer. The paths to the climbs are, in fact, well-worn and start from obvious gaps in the vegetation by the side of the old road, now a grassy path. The best plan is to identify the upper section of the climb from the main road, cross the ditch between the new and the old road by the closest of the small footbridges and then to follow the path nearest to the route up through the vegetation.

There are two recognised descent routes, Belshazzar Gully near the right end of the crag and a very steep path at the left end of the crag above Bwlch y Moch Farm. Both ways are well-worn and are easily located by following a path along the top of the cliff. When following this path keep to the cliff side of the fence. On no account should this fence be crossed, or, a descent made through the field or orchard of Portreuddyn Farm, nor through the grounds of Portreuddyn Castle. This is private land, there is no right of way and climbers on this land in recent years have given rise to serious complaints.

## Grasper Buttress

The first routes on Grasper Buttress are gained by following a path up rightwards through the trees from the last building along the roadside. The other path, which leads back left behind the building is, in fact, the descent for the routes hereabouts. The foot of Grasper Buttress is defined by an area of slabs below some overhangs. The first routes start some way up on the left.

**Gilljo**   210 feet   Very Difficult                                    (27.4.68)
A reasonably good route, not just if you've done everything else here at this grade. Start about 70 feet up and to the left of the lowest point of Grasper Buttress, level with the left-hand of two overhangs above and to the left of the start of *Valerie's Rib*.
**1** 110 feet. Move right onto the slab above the overhang to a rounded rib, follow the shallow depression on the right, moving

to the right at the top to avoid the overhang. Belay at the large ledge.

**2** 100 feet. Ascend the right-hand side of the slabby rib above to the foot of a broken corner. Climb the corner to a ledge, go up a short crack, trend right and finish up a short steep wall.

### Rip Torn   180 feet   E2                                    (4.96)

The first pitch provides most of the interest. Start as for *Valerie's Rib*, below the left-hand of two overhangs, atop a blocky pinnacle.

**1** 110 feet. 5c. Go straight up to the first overhang and move left until it is possible to heave round on jugs and gain the base of a rounded rib; *Gilljo* crosses here. Continue up the slabby rib to gain the base of a shallow groove at the centre of an overlap and pull up into it. A difficult sequence then leads onto a ledge; finish direct via a short crack.

**2** 70 feet. 4c. Take the edge of the rib above until a move left gains a slab and the top of the pinnacle. The obvious crack in the wall above leads to the top.

### Valerie's Rib   220 feet   Hard Severe                       (12.7.51)

A bright open climb with a bold second pitch. Start about 60 feet up and on the left of the lowest point of Grasper Buttress at some blocks, below an overhang and level with another roof out to the right.

**1** 30 feet. Move up and then trend diagonally right to a ledge on the edge of the rib, in a surprising location.

**2** 100 feet. Climb straight up to the base of a groove. Step right and, keeping to the right of the rounded slabby rib as much as possible, reach a ledge and a nose of rock. The crack to the right of this nose leads to large vegetated ledges. *Valerie's Rib Direct* takes the groove to the left of the rib.

**3** 90 feet. Scramble up to the right to a ledge and a tree above an area of rockfall. Take the crack above to another tree, proceed left and continue up the broken crack above to finish. It is possible to move right above the area of rockfall to gain the original layback crack.

### Valerie's Rib Direct   270 feet   Severe                     (1964)

An easier, but pleasant, variant on the original. It is best to start just left of *Valor* making a much longer first pitch.

**1** 80 feet. Climb the slabby corner just left of the toe of the buttress to gain a blocky ledge; the proper start of *Valerie's Rib*. Move up and trend diagonally right to a ledge on the edge of the rib or, even more direct, take the thin groove above the blocky ledge at Hard Severe.

**2** 110 feet. Climb up to reach the base of an open groove just left of the rib. Go up the groove but step left at the top to reach a

slab to go back right to round a nose of rock. Ascend the crack
on the right to gain a large grass ledge. Fairly well-protected,
usually done in error for the original.
**3** 80 feet. Scramble up and climb the crack about 10 feet to the
left of the usual layback finish or, the wall and chockstone-filled
crack a little further left again.

**Valor**   230 feet   E2                                    (1964)
A memorable route with the crux exactly where it should be,
providing an exposed and difficult finish. Start at the foot of the
slabs beneath the prominent overhang at the foot of *Valerie's Rib*.
**1** 60 feet. 5b. Ascend the slabs over a little overlap to beneath
the roof. Traverse right and move up and around the right-hand
side of the overhang to the stance on *Valerie's Rib*. Alternatively,
clamber up over the roof by the crack on the left.
**2** 90 feet. 5a. Move up and right to a short groove capped by a
small triangular overhang. Climb this and a short ramp, go
diagonally right and then traverse left 20 feet to a tree belay.
**3** 80 feet. 5c. Traverse right across the rockfall-affected area to
reach the layback crack, climb this and go up the smooth slab on
the right to a small exposed ledge. Climb the steep wall and the
slanting groove above to a good ledge and belay. Climb the
easy wall on the left to the top.

**The Pink Fridge**   80 feet   E3 5c                        (4.83)
A diverting route up a series of cracks in an overhanging wall.
Start about 20 feet to the right of *Valor* at a short chimney below
a vegetated groove. Ascend a blocky fin to reach the base of a
steep crack and follow this line up the wall, escaping left onto
easier ground just before the top of the wall. Move diagonally
right to finish off as for *Valor* pitch 2.

To the right of the *Valerie's Rib* area is a steep wall leading to a
series of grooves. The base of the wall is best gained from the
start of *Kestrel Cracks*. A short blocky corner, the start of *Clean
Edge*, leads to easy slabs which can be climbed to the large tree
at the foot of *Clapton's Crack*.

**The Grasper**   150 feet   E2                              (2.6.61)
An excellent route with a difficult and strenuous final pitch also
involving some very wide bridging. The route takes the overhangs
on the left-hand side of the wall and goes up the more prominent
left-hand of the two grooves above. Start on a clean sloping
ledge at the foot of the wall.
**1** 80 feet. 5c. Climb a shallow groove to a narrow ledge, then
move left across a rib into an overhanging niche. Move left again
onto another rib and follow the groove to a small roof. Climb
round the roof to a good ledge on the right and then move back

## Craig Bwlch y Moch
### Left-Hand Area

1. The Grasper E2
2. Zukator E4
3. The Neb E2
4. The Plum E1

left to a thin crack, which leads to a huge spike just to the right of *Valerie's Rib*. Traverse right to a stance directly below the final groove.
**2** 70 feet. 5c. Climb the short wall and then the groove to an overhang, pull over this, then exit left and climb the sharp rib to the top.

**New Management**  150 feet  E3 6a                    (30.7.79)
Quite a tough eliminate based on *The Grasper*, with some good climbing, quite high in the grade. Start just right of *The Grasper*. Ascend the wall to a diagonal crack crossing left past *The Grasper* to reach a groove between *Valor* and *The Graspet*. Climb the groove until a move right gains the crux of *The Grasper*; continue up this route to finish.

**Zukator/Grasper Connection**  E3 5c
A combination of the first pitch of *Zukator* with the top pitch of *The Grasper* gives a really fine outing at the grade.

**Zukator**  180 feet  E4                              (10.64)
An impressive climb, with some extremely hard groove climbing on the second pitch, which takes the groove to the right of the top pitch of *The Grasper*. Start at the foot of the obvious corner of *Clapton's Crack*, to the right of the start of *The Grasper*.
**1** 90 feet. 5c. Move left into a niche and go left again around the arête to a small ledge. Climb up with difficulty to the square-cut ledge in the middle of the wall. Continue up and rightwards until beneath some overhangs level with the stance of *The Grasper*. Traverse left beneath the overhangs to reach the stance.
**2** 90 feet. 6b. Follow *The Grasper* to the groove and then step down and move blindly round the jutting corner on the right to gain a small ledge at the foot of the overhanging groove. Ascend this in safety but with great difficulty, exiting right at the top.

**The Man Who Fell to Earth**  130 feet  E4  †        (5.98)
A filler-in with some new ground and an exciting finish. Start as for *Zukator*.
**1** 70 feet. 6a. Climb up to the initial pod of *Zukator*. Move up right to a peg and climb above this on positive edges to gain the peg on *Quite Easy for Bigheads*. From this move to the belay on *The Grasper*.
**2** 60 feet. 6a. Ascend the arête between *The Grasper* and *Zukator* to an obvious cams slot. Throw yourself rightwards to gain the final 10 feet of *Zukator*.
Variation
**Direct Finish**  60 feet  E5 6b  †                   (10.99)
**2a** Climb the arête to the cams slot. Make a powerful stretch up to a finger lock in the overlap to finish in a stunning position.

Keith Robertson, solo on the fine finger crack of *Fingerlicker* E4, Craig Pant Ifan.
Photo: Robertson collection

Louise Yin on *Scratch Arête*
HVS, Craig Pant Ifan.
Photo: Carl Ryan

**Quite Easy for Bigheads**   150 feet   E6 6b        (2.6.86)
Another 'last great problem' solved by this bold eliminate. Start
as for *Zukator*. Follow the first pitch of *Zukator* to where it
traverses left into *The Grasper*. Instead of going left, make some
difficult moves up to reach the ledge below the groove of *Zukator*.
Step out right onto the arête and ascend it to join *Marathon Man*
near the top.

**Marathon Man**   170 feet   E5                      (5.6.77)
The obvious groove right of *Zukator* provides a poorly-protected,
strenuous and technical main pitch.
**1** 80 feet. 5c. Climb *Zukator* until it is possible to traverse right to
a good stance and tree belay; also the top of pitch 1 of *Clapton's
Crack*.
**2** 90 feet. 6a. Move left through vegetation to gain the obvious
groove. Climb this to overhanging ledges and move up and
slightly right to reach a small spike. Step left and climb through
the bulge, using an undercut crack, to reach a good hold. Finish
easily.
Variation
**2a** 90 feet. 6a. From the small spike step slightly right and go
straight up through the bulges.

**Clapton's Crack**   175 feet   Very Severe          (19.1.61)
A good climb with a strenuous first pitch, taking the obvious
corner to the right of *The Grasper*. Start by scrambling up to the
right from the foot of *Valerie's Rib* to gain a grassy bay below the
corner.
**1** 75 feet. 4b. Climb the pleasant corner to a large stance on the
right.
**2** 100 feet. 4a. Move up a steep wall to gain the rightward-
sloping ramp, which leads by broken slabs to the foot of a
chimney. Step onto a slab on the left and ascend the deep crack
to the top or, go straight up the chimney which is the original
line.

**The Sword**   270 feet   Hard Severe                (9.84)
A poor route which starts very low down and immediately right of
the gully leading up to *The Grasper* area, at the base of Neb
Buttress, below a broad rib.
**1** 100 feet. Climb the corner to a big overhang, proceed to the
right and continue up ribs and slabs to belay at the foot of
*Clapton's Crack*.
**2** 70 feet. Move right to blocks 15 feet right of *Clapton's Crack*
and follow the arête above.
**3** 100 feet. Follow a crack leading diagonally right until one is
able to step left onto an arête. Scale the wall to the right of the
'sword' to a bollard and then go easily up a blocky nose to
finish.

**Clean Edge**   100 feet   E2 6a                    (30.7.80)
A scrappy start leads to some absorbing and technical climbing.
Start 50 feet left of and below the start of *Kestrel Cracks* at a
large tree below an overhang. Climb the crack, moving right to
spikes. Climb the broken groove to reach a good foothold on the
right. Go up the thin crack in the middle of the wall, via some
rather problematic moves which need to be started correctly, to
finish on a large ledge. Belay on the tree well back and finish up
*The Neb.*

## Neb Buttress

This buttress is easily spotted. It is the slender tower of rock with the
huge overhang at its top which is cleft by an obvious crack, the line
of *Neb Direct.* Originally known as Dotheboys Buttress.

**Kestrel Cracks**   200 feet   Very Severe                (8.61)
This steep route takes a more or less direct line up the left-hand
side of Neb Buttress. Start at the foot of the prominent groove
capped by an overhang.
**1** 85 feet. 4c. Climb the chimney direct and turn the overhang on
the right to reach a steep crack which leads to a stance.
**2** 35 feet. Climb up the rib just on the right to the foot of a
leaning corner.
**3** 80 feet. 5a. Ascend the rather awkward corner for about 20
feet to a large spike. Step left into a small crack, ascend this and
the deep crack left again to finish.

**The Neb**   220 feet   E2                           (6.61)
A fine first pitch and two problematic cracks lead to a traverse
right underneath the obvious roof crack that dominates the
buttress. Start just right of *Kestrel Cracks.*
**1** 90 feet. 5b. Climb the right wall of the corner, trending right to
a small ledge, and proceed to climb the arête direct to a stance
at the top of the first pitch of *Kestrel Cracks.* This was the original
and better line.
**2** 50 feet. Go up a rib on the right and traverse into a grassy
bay to reach the foot of a thin, overhanging crack.
**3** 20 feet. 5c. Climb the crack; a sustained onslaught is required
to overcome this short but desperate obstacle.
**4** 60 feet. 5c. Another overhanging crack eventually yields,
allowing one to reach a slab below the large roof. Traverse
delicately right and go up a short groove to finish; good
ropework is an added advantage on this pitch.
Variation
**1a** 90 feet 5b. From the small ledge, move up and round the
arête.A steep wall then leads to a large ledge and a short
groove; this gains the stance.

**Broken Edge**   80 feet   E2 5c   (5.7.79)
A good pitch with one committing move, can be used as a top
pitch to *Dotheboys*. Start at the belay below *The Neb's* third
pitch, or start up the top pitch of *Kestrel Cracks*. Ascend the first
overhanging crack of *The Neb* and move out to the arête left of
*Neb Direct*. This is followed, in a fine position, to a difficult
mantel move near the top.

**Neb Direct**   50 feet   E3 6a   (1960s)
A stunningly situated and photogenic pitch taking the obvious
roof crack. Start at the belay at the end of pitch 3 of *The Neb*.
Climb the overhanging crack to the slab as for *The Neb*. Ascend
the roof crack above with great difficulty. A good technique will
save knuckle wear and bicep fatigue. A fine jamming pitch.

**Dotheboys**   100 feet   E1 5c   (9.6.84)
A good climb, quite hard for the grade. Start just to the right of
*The Neb*, below a corner-groove. Mantel onto a small ledge at
the foot of a smooth groove. Climb the groove for a few feet until
a swing right allows another ledge to be gained. Go up to the
right again until a move back left gains the base of a gangway;
follow this to its top. Step right to reach a small pocket, finish
easily; belay as for *The Neb*.

The next couple of routes are best located by looking across from
the top of the *Grotto/Christmas Curry* area and abseiling in. The
gully approach is very dangerous at present.

**Anagram**   100 feet   E2 5c   (3.78)
This short, steep, if rather esoteric, route on the right-hand side of
Neb Buttress gives some good climbing, quite high in the grade.
Start about 100 feet up the gully between Neb Buttress and
*Grotto* below an obvious groove. Climb the overhanging groove
to a ledge. Step right into a crack and climb this, past a ledge, to
finish up the last few feet of *The Neb*.

**Final Exam**   110 feet   E2 5c   (27.9.78)
Although wallowing in obscurity, as well as vegetation, this route
has some good climbing. Start, after a cleaning session, below
the corner of *Anagram*. Climb the short overhanging crack to an
easier chimney and so to a good ledge. Continue up the steep
crack and the niche above, with a hard exit to easier ground.

**Magic Mushroom**   100 feet   E2 5b   (3.7.79)
A rather trivial filler-in; start just left of *Grotto*. Climb the wall
leftwards on some spaced holds for 35 feet until it is possible to
step right to place protection in *Grotto*. Continue straight up the
wall above.

**Grotto**   150 feet   Very Severe                              (25.4.64)
An interesting climb, much better than its appearance would
suggest. Start by taking the first two pitches of *Christmas Curry*
and traversing left to an obvious flake belay.
**1** 90 feet. 4c. Climb straight up the wall directly above the flake.
Step left into a shallow corner, climb this for a few feet and then
move across the steep slab on the left to the foot of the obvious
groove. Move round the roof at the foot of the groove and climb
up to a second roof. Pull round this to the right and ascend a
short corner to a good spike belay or climb the crack on the left,
harder and often wet.
**2** 60 feet. 4c. Move left for 15 feet before swinging out left onto
a rib. Continue straight up until forced to move left again and so
to the top of the crag.

**Grotto Direct**   150 feet   Hard Very Severe
A surprisingly entertaining climb. Start as for *Grotto*.
**1** 90 feet. 5a. Climb straight up the wall above the flake to join a
steep crack just right of the arête. Follow this to a small ledge
then go left below an overhang to climb a short slab. This then
joins the parent route below the short corner leading up to the
spike belay.
**2** 60 feet. 4c. Ascend the steep slab and rib, above the belay
and just left of *Christmas Curry*, to the top.

**Vindaloo**   150 feet   Hard Very Severe                      (10.3.68)
A poor climb which starts at the flake at the foot of *Grotto*.
**1** 90 feet. 5b. Take the diagonal crack on the right and the steep
wall above to a small ledge. Move left to the crack on the arête
and follow it to the block belay of *Grotto*.
**2** 60 feet. 4c. Climb the obvious groove trending left at the top.

**Christmas Curry**   250 feet   Severe                         (25.12.53)
An interesting and enjoyable climb, especially with the *Micah
Eliminate*; very popular. Start at the bottom right-hand side of the
buttress, at the foot of a short slab beneath an obvious chimney.
**1** 40 feet. Scale the slab and the chimney to a tree belay.
**2** 90 feet. Climb up to the left to reach sloping ledges. Climb the
steep wall into a recess. Move up to the right on good holds until
it is possible to make a step back left onto the slab above, from
which a crack leads to a good ledge.
**3** 60 feet. Climb the slab behind the tree and step onto the wall
to the left, above a sharp-edged overhang. Good holds lead up
the steep wall to another large ledge.
**4** 60 feet. Enter the prominent corner on the left and pull left
across the rib to reach a cluster of spikes. Go up the wall above
into a groove and finish on the right.

Variations

**Micah Eliminate**   120 feet   Hard Severe                    (1954)
An excellent variation, with some bold climbing in a fine position.
**3a** 120 feet. Step right from the stance and ascend a short
groove. Continue up another groove to reach the ledge right of
the final stance of the normal route. Climb the thin crack and step
right to the arête, which is followed to the top.

**Finish of Moments**   50 feet   E3                           (1978)
A variation with poor rock and poor protection.
**4a** 50 feet. 5b. The arête left of the *Treemudrock Finish*.

**Treemudrock Finish**   50 feet   Very Severe                (1968)
**4b** 50 feet. 4c. The prominent corner taken directly to the top.

**Lleolwyr Finish**   50 feet   Hard Very Severe              (1968)
Some good moves; it ascends the wall to the right of *Treemudrock
Finish*.
**4c** 50 feet. 5b. Go straight up the middle of wall until a difficult
sequence up and right is made to gain a leftward-slanting crack
leading to the top.

**The Plum**   140 feet   E1 5b                               (12.61)
One of the Tremadog classics; a route which requires the use of
almost all forms of climbing technique; what more could you ask
for? It takes the prominent arête on the right of *Christmas Curry*.
At the foot of the arête there is a shallow corner capped by a
roof. Start at the base of the corner. Ascend the awkward corner-
crack to a step left onto the rib. Climb the rib with difficulty to
reach a small ledge below a V-groove. Go up the groove to
reach a ledge, possible stance. Climb the prominent crack to a
small ledge, step right and ascend the rib. This is difficult at first
but eases towards the top.

**Bombshell**   150 feet   Hard Very Severe 5a               (15.4.79)
A bit of an eliminate. Start just up and to the right of *The Plum*.
Traverse in from the right to gain the roof and pull over this to
reach a ledge. Follow the awkward grooves to the right of *The
Plum* for about 60 feet until a move left can be made into *The
Plum*; finish up this route.

**Molar**   90 feet   Hard Very Severe 5b   ‡                 (1964)
A poor route up the small buttress high on the cliff and to the left
of *The Fang*. It can be reached by an unpleasant scramble up the
steep vegetation to the right of *The Plum*, or from the end of the
traverse of pitch 2 of *The Fang*. Start at a tree belay at the foot of
the buttress. Climb up to a small overhang and pull into a short
chimney which leads to a ledge. Struggle through the holly above
to a crack which leads steeply to the top.

**Footless Frenzy** 200 feet E1 (1979)

A poor start leads to a good top pitch. Start on the pathway up to *The Fang,* below some obvious corners.

**1** 100 feet. 5b. Ascend the corners above, moving slightly right near the top to belay on the spikes of *The Fang.* Walk up to the *Molar* belay.

**2** 100 feet. 5a. Start off as for *Molar* but go right up obvious corners and grooves to finish up a wall. Belay as for *Molar.*

**Quimbo** 170 feet E2 ‡ (4.81)

The first pitch is rather overgrown and requires 'rediscovery'. The top pitch is a combination of two variations on *The Fang.* Start at the base of a thin crack on the left edge of the lower wall.

**1** 80 feet. 6a. Some strenuous and difficult starting moves up the thin crack allow one to gain the belay of *The Fang.*

**2** 90 feet. 5b. Follow the corner behind the stance directly to the overhang and then move left with difficulty to join the normal route. Follow *The Fang* to the end of the traverse and ascend an interesting groove to finish.

**The Fang** 200 feet Hard Very Severe (4.6.61)

A good route with both strenuous and delicate climbing. The obvious buttress between *The Plum* and Vector Buttress contains a roof with a large inverted rock spike — The Fang. Start from the foot of the gully on the right.

**1** 80 feet. 5a. Climb a leaning pinnacle just left of the gully. Move left to a short overhanging groove and ascend this to a ledge. Step back right and ascend a crack to a small stance.

**2** 120 feet. 5a. Climb up and left and after a few awkward moves step down left onto a sloping ledge on the rib. Traverse left for a few feet and then climb up until it is possible to move back right into the centre of the final slab. Climb straight up to the top with poor protection.

Variation

**The Root** 100 feet E2 5c (1994)

A spectacular addition.

**2a** 100 feet. 5c. Climb up and left until one can bridge up using 'The Fang'; a layback move right then gains a foothold on 'The Fang' itself. Move up and join *Extraction* and finish off as for this route.

**Extraction** 160 feet E2 (16.6.75)

A good companion route to *The Fang* with two hard and contrasting pitches. Start just to the right of *The Fang,* below a thin crack.

**1** 60 feet. 5c. Climb the thin crack direct to the first stance of *The Fang.*

**2** 100 feet. 5c. Go diagonally across the right wall to a small ledge on the arête. Move up a few feet to an overhung niche and then move left across the steep wall, with difficulty, to the slab of *The Fang*. Climb the right-hand side of the slab to the top.

**Striptease**   160 feet   Very Severe                                    (3.4.61)
The shallow gully to the right of *The Fang* buttress gives a strenuous and interesting climb, which is often dry, even during heavy rain. Start right of *The Fang* at the bottom of the gully.
**1** 120 feet. 5a. Climb the chimney direct over two overhangs, moving right at the second one, to a good tree belay.
**2** 40 feet. 4b. Step left onto the arête and ascend it to the top.

**Burlesque**   120 feet   E3                                         (12.4.66)
Quite a technical route, high in the grade. Start above and to the right of *Striptease* beneath the overhang.
**1** 90 feet. 6a. Climb up to the overhang and turn it on the left to gain a slab. Move right to a thin crack and enter the overhung groove on the right. Follow the groove to reach the slabs right of *Striptease*. Step right and ascend more or less directly up little slabs and overhangs. One is then forced forced onto easier ground on the right, that of *G String*, ascend this or finish via pitch 2a of *G String*. Climb up to a tree belay above and to the right of the big tree of *Striptease*.
**2** 30 feet. 4c. Climb the steep wall to the top.

**High Kicks**   130 feet   E2                                        (1978)
A bit of a filler-in but with some good moves. The 5c pitch can also be gained by ascending *Burlesque*. Start 12 yards right of *Striptease*, at the foot of a corner capped by an overhang.
**1** 50 feet. 5b. Go up *G String*, but traverse left to enter a groove and continue to belay on *Burlesque*.
**2** 40 feet. 5c. Follow the obvious groove above and to the right of the belay. This pitch can also be gained by starting up *Burlesque*.
**3** 40 feet. 4c. Finish up the wall or, end by going up *G String* pitch 2a.

**G String**   130 feet   Hard Very Severe                            (1964)
The difficult section is short but interesting. Start 35 feet right of *Striptease*, at the foot of a corner capped by an overhang.
**1** 90 feet. 5b. Ascend directly up the corner to the overhang and move left onto the arête with difficulty to pull over the overhang to a small ledge. Climb more or less directly to a tree belay above and to the right of the big tree of *Striptease*.
**2** 40 feet. 4c. The steep wall is climbed to the top.
Variation   E1                                                       (5.85)
A problematic finish.
**2a** 40 feet. 6a. Ascend the groove in the right-hand side of the upper wall; small wires essential.

**Triangulum** 160 feet   Hard Severe                    (3.57)
An intricate line avoiding the overhangs with an interesting top
pitch. Start as for *G String*.
**1** 90 feet. Ascend the crack to the overhang (often wet) then
scuttle off delicately right to a mantel move also used by *Hail
Bebe*; tree belay up and right.
**2** 70 feet. Walk left along a thorny rake, then cross a slab left to
a tree. An awkward stride back right gains a good hold; finish
over a block.

## Vector Buttress

This buttress, the scene of many an epic struggle, must stand out as
one of the most impressive pieces of rock in Wales. It lies directly
above the start of the drainage ditch crossed by a number of footbridges, approach past a sign through trees and boulders.

**Hail Bebe** 225 feet   Very Difficult                (28.3.54)
Scrappy and vegetated, but it is the easiest way up this part of
the crag and is a good beginners' route. Start at the base of the
slabby side of Vector Buttress, lower down and to the left of *One
Step in the Clouds*.
**1** 30 feet. Climb steeply up blocks to a large tree.
**2** 45 feet. Traverse left to a large area of vegetation and move
up to belay in the trees.
**3** 40 feet. Ascend and reach a crack with difficulty to another
tree.
**4** 50 feet. Scale the short crack above and move on to yet
another tree.
**5** 45 feet. Gain the slab on the right and traverse diagonally
right to a ledge and belay.
**6** 15 feet. Climb a short crack to finish.

**One Step in the Clouds** 230 feet   Very Severe   (11.5.58)
A pleasant and exposed climb which starts on the left-hand side
of the steep lower wall of Vector Buttress.
**1** 90 feet. 4b. Climb steeply up blocks to a large tree. Continue
up the wall behind the tree and then take a V-groove to a good
stance beneath the big overhangs.
**2** 30 feet. Go round the corner on the left and up the shallow
crack to a sloping ledge and tree belay.
**3** 60 feet. 4c. Climb up for 20 feet then go diagonally right off
the end of a ledge to a spike runner and make a difficult, but
well-protected, move up in a stupendous position to reach a good
stance. It is slightly easier to ascend direct, via a little groove, to
the same stance.
**4** 50 feet. 4b. Step right for a few feet on the obvious traverse
line and ascend the difficult short groove and awkward

mantelshelf above. Alternatively, climb the slabby wall direct, which is harder than the ordinary way.

The following climbs take lines up Vector Buttress proper and include some of the best routes in Wales as well as a concentration of the hardest in this guide.

**Dark Side**   80 feet   E2 6a                    (1972)
A good introduction to the more technical climbs at Tremadog. Start from the stance at the end of pitch 1 of *One Step in the Clouds*. Traverse right for a few feet and move up the wall to a thread runner. Step left and move into the overhanging chimney-groove. Climb this to where the angle eases and move left to follow the continuation groove and flake to the top.

**Sultans of Swing**   180 feet   E4                    (4.80)
A superb left-to-right girdle of the *Vector* headwall journeying through some spectacular rock scenery. Probably best done on a Bank Holiday! The unrelenting second pitch requires a determined approach, to say nothing of good rope technique. Start from the stance at the end of pitch 1 of *One Step in the Clouds*.
**1** 40 feet. 6a. Traverse right for a few feet and then move up the wall to a thread runner. Step left and move into the overhanging chimney-groove and ascend this to where the angle eases (as for *Dark Side*). Move right to take a hanging belay on the slab below the final groove of *Vector*.
**2** 140 feet. 6a. Traverse right to beneath the wide crack of *The Croaker*, difficult and committing moves then lead around and right to beneath the smooth headwall. Traverse delicately right to a good spike and climb straight up onto a detached flake which provides a good foothold. This section is part of the last pitch of *Cream*. Move up and right to a good hold on *Void* and ascend the wall and crack until about 15 feet below the top of the crack. Swing right into another crack, that of *The Mongoose,* and follow this more easily to the top.

**Diadic**   220 feet   E1                    (3.6.64)
An enjoyable and direct climb through impressive rock scenery. Start at the foot of Vector Buttress as for *One Step in the Clouds*.
**1** 90 feet. 4b. Climb steeply up blocks to a large tree. Climb the wall behind the tree and then a V-groove to a good stance beneath the overhangs (as for *One Step in the Clouds*).
**2** 80 feet. 5b. Traverse easily right for a few feet and then move up and right to reach a thread runner. Move awkwardly round the small fang of rock on the right and go straight over a bulge. Climb the groove above to reach a short slab at the foot of an overhanging crack and a junction with *Vector*. Climb the crack with difficulty, as for *Vector*, and then more easily to the last

stance of *One Step in the Clouds*.
**3** 50 feet. Climb diagonally right to the top of the crag.

## Nimbus  220 feet  E2  (6.61)

A steep and exposed route crossing Vector Buttress from left-to-right. Start as for *One Step in the Clouds*.
**1** 90 feet. 4b. As for pitch 1 of *One Step in the Clouds*.
**2** 90 feet. 5c. Go across right to a tree, step down and traverse awkwardly right to a sloping ledge at the foot of a groove. Climb this to a flat-topped spike and then move diagonally right to reach the cave of *Vector*.
**3** 40 feet. 4b. Follow the obvious diagonal line rightwards to a large stance overlooking the gully. From here, probably the best option is to finish up *The Snake*, also at E2.
Variation
**1a** 90 feet. 5a. Climb the shallow groove to the right of *One Step in the Clouds* until it is possible to step left to the good stance.

## The Weaver  210 feet  E2  (2.80)

A good climb, which crosses *Nimbus* to finish up the final groove of *Vector*. Start at the foot of the Buttress, just right of *One Step in the Clouds*.
**1** 40 feet. 5b. Climb straight up the faint groove and move right and up a short wall to the first stance of *Vector*.
**2** 120 feet. 5c. Step up and then move left for 10 feet. Climb the steep wall direct to a triangular overhang on *Nimbus*. Step right and move up a groove, go back left to reach good footholds. Follow a crack to join *Diadic* below the final groove of *Vector* and ascend this to a belay.
**3** 50 feet. Climb easily up the slab to finish.

## Bananas  220 feet  E5  (30.3.80)

This powerful climb utilises *The Weaver* to start, then attacks the spectacular flake-arête above and to the right of the wide crack of *The Croaker*. Start at the foot of the buttress, just right of *One Step in the Clouds*.
**1** 40 feet. 5b. Climb straight up the faint groove and move right and up a short wall to the first stance of *Vector*, as for *The Weaver*.
**2** 100 feet. 5c. Step up and then move left for 10 feet. Climb the steep wall direct to a triangular overhang on *Nimbus*. Step right and move up a groove and then go back left to reach good footholds. Follow a crack to reach *Diadic* at the large thread, as for *The Weaver*. Move right and go over the roof to reach a hanging stance below the wide crack on *The Croaker*.
**3** 80 feet. 6b. Climb the crack and then move up and right to the flake-arête; a knee lock allows a 'rest'. Ascend the flake-crack

above with great difficulty to a desperate mantel; finish up easy ground.

**Llanberries**   65 feet   E7 6c                                        (5.5.87)
A dynamic pitch in a fantastic position, up the wall left of *Strawberries*, 'air miles' guaranteed. Start 20 feet below the spike belay at the base of the top pitch of *Cream*, but using the spike as the belay. Climb the slab left of *Cream* to gain the base of the *Strawberries* crack. Layback the footholds of *Strawberries* to a jug using a peg, a *Rock 1* and an *RP3* for protection. Some very difficult moves up and then left may gain an even harder move, which leads to the arête. Finish up the edge.

**Strawberries**   60 feet   E6 6b                                      (3.80)
The stunningly situated crack in the *Vector* headwall gives one of the most sought-after traditional 'flashes' in Wales. Start below the top pitch of *Cream*, at the spike stance overlooking the gully. Move left as for *Cream* but continue leftwards to gain the crack. This is climbed with a great deal of difficulty, a safe but sustained sequence of 6b moves.

**Dream Topping**   60 feet   E7 6c                                     (10.84)
An amazing extension to an already difficult route which is, in effect, a direct version of *Strawberries*. Start as for *Strawberries*. Ascend *Strawberries* to the top of the first crack; a desperate sequence of moves may now allow the continuation crack to be reached. Follow this, and easier ground, to the top.

**Cream**   225 feet   E4                                               (1.5.76)
A superb route barging its way through the overhangs. A difficult second pitch gives access to the exposed series of moves on the headwall. Start at the foot of the buttress, just right of *One Step in the Clouds*.
**1** 40 feet. 4c. Climb the groove to a spike belay on the right; the first stance of *Vector*.
**2** 80 feet. 5c. Climb above the spike to cracked blocks level with the ochre-coloured slab of *Vector*. Step round and down to the left and climb up the short wide groove to join *Nimbus*. Move left onto a wall and move up to a roof. Traverse right to a belay in the cave of *Vector*.
**3** 40 feet. 4b. Traverse right along the obvious break to a stance overlooking the gully, as for *Nimbus*.
**4** 65 feet. 6a. Step left across the wall onto a spike and clamber up onto a detached flake, which provides a good foothold. Continue up the wall and crack above until better holds lead up and left to the top. A superb pitch.
Variation
**2a** 70 feet. 6a. Climb above the spike to cracked blocks level

with the ochre-coloured slab of *Vector*. Move left and layback
with great difficulty to join *Nimbus*. Follow *Nimbus* to the cave
belay of *Vector*.

**Vector**   250 feet   E2                                    (26.3.60)
The original route of the buttress gives steep and intricate
climbing through impressive overhangs; a truly tremendous climb,
one of the best at Tremadog, now sadly spoilt by overuse. Start at
the foot of the buttress, by a large flake right of *One Step in the
Clouds*.
**1** 60 feet. 5a. Climb a short groove and step right onto a slab.
Move delicately left to another short groove which leads to a
small stance with a spike belay.
**2** 80 feet. 5c. Move right awkwardly across the wall to the
bottom of a diagonal crack. Climb the crack to a large spike on
the right. Step left from the top of the spike and make some hard
moves to reach the foot of the ochre-coloured slab. Climb up this
and over a bulge, step left into a groove and follow this to the
large roof. Traverse left to a cave to belay.
**3** 60 feet. 5b. Move left out of the cave and pull over a small
overhang. Traverse left and then make an awkward move up to
the foot of an overhanging groove. Climb this strenuously to
reach the last stance of *One Step in the Clouds*.
**4** 50 feet. Climb the slab diagonally right to finish.

**The Croaker**   70 feet   E2 5c   ·                          (1.4.64)
Absorbing climbing in a fine position, somewhat easier now with
the disappearance of a block which has removed the need to
perform the difficult mantel. Start from the cave stance of *Vector*.
Move left from the cave and up onto the slab as for *Vector*. Climb
up to the wide crack in the overhang above, ascend the crack
and move left to reach a second overhang. Climb this, once the
scene of many a failure, to reach the stance on *One Step in the
Clouds*.

# Craig Bwlch y Moch
## Vector Buttress

1. Dark Side E2
2. Nimbus E2
3. Diadic E1
4. Cream E4
5. Vector E2
6. Void E4
7. The Atomic Finger Flake E4
8. Bananas E5
9. Llanberries E7
10. Strawberries E6
11. The Snake E2
12. The Mongoose E5

**The Atomic Finger Flake**   150 feet   E4   (2.3.80)
The second pitch takes the ludicrously overhanging flake on the underside of the ochre-coloured slab and requires forceful climbing. The prospect of coming off is quite distressing for the second. Start just right of *Vector*.
**1** 60 feet. 5b. Climb up the face of the slab between *Vector* and *Void* until forced into the latter.
**2** 90 feet. 6a. Climb the very shallow groove to the right of the belay and ascend more easily to a vegetated ledge on the right. Climb up to a bulge and then make some very hard moves left across the overhanging wall to reach the base of the flake. Climb the flake to a ledge on the left and then make an awkward move over the bulge on the right to gain a groove. Follow this and then easier ground to the large ledge overlooking the gully.

**Swift Undercut**   90 feet   E7 6c   (11.90)
This outrageous addition takes the underside of the ochre-coloured slab to give extraordinarily powerful climbing in a ridiculous position. Start at the first stance of *The Atomic Finger Flake*. Move up from the shallow groove to a spike and onto the underside of the slab. Move up and left past three pegs, eventually heel hooking the edge of the slab; pull round and breathe a sigh of relief. Either finish up *Strawberries* or jump off into the *Void*.

**Void**   200 feet   E4   (1975)
An excellent climb with a superb and technical culmination up the *Vector* headwall. Start at the base of the groove directly below the ochre-coloured slab.
**1** 45 feet. 5b. Climb the groove to a belay below the large spike on pitch 2 of *Vector*.
**2** 85 feet. 5c. Climb up onto the spike. Step left from the top of the spike and make some hard moves to reach the foot of the ochre-coloured slab. Ascend this and go over a bulge, step left into a groove and follow this to a large roof; *Vector* goes left from here. Traverse right onto an overhung ledge and reach a hidden crack further right. Climb this to the large ledge overlooking the gully.
**3** 70 feet. 6a. Directly above the belay is a fine pod, guarded by an overhanging crack. Enter the pod and climb it until it is possible to move left onto a good hold. Climb the wall and crack above directly to the top. A strenuous and sustained pitch.

The following two routes start from the large ledge overlooking the gully gained either by *Nimbus* or *Grim Wall*.

**The Mongoose** 80 feet E5 (5.77)
The right edge of the *Vector* headwall provides an extremely hard
and bold pitch which should be led without placing any runners
in *Void*. Start from the large ledge overlooking the gully.
**1** 20 feet. 4c. Climb the slab to a belay next to the pod in the left
wall.
**2** 60 feet. 6b. Climb into the pod and exit left to a resting place.
Climb straight up the wall and crack to the top; a serious pitch.

**The Snake** 90 feet E2 (1.6.75)
Although somewhat overlooked this is a good way to finish off
*Nimbus* or to reach the top having failed on the headwall pitch of
*Void*. Start from the large ledge overlooking the gully.
**1** 20 feet. 4c. Climb the slab to a belay next to the pod in the left
wall.
**2** 70 feet. 5c. Climb into the pod and exit left to a resting place.
Follow the obvious traverse line left, crossing *Void*.

## Shadrach Buttress

Vector Buttress is bounded on the right by a steep vegetated gully.
Right again is a fine steep wall, which is climbed by a number of
good routes. An obvious chimney (the first pitch of *Shadrach*) is a
very good landmark. Most of the routes on Shadrach Buttress are
gained by taking a path leading round below Vector Buttress, then
going up a rock step to reach an arboreal ledge system near the
foot of the obvious chimney.

**Grim Wall Direct** 180 feet E1
A fine eliminate taking the left-hand side of the steep wall, giving
sustained climbing. Start immediately right of the vegetated gully,
before the rock step in the path
**1** 100 feet. 5b. Climb the striated crack onto a slab above and
move diagonally left to a bulge. Go over the bulge to reach a
slab. The slab leads with some difficulty to a large stance and
tree belay.
**2** 80 feet. 5b. Follow cracks in the prominent rib above to a
steep pull through a bulge, then step into the shallow groove
system on the right, below a small overhang. Surmount the
overhang and continue up the groove to a step right at its end.

**Leg Break** 170 feet E3 (1976)
A vicious eliminate, with some poorly protected climbing. Start at
the shallow groove 20 feet right of *Grim Wall Direct*, at a tree.
**1** 95 feet. 5c. Climb the shallow groove and move up into
another shallow groove. Step right and ascend the front face of
the flake to the *Grim Wall* hand-traverse. Continue directly up the
middle of the thin slab to an easier slab. Traverse left to the
stance of *Meshach*.

**2** 75 feet. 6a. Climb up onto the block and move diagonally right with great difficulty to the obvious break in the overhang. Pull over the overhang and move diagonally left, crossing *Meshach*, to climb a thin crackline slightly leftwards to the top.

**Grim Wall**   180 feet   Very Severe                    (3.57)
A fine route with a steep top pitch. Start below the obvious chimney of *Shadrach*.
**1** 100 feet. 4b. Climb up and slightly left to gain a scoop and then go left again to a sharp flake. Hand-traverse the flake to reach a corner on the left. Ascend this and then the rib on the left to reach a ledge below the final wall.
**2** 80 feet. 4c. Climb up daigonally to the right and pull over a small overhang to gain a small ledge on the left. Traverse left to a cracked rib and climb this steeply to the top.

**Meshach**   190 feet   Hard Very Severe                (7.62)
A Tremadog favourite, with excellent climbing on the second pitch. Start below the obvious chimney of *Shadrach*.
**1** 110 feet. 4c. Climb up the slabby rake leading left to a ledge, gain a scoop above to then take the shallow groove on the right, which leads with a step right to a good ledge. Move up the wall above for a few feet to join *Shadrach*, which is followed for a few feet until it is possible to step down to the left into a small niche. Climb the wall on the left to a good spike and traverse left to a corner. Continue to the large stance in the gully, at the end of pitch 1 of *Grim Wall*.
**2** 80 feet. 5a. Climb up diagonally right and go left over the overhang to a small ledge. Step right above the overhang and ascend the wall above trending rightwards past a crucial peg. Continue to the top moving first left and then right to finish.
Variation
**Rattlesnake Finish**   70 feet   E2                    (29.8.78)
**2a** 70 feet. 5c. As for *Meshach* pitch 2 to just past its crux, climb up for 10 feet and take the thin crack diagonally up left with the crux at the top.

**Blinkers**   160 feet   E2                              (9.78)
An eliminate with a very contrived first pitch. Start as for *Shadrach*, at the obvious chimney.
**1** 85 feet. 5b. Climb straight up to a prominent overhang just left of the *Shadrach* chimney. Pull over the roof to join *Shadrach* which is followed to a belay.
**2** 75 feet. 5b. Traverse diagonally left for a few feet to a poor flake at the start of the traverse of *Meshach*. From there ascend straight up the wall above to the widest point of the roof. Pull over this using a flake crack. Climb diagonally left to cross *Meshach* and climb the final wall to finish at its highest point.

Variation
**2a** 70 feet. 5a. From the stance climb the shallow groove on the left to finish up twin cracks.

One of the best hybrid pitches on the Shadrach Buttress is to climb *Leg Break* as far as the good spike on pitch 1 of *Meshach* and then continue up pitch 2a of *Blinkers*. This gives a really good pitch at E1 5b; highly recommended.

**Shadrach**   170 feet   Very Severe                    (13.5.51)
Another good and popular climb with a tricky top pitch. Start at the obvious chimney .
**1** 60 feet. 4b. Climb up the outside, or the inside, of the chimney, all rather strenuous, to a block belay.
**2** 50 feet. 4b. Step left and climb onto a flake, then climb the wall above to a belay at the foot of a huge block.
**3** 60 feet. 4c. Climb up onto the top of the block. Climb awkwardly into the shallow groove above and after a few feet step right to finish up the wall.

**The Brothers**   190 feet   Very Severe              (9.6.57)
A companion route to *Shadrach* and just as agreeable. Start below the chimney of *Shadrach*.
**1** 90 feet. 4b. Climb the crack to the right of the chimney and then step down and ascend diagonally rightwards to a ledge and belay below an overhang at the foot of the final steep wall.
**2** 50 feet. 4b. Traverse left under the overhang and across a short groove, then climb up to the right-hand side of the huge pinnacle block of *Shadrach*.
**3** 50 feet. 4c. Climb up onto the top of the block. Climb awkwardly into the shallow groove above and after a few feet step right to finish up the wall; the third pitch of *Shadrach*.
Variations
**The Brothers Direct Finish**   70 feet   E1          (1968)
**2a** 70 feet. 5b. An interesting pitch. From the belay above pitch 1 of *The Brothers*, move right of the overhang to the foot of a crack system and climb this to an obvious undercut at an overlap. A long reach gains rounded holds and easier ground.
**The Brothers Independent Finish**   50 feet   Hard Very Severe
                                                        (9.64)
**3a** 50 feet. 5a. Step down and right off the right-hand side of the pinnacle block of *Shadrach* onto the wall itself. Climb up to a small overhang and use a slot in this to reach over to gain good holds above. Continue easily to the top.

**Oblatron**   160 feet   E3                            (5.79)
A rather contrived first pitch with a short crux providing only fleeting interest. Start as for *The Brothers*, below the wide crack.

**1** 80 feet. 5c. The arête left of *The Brothers* is climbed, moving right at the top onto a slab. Belay below an obvious overhang below the final steep wall.
**2** 80 feet. 5c. Go up and right to a flake and pull through the overhang to reach a crack, follow the crack stepping left at its end. Move up and back right to reach an overlap and a ledge above; finish easily.

**Emily Street**   150 feet   E2                                    (5.9.80)
Fairly high in the grade, the main pitch is quite bold. Start as for *The Brothers*.
**1** 60 feet. 5c. Climb up onto the slab right of the wide crack on *The Brothers* and move up into a slim groove curving rightwards and follow this to an overlap. Precarious moves right lead to another slabby groove and a move up left to belay on *The Brothers*.
**2** 70 feet. 5b. As for *The Brothers Direct Finish*.

**Carlo**   120 feet   E1                                          (1969)
Takes the line to the left of the big rectangular overhangs. Start as for *The Brothers*.
**1** 70 feet. Climb onto the slab as for *Emily Street*, step right again and tackle the bottomless chimney above to move left to belay as for *Oblatron* below an overhang
**2** 50 feet. 5b. Move up diagonally rightwards to stand on the detached block. Step off the block onto the wall behind and ascend the crack which becomes a corner at the overhang to grapple with some trees to finish.

**Sometimes**   160 feet   E3                                     (25.5.79)
A right-to-left girdle of Shadrach Buttress covering some good ground. Start as for *The Brothers Direct Finish*.
**1** 60 feet. 5b. Ascend *Brothers Direct* until level with the top of *Shadrach* pinnacle; traverse across to this.
**2** 100 feet. 6a. Follow *Shadrach* for 20 feet until level with the obvious traverse-line below the long overlap on the left; follow this to a point just before a gap in the roof. Pull up through the roof and take the diagonal crack leading leftwards into *Grim Wall Direct*. Move up 10 feet and go left into *Grim Wall* and finish up this.

## Slips Area

The next routes all start below Shadrach Buttress proper. They are reached by following the road as far as the first footbridge across the drainage channel and heading off up through the trees. Once in amongst the shrubbery look out for some mossy slabs leading up to the base of a large boulder-choked chimney. This is the initial pitch of *Nifl-Heim* as well as two obvious grooves higher up to the right which are the starts of *Venom* and *Leg/First Slips*.

**Semper Dexter Nil Sinister**   110 feet   E1 5c        (5.5.91)
Difficult to find. Start about 40 feet down and round to the left of *Bashi Bazouk* below two sets of rightward-trending overlaps. Ascend the damp corner and negotiate the first overhang on jugs to follow a rightward-trending crack and continue to the very edge of the arête, a long reach through the overhang provides the crux, moving left before this reduces the grade. A short chimney to the right of a large block leads up to the *Shadrach* area.

**Bashi Bazouk**   90 feet   E1 5b        (5.5.91)
Good climbing which starts as for pitch 2 of *Nifl-Heim*, on top of the flat ledge at the base of the shallow corner. Follow *Nifl-Heim* to the base of the easy ramp and keep on climbing the open groove until some difficult moves allow one to swing up and left onto a slab. At the top move right to a large tree, or, continue up a short prickly chimney as for *Semper Dexter...*

**Nifl-Heim**   210 feet   Very Severe        (27.9.55)
The route contains some good and varied climbing. The first pitch may well provide the crux to some. Start at an obvious chimney above the vegetated slabs.
**1** 40 feet. 4a. Climb the chimney to a large flat ledge with a large flake belay under the overhang.
**2** 60 feet. 4c. Walk left and climb a shallow corner and then a narrow ramp leading to easier ground on the right. Trend up and right to a good tree belay and a junction with *Leg Slip*.
**3** 80 feet. 5a. Climb straight up for 15 feet to a horizontal crack. Traverse horizontally left with difficulty to reach a tree and then ascend more easily to another tree belay below the final wide crack.
**4** 30 feet. 4c. Climb the crack and scramble up the slab to finish.
Variation
**2a** 40 feet. 4c. Climb the overhang just to the right of the flake belay — good moves on good holds — then continue to the tree belay.

**Pizzle Puzzle**   165 feet   E3        (5.5.91)
Very much an eliminate. Start immediately right of the obvious chimney of *Nifl-Heim*, at the base of a green wall.
**1** 105 feet. 5c. Some long reaches up the poorly protected wall allow one to move right to gain *Pretzl Logic* at the overhang. Head on up to the sloping ramp, possible belay. Climb the short wall above, just to the right of the V-chimney of *Pretzl Logic* to gain the tree at the end of the traverse on pitch 3 of *Nifl-Heim*.

**2** 60 feet. 5c. Move up vegetated slabs to finish up the crack and overhang of *Pretzl Logic*.

**Pretzl Logic**   170 feet   E2                          (7.74)
The best line up the rock between *Nifl-Heim* and *Venom*. The second pitch is now harder with the loss of a block, producing a varied and sustained outing. Start at a small groove 15 feet left of the start of *Venom*.
**1** 55 feet. 5c. Climb the groove to the overhang where difficult moves then lead up to easy slabs, go up these and then left to the tree belay of *Leg Slip*.
**2** 70 feet. 5c. Climb the steep V-chimney on the left and go up to the belay below the crack of *Nifl-Heim*.
**3** 45 feet. 5c. Step left and pull into the steep corner-crack. Climb this and the overhang above to a steep finishing crack; a gritstone style pitch.

**Venom**   180 feet   E3                          (27.4.76)
Despite being a rather contrived line it does give some steep and interesting climbing. Start at a smooth groove, up and to the right of the chimney of *Nifl-Heim*.
**1** 50 feet. 6a. High in the grade. Climb the groove with great difficulty to a small stance on the left under the roof and a junction with *Leg Slip*.
**2** 85 feet. 5b. Step left and climb straight up the steep wall. At a small overhang either make a bold move left to easier but scrappy ground or step right to continue up the wall with some good climbing and protection finally moving left to the trees. Climb up to below the wide crack of *Nifl-Heim*.
**3** 45 feet. 5c. Step left and pull into the steep corner-crack below the large rectangular overhangs. Climb this and the overhang above to a steep finishing crack as for *Pretzel Logic*.

**Timeslip**   150 feet   E3 6a                          (28.8.78)
Despite its eliminate nature the route does provides some good situations. Start as for *Venom*. Ascend the wall to the left of *Venom's* first pitch to an overlap and make some hard moves left to gain the arête and follow this to the stance of *Leg Slip*; possible belay. Climb the wall as for *Venom* but at the small

# Craig Bwlch y Moch
## Slips Area

1. Pizzle Puzzle E3
2. Nifl-Heim VS
3. Pretzl Logic E2
4. Venom E3
5. Leg Slip E1
6. First Slip E1

overhang move right to the arête, move up and step left again to finish up the final wall in a fine position.

**Certain Slip**   150 feet   E3 6a                           (1977)
An eliminate that follows *Venom* until it is possible to traverse right round the arête into *First Slip*. Climb up this and pull through the overhang and move left towards *Leg Slip*. The slab on the right is then climbed to a small overhang, which is turned on the left.

**Leg Slip**   145 feet   E1                                  (13.3.60)
A good sustained route which takes the left-hand of the two obvious groove-lines on the right edge of the buttress. Start at an obvious groove capped by a roof up and to the right of the chimney of *Nifl-Heim* and just right of *Venom*.
**1** 50 feet. 5a. Climb the groove until it is possible to escape left and reach the top right-hand end of a sloping ramp and a small stance under the roof.
**2** 95 feet. 5b. Pull through the overhang on the right to reach the obvious groove. Bridge up this until it is necessary to move right onto the rib and back left into the groove again. Climb the groove to the overhang, move left with difficulty to gain easy ground and a tree belay. Scramble up to a grassy ledge and then climb the easy-angled slab to the top.

**First Slip**   160 feet   E1                                (13.3.60)
A thin and precarious climb taking the right-hand of the two obvious grooves. Start as for *Leg Slip*.
**1** 110 feet. 5c. Climb the groove to the roof and traverse right to gain a ledge at the foot of the right-hand groove. Climb this with difficulty to a good ledge.
**2** 50 feet. 4b. Climb the flake above and then a series of ribs. Scramble up the slab to finish.
Variation
**Leg Break Finish**   70 feet   E2                           (3.68)
**2a** 70 feet. 5c. From the ledge below the right-hand groove of *First Slip* move left and go up to a crack. Follow the crack and a slab to a large overhang just right of *Leg Slip*. Move right under the overhang and bridge, with difficulty, up and to the right. Go back left under the larger overhang above and up the groove to the left with difficulty. A wall and cracked groove lead to the top. The original route stepped left using sidepulls from the upper right-hand groove of *First Slip* onto the slab.

**Freudian Slip**   190 feet   E2                             (16.7.78)
A bold little number. Start below the arête just right of the first groove on *Leg Slip*.
**1** 80 feet. 5c. Climb the arête to the foot of the thin groove of

*First Slip*. Step right to belay at a tree.
**2** 110 feet. 5b. Follow the slab behind the belay until it is possible to gain a groove on the right wall. Go up this, past a protection peg, to an easier crack, which leads to the top.

**T.I.S.**  120 feet  Hard Very Severe  ‡          (18.4.81)
A rather vegetated route which needs regular cleaning. Start to the right of the final pitch of *Freudian Slip,* below a prominent corner-crack.
**1** 60 feet. 5a. Climb the corner and layback up to a bulge, pull through the bulge to reach ledges and a tree belay.
**2** 60 feet. 4b. Follow the corner directly behind the tree to an overhang and step left to finish up slabs.

**Slip Shod**  30 feet  E1 5b          (14.5.93)
Ascends the clean-cut arête 20 feet to the right of *Freudian Slip;* poor protection.

Several routes have been made in the vegetated area to the right; **Breeze Buttress**, a rather overgrown V Diff being one of them. They are not particularly worthwhile and are only reached after an unpleasant and very painful approach.

High up in the trees to the right of the Slip climbs is a small tower split by a groove. The two climbs on this buttress start from a ledge that is best reached by abseiling from the top. This will also allow one to re-clean them.

**The Jackal**  100 feet  E1 5b  ‡          (1979)
Start just a little to the left of *Slipway*. Climb the crack and groove system up the centre of the buttress.

**Slipway**  100 feet  Hard Very Severe 5a  ‡          (3.70)
Short but interesting. Start from the grass ledge at the base of the left-hand groove. Climb directly up the groove to the top.

Down and to the right, amongst the trees, is a somewhat paler area of rock. The large boulder field beneath is witness to the huge rockfall that took place on what was once Ivy Buttress. Two routes tentatively climb the rock scar, both are desperate to reach.

**Solitaire**  100 feet  E1 5b  ‡          (1979)
Quite scary climbing which starts just left of centre of the area of rockfall. Climb up a groove, then follow crack systems to the top, with fingers crossed as much for luck as for jamming.

**Crazy Diamond**  100 feet  E1 5b  ‡          (1979)
Another frightening route, slowly losing its patina of looseness.

Start at the lowest point of the rock near the middle of the buttress. Ascend, with trepidation, the shallow groove in the centre of the buttress.

## Oakover Buttress

A rather forgotten area, with its top just jutting above the trees, up and to the left of Merlin Buttress. Dominated by the *Oakover* slab, this section of cliff is gained by ascending the usual descent hereabouts, namely that of Belshazzar Gully. Follow the gully to about one third of the way up and fork off to the left to gain the base of the obvious slab.

**Knell for a Jackdaw**    150 feet    Severe    (5.6.55)
A poor climb with an interesting first pitch up the small buttress immediately left of the *Oakover* slab. Start at the left end of the ledge at the foot of a groove and overlooking the huge rockfall.
**1** 60 feet. Climb the groove, trending right in the upper part, and make an awkward layback to finish.
**2** 30 feet. Step up left into the corner with large blocks and ascend to the trees above; escape possible.
**3** 20 feet. Follow the buttress edge on the right to a tree belay.
**4** 40 feet. Climb the crack to finish.

**Hedera**    130 feet    Hard Very Severe    (31.3.64)
A good route, although sometimes affected by seepage. To the right of *Knell for a Jackdaw* is a large slab bounded on its left by a curving corner. Start at the foot of the large right-facing corner.
**1** 40 feet. 4b. Climb the awkward corner crack to a tree belay.
2 90 feet. 5a. Climb the corner, past a small tree, to the overhang. Move right for a few feet and continue up the crack to the top.

**Oakover**    180 feet    Very Severe    (5.6.55)
A good and varied route which breaks out of the corner onto the slab. Start at the foot of the corner, as for *Hedera*.
**1** 40 feet. 4b. Take the first pitch of *Hedera*.
**2** 100 feet. 4c. Traverse out right onto the slab and go up with difficulty to a ledge. Continue rightwards and up with some hard moves to gain a ledge below the prominent oak tree. Move into the groove on the right and go up through the trees.
**3** 40 feet. 4b. Ascend the crack to the top.

**Bloodsucker**    150 feet    E2 5c    (Spring 78)
Start just right of *Oakover* at the base of the slab. Ascend the slab direct on good positive holds until the base of a narrow ramp-line leading leftwards is reached. Follow this with increasing difficulty until a long reach can be made into the wide crack

of *Hedera*. Step up through the overhang into the upper groove system (vegetated) and follow this to the top, or layback up rightwards to finish as for *Heartline*.

**Heartline**   170 feet   E3                                    (27.8.78)
A bold route with some excellent climbing. Start below and left of the right-hand arête of the *Oakover* slab.
**1** 120 feet. 5c. Climb up right to the rounded edge of the slab, move up — without the use of the tree — until it is possible to make some difficult moves diagonally left on small flaky holds. Go up again to reach the base of a shallow dark ramp-line leading leftwards, step right and continue direct on spaced holds to the base of an obvious corner. Belay on the large oak in the corner.
**2** 50 feet. Scramble up the blocks behind the trees to reach the top.

**Axeminster**   120 feet   Hard Severe   ‡            (15.4.68)
A rather scrappy climb up the groove system on the right-hand side of the *Oakover* slab. Start at the foot of a flake crack below a leaning corner.
**1** 30 feet. Climb the easy flake-crack for 15 feet to a tree, traverse right and climb a crack to a ledge on the edge of Belshazzar Gully.
**2** 60 feet. 4a. Ascend the slab above and make an awkward move into a groove. Climb the crack on the right until it is possible to move back left to a tree belay.
**3** 30 feet. Climb the groove easily to the top.
Variation
**1a** 90 feet. The leaning corner can be climbed to link either with *Oakover* or to trend rightwards to rejoin *Axeminster*.

Up to the right of *Axeminster* is the upper section of this buttress, this continuation forms the upper left wall of Belshazzar Gully.

**Föhn**   80 feet   Hard Severe 4b                    (26.5.79)
A good start leads to rather broken rock, large tackle protects. Start about 100 feet down Belshazzar Gully below the front edge, or 'prow', of this small buttress. Grapple with the steep crack snaking up the front end of the 'prow' and take another crack to a large ledge. Climb the short wall to finish.

**Chinook**   100 feet   Hard Severe 4c               (25.3.64)
Once again an entertaining start; the lower down you begin, the harder it is. Start at a crack in the steep wall to the right of the 'prow'. Take the overhanging crack to a small tree and then the short corner on the right to another tree. Clamber up the edge to finish.

# Merlin Buttress

This is the closest buttress to the road. The start of *Belshazzar* can be found in the dank bay on the left. After the slabby arête comes a clean wall, to the right of which is an area of rockfall above a large slab. The start of *Merlin* itself and the diamond-shaped *Geireagle* wall are right again, with the slab of *Oberon* below.

**Down to Earth**   90 feet   E2                                    (10.94)
A filler-in with one hard move. Start just left of *Belshazzar* behind the tree at the left edge of the green wall.
**1** 40 feet 4a. Follow the groove, rib and slab above to the large tree belay on *Belshazzar*.
**2** 50 feet. 5c. Step left and head for the obvious thin crack, via a long reach for a flake crack; thread. Interesting moves lead to a good hold; entering the short groove above proves to be the crux. Head up to some trees level with the steps in Belshazzar Gully. Scramble across to the steps when finished.

**Re-entry**   110 feet   E2                                        (7.81)
The rather fingery but well-protected first pitch can often be damp and so may seem a touch hard for the grade. Start below the green wall to the left of the initial cleft of *Belshazzar*.
**1** 40 feet. 5c. Ascend the steep wall, via some diagonal cracks, moving left near the top to a ledge and a tree belay.
**2** 70 feet. 5a. Above is a small overhang; surmount this and move right to a ledge. Go left to gain, then climb, a short curving corner crack until it is possible to follow the arête.

**Belshazzar**   215 feet   Hard Very Severe                       (23.7.51)
After a usually dank start the climb improves to give some good situations. Start at the foot of a crack in the secluded bay just to the right of the foot of Belshazzar Gully.
**1** 45 feet. 4c. Climb the crack and layback through the bulge to a ledge and a tree belay; fairly strenuous.
**2** 120 feet. 5a. Traverse right for a few feet and ascend the wall to a ledge. From the right-hand end of the ledge climb a slab and then move round the rib to a groove. Climb this to a ledge on the rib. Move onto the face on the right and traverse across this into the corner of *Rienetta*. The wall direct is 5b.
**3** 50 feet. 4b. Climb the corner and crack above, moving left to finish.

Unfortunately, just to the right of *Belshazzar*, there has been a significant amount of rock movement. At the bottom of the cliff huge blocks have slid down and away from the rest of the face, making the start of one long-forgotten route a much harder and potentially lethal undertaking. The route in question was called *Cam Fawr*. Additionally, a little further to the right, blocks have also 'fallen out' below the next route, namely *Earthsea*. If you have any doubt about this line do not climb it.

To the right of the rockfall the crag forms a big recess. The left wall of this recess contains a number of interconnecting pitches. The following routes probably offer the most rational combinations, but they can be varied at will. An obvious feature is the slabby ramp which cuts the wall diagonally from left to right.

**Earthsea**  140 feet  Hard Very Severe  ††        (7.2.78)
A rather contrived route. Start at a large tree below the slabby ramp.
**1** 80 feet. 5a. Scramble up onto the ramp. The steep wall on the left is split by two grooves, the second of which contains a tree. Follow the first groove, step left and move back right to gain easier ground. Climb up and right to gain a diagonal crack in the steep wall. This leads to a large ledge with belays well back.
**2** 60 feet. 4a. Move right and follow the edge of the steep wall to the top, or scramble up the easy slabs.

**Daddy Cool**  130 feet  E2        (15.1.78)
An intricate route, one of the best hereabouts. Start by scrambling up the ramp to the tree in the second groove, there is no ledge at the tree so roping up might be awkward for some.
**1** 65 feet. 5c. Move up the ramp for a few feet and step back left onto a pedestal below the obvious diagonal crack. Climb up past the crack to the overhang, pull over this and then go back left to the large stance of *Earthsea*. Either finish up *Earthsea* or continue by:
**2** 35 feet. 5a. Move up and right onto the steep wall and follow the obvious traverse line into the corner, as for *Belshazzar*.
**3** 30 feet. 5c. Ascend the steep, clean corner just left of the finish of *Rienetta*, as for *The Sting*.

**Salamanda**  160 feet  Hard Very Severe        (24.1.78)
A good top pitch. Start at the foot of the blunt rib that leads up to the slabby ramp.
**1** 90 feet. 4c. Climb the rib and then follow the ramp to where it ends at a tower with block belays. A poorly protected pitch.
**2** 70 feet. 5a. Climb straight above the block, past a small overhang, to a narrow ledge. Continue directly up the wall to finish by a steep crack.

**The Sting**  140 feet  E2        (5.1.78)
A hard corner on the second pitch gives a cracking finish. Start beneath the slabby ramp.

# Craig Bwlch y Moch Merlin Buttress

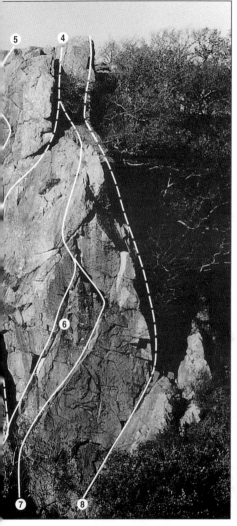

1. Belshazzar HVS
2. Daddy Cool E2
3. Salamanda HVS
4. Merlin VS
5. Merlin Direct
Finish HVS
6. Vulture E4
7. Geireagle E3
8. Y Broga HVS

**1** 75 feet. 4a. Climb the corner-crack of the slabby ramp to the stance at the top of pitch 1 of *Salamanda* or climb pitch 1 of *Salamanda*.

**2** 65 feet. 5c. Move across to the ledge in the corner on the right below an overhang. Climb left into the groove with difficulty and go up this to a ledge below the clean-cut yellow corner just left of *Rienetta's* top pitch. Climb the corner to finish.

**Heartbreak Hotel**   150 feet   Hard Severe        (24.1.78)
A poor route. Start at the base of the recess and climb the angle of the recess to belay at 100 feet to finish up the last pitch of *Rienetta*.

**Rienetta**   200 feet   Hard Severe   ††        (8.3.52)
Not a very good route; it has been much affected by rockfall. Though not quite the same as the original line, it still tackles the large open corner in the centre of Merlin Buttress. Start at a chimney just to the right of the foot of the spur which comes down close to the road.
**1** 40 feet. Climb the chimney to a recess and move left to a tree belay.
**2** 80 feet. Climb the easy slabs trending right to the flake belay of *Merlin*.
**3** 30 feet. Traverse left across a corner and move out to a crack, which leads to a belay. Care is required with loose rock on this pitch.
**4** 50 feet. Ascend the corner and crack above, moving left to finish.

**Dragon**   170 feet   E2        (4.10.74)
A very hard corner-crack on the second pitch is the main feature of this route. Start 10 feet to the left of and below the broken blocks at the start of *Merlin*.
**1** 90 feet. 4b. Climb diagonally left over the arête and into the bottomless chimney. Ascend the chimney to the roof, step left and go up easily to the large flake belays of *Merlin*.
**2** 80 feet. 6b. Move up and left into the overhanging corner; a desperate move up the crack gains the ledge. Move up and left as for *Merlin Direct* to finish straight up the slabby wall.

**Merlin**   160 feet   Very Severe        (15.4.56)
A good climb — steep and open. Start to the left of the prominent *Oberon* slab, by a pile of blocks below a steep groove capped by an overhang. The route originally took the groove throughout, the bottom of which is now 6a.
**1** 80 feet. 5a. Step up leftwards and then go back up right to reach two cracks leading diagonally rightwards into the groove; the upper crack is easier at 4c. Climb the groove above until it is

possible to pull out left beneath the overhang, trend left across the slab to belay below the steep wall at some 'hollow' flakes.

**2** 60 feet. 4b. Difficult moves up the slab gain the obvious crack above. Clamber up this to a step right onto the wall, then go up to a ledge. Traverse the slab on the right into a groove and follow this to a belay.

**3** 20 feet. 4a. Climb the steep corner above to finish.

Variation

**Merlin Direct Finish**   80 feet   Hard Very Severe   (1959)
A superb airy pitch, the top moves of which still see a fair number of wobblers.

**2a** 80 feet. 5a. Climb the slab and crack as for the original pitch, but traverse left and go up to gain another crack. Where this gets difficult, arrange protection and move left once again to gain a further crack and ascend this via a couple of long reaches to the finishing moves.

**Vulture**   100 feet   E4   (5.5.75)
A sustained and strenuous crack climb involving some very precarious laybacking and a technical finish. Start as for *Merlin*, at the base of a vertical groove, which has been affected by rockfall.

**1** 80 feet. 6a. Climb the groove direct or take the easier *Merlin* start to gain the ramp-line of *Geireagle*. Step right onto the ramp and take the steep layback crack above the ramp. This leads to a triangular niche and then a junction with *Geireagle*. Move left to the arête and ascend the overlap onto a slab below the final corner of *Merlin*.

**2** 20 feet. 4a. Climb the corner to finish.

Variation

**Vulture Direct**   100 feet   E4 6a   (19.9.82)
**1a** A vicious continuation. Follow *Vulture* to where it joins *Geireagle* and continue up the obvious crack above and left of the ledge on *Geireagle*.

**Geireagle**   130 feet   E3   (27.2.66)
A steep, sustained and fingery climb. Start below the vertical groove of *Merlin* — the scene of a rockfall.

**1** 110 feet. 5c. Either climb the groove direct (6a) or follow the present route of *Merlin* to the base of an obvious ramp-line crossing the wall on the right. Follow the ramp-line to its end and make some hard moves up to a good ledge. Move up left and make a long reach to the arête. Climb the overlap onto a slab, and take a stance below the final corner of *Merlin*.

**2** 20 feet. 4a. Climb the corner above to finish.

**Y Broga**   140 feet   Hard Very Severe   (5.62)
An interesting little route with a smooth and difficult first pitch.

Start just to the right of the blocks of *Merlin*, at the corner formed on the left side of the obvious slab.

**1** 50 feet. 5a. Ascend the corner to a big ledge, a large selection of big protection devices is rather useful, as are a variety of unusual climbing techniques.

**2** 60 feet. 4b. Climb the steep wall on the left to a small ledge and continue up to another ledge, from which a groove leads to a tree belay.

**3** 30 feet. 4c. Go up the slab for 10 feet and then step onto the arête and finish up this.

Variation

**O Brother**   60 feet   Very Severe                    (16.6.96)

**2a** 60 feet. 4b. Ascend the crack to the right of the original route.

**What's in a Name?**   140 feet   E3

A very slight route, which just about manages to cover enough new ground. Start as for *Y Broga*.

**1** 50 feet. 5a. Climb the initial slabby corner of *Y Broga*.

**2** 60 feet. 5c Move up a few feet until a swing out onto the wall on the left allows one to gain the ledge of *Geireagle*. Climb the groove above to regain *Y Broga* and follow this to the tree stance.

**3** 30 feet. 4c. As for pitch 3 of *Y Broga*.

**Oberon**   170 feet   Severe                    (11.55)

A worthwhile climb, particularly for beginners. The grade is upped for the, now, very polished first pitch. Start at the foot of the slab, just left of centre.

**1** 50 feet. Climb up and go across to the right edge of the slab, then move back left to the centre to reach the top of the slab. Belay at the foot of a chimney.

**2** 60 feet. Ascend the overhanging chimney above and then follow a continuation which leads to an easy slab and a large tree belay.

**3** 60 feet. Ascend the corner behind the tree to the foot of a steep crack and finish up this.

Variation   110 feet   Hard Severe                    (1955)

Not actually a variation; this is, in fact, the original line of *Oberon*.

**2a** 90 feet. Scale the initial chimney and from its continuation, make a high step left and traverse out to the edge and a slab on front face of the buttress. Belay below a steep corner.

**3a** 20 feet. Finish up the short, but steep, top corner of *Merlin*.

A short route was seemingly climbed up the wall to the left of the top corner of *Trivial Pursuits*. A peg was in place but is now gone.

Pete Robins tackling the fine
jamming pitch of *Neb Direct* E3,
Craig Bwlch y Moch.
Photo: David Simmonite

Pete Robinson climbing *Micah Eliminate* Hard Severe, Craig Bwlch y Moch.
Photo: Carl Ryan

Louise Yin climbing the
classic *One Step in the
Clouds* VS, Craig Bwlch y
Moch.
Photo: Carl Ryan

Airlie Anderson on Cream
E4, Craig Bwlch y Moch.
Photo: David Simmonite

**Trivial Pursuits**   40 feet   E3 6a                                (1994)
Sustained climbing taking the thin crack in the steep wall left of
the final corner of *Oberon*. Start at its base, step left into the
crack and follow it diagonally right to the base of a groove. Enter
the groove and finish by a swing out left at the top.

**Emotional Crisis**   50 feet   E4 5c                               (4.83)
A rather bold offering taking the obvious arête to the right of the
final pitch of *Oberon*. Start right of *Oberon's* second stance. Two
possible starting options lead to a crux bulge at about 15 feet,
pass this and swarm up the arête direct; don't bother to stop for
gear.

Level with the top pitch of *Oberon* and just to the right is a very
small buttress. Apparently this is the location of a short climb of
about V Diff in standard.

Very near to the old road, on the underside of the *Oberon* slab,
is a short, clean bouldering wall containing an obvious crack
slanting up from left to right.

## Boo-Boo Buttress

To the right of Merlin Buttress, level with a roadside sign, is an
area of vegetated slabs which were once known as the Far
Eastern Slabs. These can be climbed almost anywhere at up to
about Diff in standard and give a good introduction to beginners.
A crack on the right-hand side gives probably the best line.
Continue a little further along the old road and this will bring you
to a path leading up to the starts of the next few routes.

**Boo-Boo**   200 feet   Very Difficult                          (24.3.61)
A pleasant little climb, the only one really worth doing on these
slabs. The route takes the arête on the right-hand side of the
slabs. Start at the foot of the arête.
**1** 50 feet. Step round the arête to the foot of a steep corner.
Climb the corner-crack to a tree belay.
**2** 50 feet. Scale the corner behind the tree to the overhang. Pull
round to the right onto the slabs above. Continue up these to a
large ledge.
**3** 100 feet. Climb the crack behind the large detached pinnacle
and make a difficult step off this onto the slabs above and ascend
these to finish.

From the foot of the arête of *Boo-Boo* scramble up and right for
about 50 feet to reach the base of a steep wall. The first of the
variation routes starts about 20 feet to the left of the obvious overhanging chimney, which provides the start of both *Starship Trooper*
and *Hot Rats*.

**Starship Trooper**  90 feet  E4 5c                    (29.4.78)
A very bold route with some spaced and poor protection. Start
about 50 feet up and right of *Boo-Boo*, beneath an overhanging
crack leading up to a ledge. Climb up into the crack and move
left onto a small ledge. Move up leftwards from the small ledge to
reach a loose flake runner and a wire out to the left. It is then
possible to step right to clip a poor *RURP* peg under the overhang. Continue up the wall above the flake to reach sloping
ledges. Shake your way up and then right to a groove, which
leads to a slab to finish.
Variations
Although both of the following routes were claimed as being
independent they are in fact alternative starts to *Starship Trooper*.
**Tweek**  100 feet  E4 6a                            (27.8.80)
Quite technical; start below a short corner to the left of the
overhanging chimney. Ascend the corner with difficulty until a
traverse rightwards can be made into *Starship Trooper*.
**Rock on Tommy**  100 feet  E4 6a                     (6.6.80)
Rather enigmatic. Start below the obvious ramp-line a little to the
right of the above route. Follow the ramp and move left to reach
a good flake layaway, climb this and finish as for *Starship
Trooper*.

**Hot Rats**  100 feet  E4 6a                         (24.7.78)
Intricate and interesting climbing but again with poor protection.
Start as for *Starship Trooper*. Climb up into the crack and exit left
to a small ledge. Climb the steep wall for 10 feet and traverse
right on positive holds to a good ledge below the overhang.
Swing round to the right of the overhang and climb the wall and
arête with difficulty to a large ledge. Move left to climb the thin
crack and overhanging corner to the top.

Further to the right is a very confused area of vegetation and rock.
The original route in this section of cliff was *Savage Man*.

## Savage Man Sector
This area is best gained by heading for the blocks below *Yogi*, then
skirting down and left and then back up below the base of the slabs
to reach a short clean wall with an obvious ramp-line; the start of
*Geronimo*.

**Marino**  180 feet  Very Severe  ‡                   (6.5.83)
A rather disjointed and arboreal line up the buttress left of
*Savage Man*. Start below a vegetated overhanging corner-crack
left of the clean wall of *Geronimo*.
**1** 70 feet. 4b. Go up to the corner and climb it, exiting left at the
top. Continue up an arête to belay on a huge block

**2** 50 feet. 4b. Step off the block to the right and climb a crack to a large ledge; a ramp-line then leads to a tree belay.
**3** 60 feet. 4b. Traverse right to an arête below a small overhang, then gain a chimney which is followed to the finish.

**Geronimo** 170 feet E1 ‡ (25.7.83)
This route has an interesting start, however, suspect rock and vegetation detract somewhat. Start at the base of a clean wall with an obvious narrow ramp leading up rightwards.
**1** 70 feet. 5b. Gain the base of the narrow, slanting gangway. Very precarious moves lead to a thin crack leading up the wall. Follow the crack to a tree belay.
**2** 40 feet. 4c. Move up and step right to a small corner, go right again on good holds to reach a large ledge.
**3** 60 feet. 4c. Tackle the chimney, swinging out to the right near the top and follow easy ledges to finish.

**Savage Man** 60 feet E4 6a (1979)
A strenuous and rather friable route best gained by abseil so that an inspection can be made as to the state of the rock. Start on an ivy-covered ledge at the base of a white wall, to the right of the obvious chimney, the final pitch of *Geronimo*. Go straight up via small cracks, difficult moves up and left lead to a crack. This leads diagonally back up to the right to gain a niche; finish up blocks.

Below and to the right of *Geronimo*, to the left of the huge overhangs of *Gwaed*, is an area of slabbier rock. In some places the vegetation is quite profuse and this makes it a suitable site for budding botanists to brush up on their science. The slabs are best gained by dropping back down from the bower at the foot of *Chwys* and skirting left along the bottom of the slabs below the huge overhangs of *Gwaed*.

**Borneo** 150 feet Hard Severe ‡ (26.2.84)
A rather aptly named route, with the rock hidden under vegetation — it improves little with height. Start at the foot of the wide overgrown ramp-line just right of *Geronimo*.
**1** 40 feet. Climb easily up the ramp-line to reach a ledge and tree belay to the right.
**2** 110 feet. 4b. Move up the right-hand side of the ramp, then go over to the left for 20 feet to set up protection and finish up a chimney. Take care with some of the blocks on this pitch.

**Omo** 140 feet Hard Severe 4a ‡ (14.6.86)
Very vegetated; it scales the left-hand side of the slabs to the right of the overgrown ramp-line. Start up and left of the mossy V-recess. Climb up the left-hand side of the slabs to reach a short

corner at a bulge. Move up to the left past an overlap and climb slabs to reach the top.

**Cnychwyr**   140 feet   Very Severe                         (6.5.85)
A greasy start leads to a clean, steep finish. Start at the base of a rib leading up to thin cracks, just left of a large tree at a mossy V-recess.
**1** 70 feet. 4b. Follow the crack system up the slab, keeping to the left of a heathery cleft and reach a stance and belay above an oak tree.
**2** 70 feet. 4c. Continue in the same vein to gain a rightward-trending crack. Above is a steep wall. Go right beneath this to some cracks, move out leftwards across the steep wall to reach a small groove with a ledge above and then take the wall direct.

**Tree Radical**   80 feet   Hard Very Severe 5b        (28.8.97)
A filler-in; at least a grade easier if a lunge for the obvious branch is made. Start at the tree belay of *Cnychwyr*. Climb the slab above to gain a short, white wall with a small, triangular overhang near its centre (top). Move up left of this overhang, past a tree, to reach the base of a groove. Step left into another groove to avoid loose-looking blocks and finish up this.

**Rio**   140 feet   Hard Severe                             (6.4.84)
A clean upper section makes up for the start. Start down left of the huge overhangs of *Gwaed*, behind a large tree at a mossy V-recess in the base of the cliff.
**1** 60 feet. 4a. Move up right across the mossy slab to the right-hand end of a short wall, scale this and go up and follow the heathery cleft to a tree.
**2** 80 feet. 4a. Continue up slabs to reach a wall, as for *Cnychwyr*, and follow a diagonal line up and right skirting the steepest section of rock to gain a wide crack. Ascend the crack, finishing just to the right of a perched block.

A little further along the old road, above some huge boulders, is an area of slabs, ribs and wall. These are the last gasps of the Bwlch y Moch crags and are based around the rib of *Yogi*.

## Yogi Area
The first routes are to be found by taking a narrow path through the left-hand side of the boulders to a fairly flat bower below an obvious groove system and a rectangular double overhang halfway up an area of slabs. The groove system is the location of *Chwys*, whilst the double roof is part of *Gwaed*.

**Gwaed**   130 feet   E1                                    (25.1.81)
An entertaining route; the difficulties are short but commitment is
still required. Start at a tree at the base of a crack leading up to
the huge overhang 20 feet left and 15 feet above the start of
*Chwys.*
**1** 80 feet. 5b. Climb the short jam crack to a slab and follow the
thin crack to the first roof. Difficult moves over the initial overlap
allow precarious progress to be made into a hunched bridging
position. The confident will launch out left around the rib, a semi-
mantel will, hopefully, allow some jugs to come to hand. Move to
slabs and belay at a ledge above.
**2** 50 feet. 4c. Ascend the delightful flake line on the left-hand
side of the upper slab to reach trees.

**Placebo**   120 feet   E3 5c                              (1985)
If not verging on, then at least climbing, the ridiculous. Originally
ascended following an old description of *Penicillin*. Start as for
*Gwaed* and go up right to climb the arête left of *Chwys*, then step
left to pull through the double overhang, via a large 'hollow'
flake. This gains the crux ramp of *Chwys*. However, do not follow
the ramp but pull through the overhang above as close to the
arête as possible. Finish up the slabs.

**Penicillin**   120 feet   E3 6b                          (3.80)
An eliminate line with some very technical climbing. Start as for
*Gwaed*. Climb the arête left of *Chwys* to step right below the
base of the ramp on *Chwys* and ascend the overhanging wall on
the right, with quite some difficulty, to reach a groove. Entering
the groove is also problematic. Finish up the slabs.

**Chwys**   130 feet   E1                                   (29.4.67)
A good and sustained first pitch. Start at the foot of a broken
groove 30 feet left of the polished arête of *Yogi*.
**1** 80 feet. 5b. Climb up easily to the foot of a smooth, shallow
groove. Follow this and climb over the bulge and move left onto
the steep wall. Move up and then climb diagonally left up to the
steep ramp and over the overhang at its end. Continue to a grass
ledge and belay.
**2** 50 feet. 4a. Finish directly up the pleasant slabs.

**Sheer Kahn**   100 feet   Hard Very Severe 5a  ‡    (6.80)
A rather nondescript climb. Start about 20 feet left of the arête of
*Yogi* at the base of a slabby rib below a large, vegetated corner.
Follow the corner to the top with a couple of excursions out to the
right.

**Sheer Resist**   50 feet   E4 6b                         (29.5.82)
A good, short testpiece which climbs the left wall of the large

corner. Start about halfway up the corner of *Sheer Kahn*. Traverse out left onto the wall, then go up rightwards to reach a steep crack. Some stiff moves up the crack may allow one to attain a hard exit out and to the left at the top.

By following the path from the old road to the right of the huge boulders one can quickly gain the base of the polished arête of *Yogi*. A good spot from which to locate the other routes in this vicinity.

### Smarter than the Average Bear   125 feet   Very Severe
(26.3.88)

An oft-climbed and claimed route. Starting directly under the tree brings the grade for pitch 1 down to 4a. Start as for *Yogi*.
**1** 50 feet. 4c. Ascend the thin crackline left of the arête and continue directly through the bulge just to the right of the tree. Go up to belay as for *Yogi*.
**2** 75 feet. 4c. Clamber up vegetated ledges to the slab just left of a diagonal layback crack, finish up the slab or take the crystal crack.

### Yogi   120 feet   Very Severe
(24.3.61)

Still a good little climb, despite the polish. Although low in the grade, the apparent lack of protection or even just a touch of dampness may make it seem harder. Start at the clean arête behind and to the right of the huge block by the old road.
**1** 50 feet. 4a. Climb the steep, lower section of the arête on the right for 10 feet and pull round left onto the slabs and the thin crack. Move back right towards the arête and climb straight up to reach blocks and a large ledge above.
**2** 70 feet. Regain the rib and continue for 30 feet to where a step left can be made onto a small grass ledge at the foot of the final clean slab. Ascend the right-hand side of the slab to the top of the cliff
Variation
**2a** 70 feet. 4b. Trend left up ledges to reach the base of a slanting layback crack — the crystal-filled fissure — leading back up to the right. Delightful moves up this feature lead to the top.

### Mr. Ranger   120 feet   Hard Severe
(1964)

Another regular in the new routes book. Start just round and to the right of the arête of *Yogi*.
**1** 50 feet. Ascend the vegetated slabs to a small block, move left to gain a crack and follow this to the stance on *Yogi*.
**2** 70 feet. Climb the rib and slab above as for *Yogi*.

To the right is a final, slim tower of clean rock with an obvious overhang at half height. This is the last gasp of the Bwlch y

Moch cliffs before the vegetation totally closes in. The routes are gained by walking about 13 yards right from the foot of *Yogi* to a small bower at the base of a clean-cut corner.

**Tro**   80 feet   Hard Severe 4a                                    (12.12.60)
The easiest way up this section of cliff on good steep rock. Start below a clean-cut, rightward-facing corner at the base of the tower. Ascend the corner to a ledge and move up left to reach broken ground. Follow this to the wide crack and take this to the top.

**Dagrau**   80 feet   E1 5b                                    (4.4.83)
A good little route on which to end a day; small wires protect the crux. Start below a clean-cut, rightward-facing corner at the base of the tower. Ascend the corner to a ledge, step right to a thin crack and follow this to a sentry-box niche in the overhang. A couple of difficult moves allow some jugs and better protection to come to hand; stepping right at the overhang brings the grade down. Finish up the right-hand side of the wall.

**Llafur**   85 feet   E1 5b                                    (4.96)
Very much an eliminate splitting the two previous lines. Start just down and right of *Dagrau* at the base of a short corner. Scale the corner to a jug and a thin crack leading up to a vegetated ledge, step left and ascend the next corner. Move back right to gain the foot of a short crack, left of the obvious niche. Attain the jutting block above and follow the wall just right of the wide crack of *Tro* to gain a bower.

# Moel y Gest

The hill of Moel y Gest stands above Porthmadog, it forms a narrow rocky ridge, with two distinct summits. The higher summit is at the western end. The north flank has been quarried and provides some steep and serious routes. The south flank is made up of several buttresses, with many fairly amenable routes. It is hoped that this venue is not to be overrun by outdoor establishments as has happened with some areas in this guide.

## The South Flank

Most of the routes on the south side were climbed in the early 50s and were sadly omitted from previous CC guidebooks. As the Tremadog cliffs do not really lend themselves to easier grade routes it is hoped that the inclusion of Moel y Gest will offer those who prefer their climbing less 'extreme', an alternative venue. Also, there are many opportunities for bouldering on this sunny flank.

# MOEL Y GEST

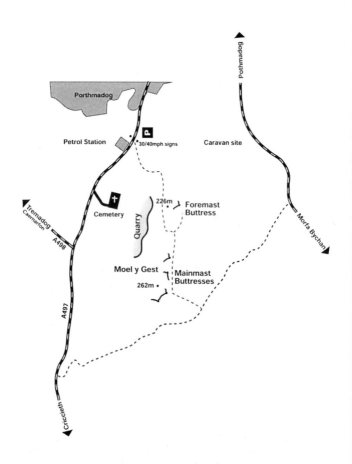

All the early route names have a nautical bent, derived from the original pioneer's likening of the south flank to a massive sailing ship, with the bow pointing eastward. Therefore, the eastern summit becomes the Foremast and the western hill, where the main climbs are situated, the Mainmast. The routes are described starting with Foremast and working from for'ard aft (westward for those who haven't found their sea legs) or from right to left, for those who don't know their compass directions.

Access to the south side is best gained by following the footpath leading up from the A497 Porthmadog to Criccieth road. One can park at a small lay-by near the 30/40 mph signs. Follow the path past an old quarry to a stile, go up to a col then turn right. After a second stile, head for the western summit of Moel y Gest, then drop down to a col, drop down again to a stone wall on the southern flank, the cliffs of Mainmast are to be seen on the right, the rocks of Foremast on the left. Allow half an hour for the approach.

## Foremast Buttress

OS Ref. 557 386

After dropping down to the stone wall, contour round left (east) to locate the cliff, then head for its base.

**Forestay**   120 feet   Very Difficult   (1945-50)
A fairly varied route; start below a heathery wall which provides a warming up pitch. About 30 feet above, the toe of the ridge comes down. An easy slab leads to a ledge, climb straight up to a mantelshelf which is followed by an 8-foot crack to a large nook. Step out to the left on a cracked slab and go up to a narrow ledge, from where a short vertical chimney leads to the sharp crest of the arête, finish up this.

**Bulwark Slab**   130 feet   Very Difficult   (1945-50)
A delicate introduction to slabs. Start on the right of the start of *Forestay* and 20 feet lower. The slab rises under the east wall of the ridge. Fairly easy climbing up a smooth slab to the large flat break under the wall of *Forestay* is followed by a delicate slab. Scramble left on the crest above to reach a belay.

**Cutlass**   75 feet   Very Difficult   (1945-50)
Good climbing; start on the left of *Forestay* and 30 feet above its foot. There is a smooth blade of rock rising out of thorny bushes. Climb the blade to a vertical pillar. Ascend the pillar on good holds, to a niche, then make an exit on the right and traverse left above the niche to reach a belay.

**Binnacle Pinnacle**   75 feet   Difficult   (1945-50)
Steeper than it looks. Start about 100 feet left of *Forestay* and 30 feet above its foot, at a steep slab with a slanting ledge on its

right. Go up the slanting ledge and step left onto the steep slab
and follow this to a ledge. The right-hand of the two cracks is
climbed to a nook followed by a step right onto the little wall to
finish on good holds.

To reach Mainmast Hill contour round Foremast Hill to the left.

**The Gun Turret**   50 feet   Severe                    (1945-50)
A good little buttress, about 100 feet above the stone wall. Start
at the lowest point of the steep tower. Step up to the left then
mantelshelf on to a ledge below the nose. Climb up to an
insecure boulder, move round on the right and go up a thin slab
to the top.

The col divides the two 'masts', many short climbs can be done
here. The area of rock after the col is the start of Mainmast; the
routes are described from right to left; i.e. as one approaches them.

## Mainmast Buttress                           OS Ref 554 388

A stone wall can be seen running along the foot of the Mainmast
buttresses. The first area of rock is in three sections and is rather
overgrown at its far left-hand end. At its right-hand end there is a
rather wandering route.

**Bulkhead Route**   85 feet of climbing   Difficult   (1945-50)
Rather rambly; start at some detached flakes a few feet above the
stone wall. Move up steeply on good holds, first left, then right for
35 feet. Traverse left at the top to belay. Easy scrambling up the
slabs above for 100 feet brings one to Scupper Crack (30 feet).
Step into the crack from the left, it proves harder than it looks.
Straight above is a short wall, Scupper Wall (20 feet), ascend
this wall to the top.

The slabs to the left are the location of the next couple of routes,
both start near the pale section of rock covered with white lichen.

**Fflat Huw Puw**   50 feet   VS 5a                      (14.6.99)
Short but surprisingly good climbing. Start just right of the pale
area of rock and take the crack slanting up right. Continue by
following its vertical continuation.

**Mynd i Forio**   50 feet   VS 5a                       (14.6.99)
A pleasant enough climb; start just left of the pale area of rock
below a triangular niche. Climb past blocks to layback onto the
slab, head for and mantel into the niche; an easy crack leads to
the top.

**Avast Behind**   80 feet   Hard Severe 4b          (28.7.99)
Good climbing which eases off in the upper half. Start below a
vertical crack leading up to a shallow groove. Climb the wall left
of the crack until it is possible to swing right and gain the base of
the groove. Step up into the groove and climb this to easy
ground; scramble up to reach good belays.

**Sea Fever**   80 feet   Hard Very Severe 4c          (28.8.99)
Start at the bottom of *Avast Behind* and make a rising traverse left
of some overhangs to a good fang. Go up to a ledge below a
forked crack (first good gear). Climb to the right of the crack to
the top; belays well back.

**Yellow Fever**   80 feet   Very Severe 4c          (28.8.99)
Start 12 feet left of the previous two routes. Climb up on small
holds to an earthy ledge below a short corner. Climb the corner,
exiting right, and continue up on rounded holds to the top; belays
well back.

The next routes climb the slim recessed area to the left.

**Shiver Me Timbers**   90 feet   E2 5c          (28.7.99)
Ascends the shallow groove system to the right of the corner;
quite high in the grade due to the flaky nature of the rock. Start at
the right-hand side of the recess. Ascend the groove to a small
overlap, move left then back up diagonally right to reach easier
angled rock. Follow the continuation groove to a grassy bay;
finish up the slabs to the right of the corner.

The central buttress is rather broken and vegetated. However, it is
certain that routes will be climbed therein the future.

The left-hand section is made of good rock once again. However, a
large ledge at about 50 feet detracts somewhat, as the climbing
above is easier.

**Oh Captain, My Captain!**   110 feet   E1 5b          (22.5.99)
It may be slightly harder for the short. Start atop a large projecting flake, ascend the pillar just left of a corner and go past
hollow flakes to trend leftwards to an awkward pull onto a
heathery ledge. Climb the wall just right of the thin vertical crack,
above the ledge, scrambling remains.

**Antur Madog**   110 feet   E1 5b          (22.5.99)
This route looks much harder than it is. Start at a squarish block
and climb the shallow groove to gain a downward pointing
spike, use this to enter the groove slanting up right. Step left onto

the slabby wall then head straight up to the ledge. Go up just left of the thin vertical crack above the ledge; scrambling remains.

**Cantre'r Gwaelod** 110 feet Hard Very Severe 5b (22.5.99)
One short, hard section; start below the left-hand of the two downward pointing spikes. Climb to the spike and pull up onto the upper slab and head for the inverted V-notch and gain the ledge. Finish off as for *Antur Madog*.

**Look Back in Anchor** 110 feet Severe (22.5.99)
The easiest line, although on first appearance, it seems far harder. Climb straight up on slopers to reach the overhang formed by a large block, step left and go up cracks to the ledge; finish for *Antur Madog*.

A rambling route, now overgrown, **The Chains** 100 feet Very Difficult (1952), starts by a boulder and follows the right-hand side of a little rock tower.

Return to the stone wall again and move west along it, the four higher buttresses of Mainmast are seen above. The first and most easterly of these is lower than the others and has a steep 30-foot wall. **The Brow** (Moderate), is just above on its right. The buttress itself, identifiable by a curious perched flake, gives a good climb.

**Signal Bridge** 120 feet Very Difficult (1945-50)
Artificial, but pleasant; start at the foot of the buttress on the right. A vertical flake of rock is lodged on the nose of the buttress just above the start. A delicate move straight up leads to the perched flake. Go a few feet to the left and step out on a fine slab. Step out left again up the buttress edge on large rounded holds. There is easy ground on the right, but the left edge provides more climbing until easy scrambling ends the climb.

**Sailor Bob's Furry Spru Stool** 70 feet Hard Very Severe 5b (22.5.99)
This route ascends a clean slab to the right of the gully giving gritstone style climbing. Mantel up the slab and arrange gear in a crack on the right, step back left and climb the slab on the left, or tackle it direct at a slightly harder standard. Pleasant moves lead to the top.

The massive buttress overhanging the Signal Bridge, with a steep headwall, is the Bridge. The gully on the left separates the Signal Bridge from the higher Bridge. It gives two diverting little routes, one on the left or port side, and one on the right or starboard side.

**Port Gangway** 70 feet Difficult (1945-50)
Start by scrambling 50 feet up the gully and gain the top of a

large semi-detached block on the left. Traverse a line of flakes into a niche under a square-cut block, pull up over this to a grassy ledge and follow the ridge to the top.

**Starboard Gangway**  85 feet  Difficult  (1945-50)
Start in the gully bed at the foot of a flake block. Gain the top of the block and climb the crack above to a niche. A long stride out to the left reaches the gully bed which is then climbed straight up to finish.

The broad ledge to the southwest of The Bridge face is Monkey's Island. Two routes use this ledge.

**Monkey's Island Direct**  130 feet  Severe  (1945-50)
Good climbing; start at the lowest point of the buttress. Go easily up to a ledge under a square-cut overhang, a sideways mantelshelf leads to a small ledge. Traverse left and then go up on good holds to a heathery ledge. The steep slab at the right end of the ledge is climbed on small holds. An awkward move at the top leads to an easy glacis. Climb the wall straight above the boulder.

**Monkey's Island Superdirect**  120 feet  Severe  (1952)
A good addition, covering interesting ground which starts immediately to the right of the foot of Wardroom Gully. Go up to the heather platform of the Monkey's Island then take the left-hand steep rib to finish.

**Monkey's Island Ordinary**  120 feet  Difficult  (1945-50)
Start on the left of the buttress at the foot of a short chimney.
**1** 65 feet. Climb easily up on the right of the chimney and then take a line of weakness in the slab on the right. Belay well to the left in wardroom Gully.
**2** 60 feet. Gain the bulge in the centre of the wall above and climb a little crack to the easy glacis. Traverse easily off to the left or climb the wall on the left.

The Wardroom area is to be found to the left and is gained up the obvious gully, Wardroom Gully, which contains a rowan tree.

**Cat o' Nine Tails**  60 feet  Very Severe  (22.5.99)
A pleasant little route which starts behind a rowan tree in the gully. Go up towards a small overhang at the base of a rounded rib. Pull up left and ascend slabs to a ledge to finish up a final little tower.

**Wardroom Deckhead**  25 feet  Very Difficult  (9.52)
Climb a short, steep wall to the right of the chimney on the right of the gully.

**Wardroom Hatch**   25 feet   Difficult                    (9.52)
Ascends the steep chimney to the right of the gully. A through
route can be made by the thin.

**Wardroom Slab**   35 feet Severe is the slab left of the next gully,
followed direct.

**Jacob's Ladder**   35 feet   Hard Severe                  (1952)
This takes the steep crack on the left wall above Wardroom Slab.

The Mainmast buttress, on the left of Wardroom Gully has a heather
ledge on its upper face, the Crow's Nest and an easy climb up its
right-hand edge.

**Crow's Nest**   140 feet   Difficult                     (1945-50)
Fairly reasonable climbing which starts at the lowest point of the
Mainmast. A short slab and easy blocks lead to a big ledge. A
long stride and a rounded mantelshelf lead to the Crow's Nest.
Climb up the corner for about 10 feet then traverse out to the
right and pull up over the nose. An easy slab finishes the climb
almost on the crest of the mountain.

**The Catwalk**   70 feet   Difficult                      (1945-50)
Start 60 feet to the left of the start of Crow's Nest and 20 feet
higher. A triangular flake with an overhanging ledge on its apex
lies against the wall. Starting on the left of the flake, 'catwalk' up
its edge to a stance at the apex. Climb the steep wall directly
above. Step right at 25 feet to continue to a good ledge and
belay.

Between *The Catwalk* and a vegetated buttress on the left is an
overgrown gully, Mizzen Gully. The broken buttress is the Mizzen
Mast which has two scrambly routes. **Mizzen Shrouds** 105 feet
Difficult (1945-50) takes the ivy direct followed by a corner while
**Mizzen Top** 75 feet Difficult (1945-50) takes the corner and wall
100 feet left.

The rocks now peter out into a steep, broken slope some 70 yards
across, down which comes a path from the summit. Going down
westward across this slope a steep corner begins a further rank of
more broken and heathery crags, often loose but giving one or two
worthy routes. The corner itself, which has a projecting loose spike
halfway up is **The Davit**, and the slab on its left is **Davit Slab**;
both are about Moderate. Going further to the left along the base
of the crags for 70 feet, one sees a small projecting rock overhead.

**Sextant**   80 feet   Difficult                          (1945-50)
Start at an ivy-crowned slab directly beneath the projecting rock

and climb up to a ledge above it. The wall above is climbed on the left, followed by a slab and a little tower.

**Belaying Pin**   85 feet   Very Difficult               (1945-50)
Start 35 feet to the left of the start of *Sextant*. There is an oak tree growing against a slab on the right. Go up the broken ridge left of the slab to a heathery ledge. Step round the corner on the left and climb the steep slab to a cleft. Gain the flat top of the Belaying Pin and climb the airy and rounded slab on the left.

About 25 feet to the left of the Belaying Pin is a short and very overgrown gully, Galley Gully. Another 25 feet to the left of the gully a vegetated buttress sends down a steep little nose and gives a pleasant climb.

**Crosstrees**   100 feet   Very Difficult               (1945-50)
Start at the toe of the buttress and make an awkward move up to the right and then follow a corner on the left to the airy Crosstrees platform. Go straight up, climbing the final tower direct.

Across a grassy slope on the left is a 20-foot blade of rock, **The Bosun's Knife** Difficult (1945-50) follows its edge. Immediately above this, and almost on the crest of the ridge, are two little rock faces, the After Turrets, with many short problems on them.

Below, the southern face of Moel y Gest ends in a broken rocky corner with a perched boulder in the shape of a Sea Lion at its foot. The stone wall turns up to the right and contours the western or after-end, overlooking Criccieth and the Lleyn Peninsula. About 100 yards north of the corner the stone wall ceases at a projecting buttress which drops to below the level of the wall. There are two short climbs there.

**Poop Arête**   50 feet   Difficult               (1945-50)
Start by crossing the wall and traversing below it to a little gully. The corner of the rock beyond is splintered, climb the broken corner to a large ledge. The right-hand edge of the arête is quite airy.

**The Fairleads**   35 feet   Very Difficult               (1945-50)
Start 20 feet left of *Poop Arête* where a chimney splits the wall. Climb the chimney followed by either of the steep cracks.

## Moel y Gest Quarry
The cliff is situated high on Moel y Gest on the opposite side of the valley to Craig y Castell, about a mile from Portmadog on the Criccieth road. The best approach is from the north. Park at a small layby near the 30/40 mph signs on the Porthmadog to Criccieth

road. Follow the path to a stile then head up to a col. From the col go right towards the summit and a stile. One hundred yards after the stile bear off right and follow a faint path below a bluff of rock which leads to the top left-hand side of the quarry. Go steeply down to the quarry base. It is also possible to approach via the cemetery adjacent to the refuse tip. An extremely steep ramp running directly down from the quarry can be followed but is strictly for masochists.

The quarry is divided into three convenient sections. The main cliff on the left is about 200 yards long and of a fairly constant height (120-130 feet). All the routes bar one described are on this section. There is a small cliff immediately above the ramp with the old winding house as a useful landmark. The right-hand section which is the highest of the three, presently has one route recorded.

There has been some debate over the years about whether to include this cliff in a *Tremadog* guide because few, if any, had shown any interest in climbing it and it was thought (rightly?) that no-one ever would. The method of recording routes on this quarry in past guidebooks has been varied and is listed below:
1970 Full description and large fold-out diagram.
1978 Topo style description with diagram reduced to one page and shortened descriptions on one page.
1983 Omitted completely with a few lines of explanation in the Introduction.
1989 The 1978 descriptions printed over two pages and no diagram.

It should be stressed that the routes described in the left-hand bay are now 30 years old, most not having had a second ascent. There are good reasons for this phenomenon. The rock is quarried dolerite and is very compact. The routes were all done using pegs for aid and protection, almost none of these are now in place. Sharp edges of rock abound so care is needed with ropes running over them. There have been recent rockfalls and almost all the routes are in a very dangerous condition. Some would probably improve if cleaned by abseil, others are just plain suicide. You have been warned. The following descriptions are included purely for the historical record, unlike the other routes in this guide we do not recommend them in their present state.

**Inferior Grooves**   95 feet   Very Severe            (11.3.67)
A rather artificial line making the best of this part of the cliff. Start at the most obvious feature at the extreme left-hand end of the cliff, a big overhang low down. The route starts some 20 yards to the right of this, immediately below a short groove which splits an otherwise featureless wall.
**1** 75 feet. Climb straight up via a scoop in the groove. Exit from

the groove left and step back right to the continuation of the groove (crux), then easily up to obvious block belays.
**2** 20 feet. Move up to an obvious exit left across a small slab, as for *Short Wall*.

**Short Wall**   95 feet   Very Severe                    (19.3.67)
A line of no particular note. Start about 25 yards to the right of the overhang at the left side of the cliff, at the base of a small easy-angled buttress capped by a pinnacle.
**1** 75 feet. Go easily up to the pinnacle and pull over a short wall, move slightly left to climb a shattered wall and up to obvious block belays.
**2** 20 feet. Move up to an obvious exit left across a small slab.

**Chough**   100 feet   Hard Very Severe (1 pt)           (6.5.67)
A rather unsatisfactory route with a comparatively easy first pitch, an abundance of loose rock and a very much harder finish. There are three white streaks on this part of the crag, the first pitch takes the line of the shattered rock just to the left of the left-hand streak.
**1** 75 feet. Climb straight up the shattered rock, past precarious spikes, and onto belays at the left-hand end of a long sloping ledge.
**2** 25 feet. Move up left over two ledges, then diagonally right past a block, use a peg to continue in the same line to the top.

**Blogg's Route**   100 feet   Very Severe (2 pts)         (5.68)
This route takes a line between *Chough* and *The Prow*, finishing in a diagonal groove. Start just to right of the line of shattered rock taken by *Chough*.
**1** 40 feet. From below precarious flakes, climb up over a shelf on the right. Traverse right and up to a wide, sloping ledge.
**2** 60 feet. Step back left and up over severely split blocks. Move up to a green groove and climb this to an awkward step out right, continue steeply to the top.

**The Prow**   110 feet   Hard Very Severe                (19.3.67)
A rather artificial line, with an indifferent start and a sensational finish. Towards the left end of the quarry there are three white streaks, only two of which reach the ground. Start at the left-hand of these, below the prow of rock on the skyline.
**1** 75 feet. Gain a ledge and move right into a crack, climb this and continue by ledges to a large bay. Exit left from this then go diagonally right to a belay below the prow.
**2** 35 feet. Move right into a clean steeply overhung corner. Climb this and continue straight up to finish just right of the prow.

**Eclipse**   120 feet   Hard Severe (1 pt)              (18.3.67)
Start 15 feet right of *The Prow*, just right of the second white streak.
**1** 50 feet. Climb straight up to a small groove, go up this to a ledge. Traverse left along the ledge and mantelshelf over the grey wall immediately above. Move right to a large ledge and belays.
**2** 70 feet. Move right to an obvious sloping red groove. Swing left from this into a bottomless groove, go up this and across a slab on the right. Break out of this on the right and move back left and up to an overhanging wall. In the middle of the wall is a bore hole. Climb the wall at this point with the aid of a sling and climb the slab to the top.

**Penumbra**   120 feet   Hard Severe              (11.3.67)
The easiest line on the cliff; it has its fair share of loose rock. Left of the centre of the cliff is a prominent overhanging arête with a large bay on its left; start immediately left of the bay.
**1** 80 feet. Climb up to a loose block on a ledge, move left and then diagonally right until it is possible to go back left to a small pointed overhang. Move left beneath this and up to a ledge and belays.
**2** 40 feet. Climb over blocks behind the belay to a wide crack in the right wall, go up this and easily to the top.

**Oblique**   140 feet   Very Severe (1 pt)              (11.3.67)
Easy, with the exception of the peg move. Start as for *Penumbra*.
**1** 100 feet. Climb *Penumbra* for 45 feet to the obvious traverse line right. Follow this to the corner and use a peg to gain a groove on the right, move up to a ledge and belay.
**2** 40 feet. Climb to a crack above and finish just right of this.

**Damocles**   130 feet   XS (2 pts)              (15.4.67)
This is almost certainly the best route in the left-hand bay, taking a challenging line on a very uncompromising piece of rock. Start 15 feet right of the prominent overhanging arête mentioned in the start to *Penumbra*, immediately right of the little fern-filled corner.
**1** 100 feet. Climb strenuously up for a few feet then move left across an overhanging rib into a shallow recess. Go up right and, with aid from a peg gain a ledge. Continue diagonally right to a stance beneath a smooth, overhanging wall. Pull over the wall, move right and up to a ledge; boulder belays.
**2** 30 feet. Move right and up into a clean groove. With aid from a peg continue up the groove to a ledge on the right. Traverse 5 feet to an overhanging crack in the wall; climb this to finish.

**Irony**   150 feet   XS (2 pts)              (6.5.67)
Another hard climb but not as worthwhile as the previous route due to a section of broken ground in the centre. The crux is

reserved until the top. Left of the centre of the cliff is a prominent, overhanging arête with a large bay on its left. Fifty feet right of the arête is a short groove at 30 feet, with a black wall on its right. Start just to the left of the groove.

**1** 70 feet. Climb diagonally right to the bottom of the groove via a large ledge. Ascend the groove, with two pegs for aid, and continue by ledges to belays on the right of a huge block.

**2** 80 feet. Traverse left behind the block, descending to a ledge and climb up left of two blocks (one on top of the other). Move right across a grey slab and mantelshelf awkwardly onto a sloping ledge, go up a short corner and diagonally right over blocks to finish.

**Fracture**   125 feet   Very Severe (1 pt)                (9.4.67)
In the centre of the cliff there is a light-coloured depression at mid-height and a pile of rubble at the base. The route takes a line on the left of the depression.

**1** 85 feet. Climb straight up for 30 feet to gain ledges on the left, move left up to a peg and use it to reach a platform above. Move left past a small tree to block belays.

**2** 40 feet. Go up diagonally right to a short steep groove, exit here.

**Scorpion**   130 feet   Very Severe                (18.2.67)
This was the first of the routes in the quarry and an aptly-named one. Start 20 feet right of *Fracture*, from a fallen block on a pile of rubble. The route takes a line on the right-hand side of the light-coloured depression.

**1** 80 feet. Pull onto a ledge, move left and trend back right to the large depression. Continue over huge blocks on the right and back left above the depression to a ledge and belay.

**2** 50 feet. Move left around the corner and up to a large perched block, climb over this and up an awkward little slab to finish.

**Oughtogo**   130 feet   Hard Very Severe (1 pt)                (2.7.67)
An eliminate with a very difficult entry. There is more loose rock than on other routes and of a scale to demand extreme caution. Start as for *Scorpion* from a fallen block on a pile of rubble some 30 feet left of the prominent corner of *Cut-throat*.

**1** 100 feet. Pull onto a ledge and climb a short, black corner, making a long reach for good holds. Use a peg placed as far right as possible to gain a sloping ledge on the right. Continue traversing to below a projecting spike, go up this and straight onto a spacious ledge, poor belay.

**2** 30 feet. Walk right for 15 feet and then trend left to a steep wall. Mantelshelf over the projecting block to finish.

**Cut-throat**   130 feet   XS                              `(19.3.67)
A strenuous first pitch of increasing difficulty. Start at the prominent crack just to the left of an obvious corner, some 40 feet left
of *The Milky Way*.
**1** 75 feet. Ascend the crack to a ledge. Move left then back right
to gain the overhanging cracks, climb these and move right,
continuing to a ledge just above and a belay.
**2** 55 feet. Exit left on good handholds and trend right to a
shattered, grooved arête, finish up this.

**Knife Edge**   140 feet   HVS (1 pt)                     (12.3.67)
An intricate line with an awkward finish. Start immediately left of
*The Milky Way*.
**1** 100 feet. Climb a small bulge, then step right to an ascending
line of shattered rock. Move left from this onto a large ledge
formed by shattered blocks below a small corner. Climb the
corner and go straight up over a series of easy-angled bulges to
a triangular sentry-box. Move left level with the sentry box and
climb a short slab topped by a wall which forms a small overhang; belay.
**2** 40 feet. Descend immediately below the belay and traverse left
to a small tree. Move round the bulge and up to a small corner,
climb this and move onto a slab, capped by an overhang.
Surmount the overhang with a peg for aid and go up a little
moss-covered slab to the top.

**The Milky Way**   130 feet   Very Severe                (11.3.67)
A well-marked line, with its share of loose rock. There has been a
rockfall on the top pitch. Start slightly right of the centre of the
crag at an obvious white quartz vein; the climb follows this line.
**1** 100 feet. Follow the quartz vein easily for 20 feet then step
slightly right up over some blocks to arrive at the top of a small
slab. Continue straight up on loose steps and up to an obvious
tree; belay.
**2** 30 feet. Immediately above the belay there is an overhanging
crack, climb this, and move right into a short groove, stepping
across to a loose triangular block. Go up this trending right to the
top.

**The Swinger**   130 feet   XS (2 pts)                   (12.3.67)
Some hard climbing and interesting situations but the rock is still
poor. To the right of *The Milky Way* is a large overhang near the
top of the cliff, below which is a distinctive pillar. The route takes
the left-hand side of the pillar.
**1** 90 feet. Go up cracks to shattered blocks and continue as far
as possible up the groove, then, with aid from a small nut, gain a
ledge up on the right. Move back left into the groove and
continue to the top of the pillar. With aid from a peg move across

the left wall and continue diagonally left to a ledge beneath the roof. Belay.
**2** 40 feet. Traverse left for 15 feet and climb up trending right above the roof to finish.

The big roofed groove between *Swinger* and *Contrast* was climbed using six pegs for aid. It is an extremely strenuous pitch and includes some hard free climbing. The line is obvious apart from one small diversion onto the right wall just below the roof.

**Contrast**   150 feet   XS (2 pts)                    (23.4.67)
High on the right-hand side of the cliff is an obvious slab. Start immediately below the left-hand edge of the slab.
**1** 70 feet. Climb easily up left, and back right, to the left-hand of two light-coloured grooves. Climb the groove with two pegs for aid to a sloping ledge and peg belay.
**2** 80 feet. Move left over blocks to a ledge. Continue up awkwardly to a protection peg above a block. Traverse right across the slab to broken rock which is climbed to finish 5 feet left of a protruding finger of rock.

**Joe Soap's Route**   125 feet   Hard Very Severe (A1)   (5.68)
To the right of *Contrast* is a very obvious steep, black groove; the route climbs this. Start directly below the groove.
**1** 85 feet. Climb broken rocks and belay on huge blocks at the bottom of the groove. Climb the groove using nuts for aid and belay on the right; junction with *Contrast*.
**2** 40 feet. Continue up loose broken rock to finish 5 feet left of a protruding finger of rock.

**Deception**   130 feet   Hard Very Severe (3 pts)     (19.3.67)
The route makes the best of a rather impenetrable section of the cliff; not sustained or particularly worthwhile. Start at the extreme right-hand end of the cliff immediately below a clean groove with an obvious niche on its left.
**1** 80 feet. Gain a ledge awkwardly and continue to the base of the groove. Climb the groove with aid from a peg and two nuts to a ledge, move left across it to block belays.
**2** 50 feet. Mantelshelf and move right over shattered blocks, move back left and straight up, finishing slightly on the right.

The next route is in the right-hand bay and is actually quite good. It takes the obvious central corner line and is reached by a scramble.

**Space Panic**   100 feet   E1 5b                        (1981)
A good well-protected pitch. Scramble 50 feet over big blocks in the right-hand bay to a large ledge below the corner. Jam the corner to a roof, traverse left into a groove and go up this to the top.

# MOEL DDU & CRAIG Y GELLI

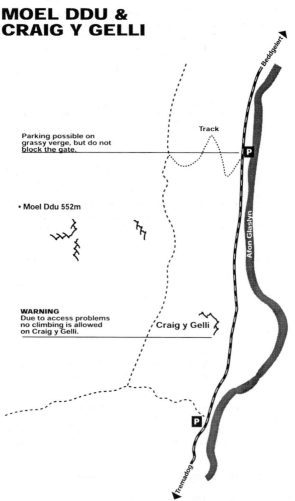

Beddgelert ▲

Track

Parking possible on
grassy verge, but do not
block the gate.

P

• Moel Ddu 552m

Afon Glaslyn

**WARNING**
Due to access problems
no climbing is allowed
on Craig y Gelli.

Craig y Gelli

P

Tremadog ▼

# Craig y Gelli (Crag of the Groove)     OS Ref 591 436

Craig y Gelli lies on the lower slopes of Moel Ddu, overlooking the A498, two miles south of Aberglaslyn Bridge, towards the end of a straight stretch of road and just before a cottage on the left. Just before the bend there is a small lay-by on the right with room for three cars. Do not park opposite the cottage. A faint path leads from the lay-by up to the right of the crag.

The main feature is a line of slabs topped by an overhang, with smaller buttresses to the right and left. The easiest descent is on the left, down a grassy slope with a short steep scramble down to the start of *Via Gellia*. A descent to the right of the crag starting at a short tree filled gully is also possible.

At the time of writing a sign at the bottom of the crag by the road warns climbers that the crag is on private property and that climbing is not tolerated by the owner. This has meant that the crag has fallen into disuse over the past few years and the climbs have become very overgrown. If the situation were to ever change and a thorough clean up operation was mounted, some of the routes are apparently well worth doing.

**Via Gellia**   120 feet   Very Severe                    (1956)
The left subsidiary buttress forms a steep slab divided from the main crag by a vegetated gully. This route takes the left edge of the slab giving a nice climb in a fine position. Start just below and left of a little overhang at the foot of the buttress.
**1** 60 feet. 4b. Go up to a detached flake then move right across a rib onto the edge of the slab. Climb the slab to a ledge and belay.
**2** 60 feet. 4b. Step onto a block out right then go up the wall above, awkward to start, to another ledge. Continue over a thin detached flake and a slab to easy ground and the top.

**Hindleberg**   80 feet   Hard Very Severe 5b          (1973)
Another interesting route. Start right of the detached flake of *Via Gelli*, below a corner. Climb the corner then step right to a crack in the slab. Climb the slab to a horizontal break then step left to a steep slab which is climbed direct, past another horizontal break, to the top.

A steep groove just left of the gully has also been climbed.

**Tornado**   150 feet   Hard Very Severe               (1962)
A scrappy and artificial climb with a few good moves. Start at the trees below the left side of the main cliff, about 15 yards right of the vegetated gully. Scramble up behind the trees and traverse right behind a block to the foot of a short steep corner below a

little overhang.
**1** 40 feet. 5a. Climb the corner to the overhang and move right strenuously to the ledge and tree belay.
**2** 30 feet. 5a. Move back left and pull over the overhang to gain the obvious ledge. Continue up the wall above to a ledge and tree belay.
**3** 50 feet. 4b. Climb cracks and ribs to a large heathery ledge and tree belay below the final chimney.
**4** 30 feet. 4a. Climb the chimney to the top.

**Cursor**   160 feet   E1                                                 (1964)
An impressive final pitch through the overhangs on the right-hand side of the main cliff. Start just to the left of the obvious tree-filled chimney.
**1** 70 feet. 4c. Climb diagonally left to a fault in the slab. Climb this to an awkward step left and a small ledge and belay.
**2** 30 feet. 4c. Climb back right into an overhanging groove, which leads to a large ledge and tree belay.
**3** 60 feet. 5b. Traverse left along the big flake to below the break through the overhangs. Climb the break until it is possible to traverse left under the final roof to easier ground.

The obvious diagonal crack through the overhang left of *Cursor* has been climbed using four points of aid.

The tree-filled gully is **Tumbleweed** Very Difficult (1955).

**Hurricane**   150 feet   Hard Very Severe                    (1979)
A good route up the extreme right-hand edge of the cliff. Start at some slabby grooves.
**1** 100 feet. 5a. Climb the easy-angled groove to a small overhang. Step right and then go back left above the overhang (crux). Continue up right to reach a crack on the right-hand side of the buttress. Climb this, moving onto the edge for a few feet before taking a stance at a tree.
**2** 50 feet. 4c. Move back out right onto the arete and climb this direct to the top.

**Pothook**   145 feet   Hard Severe                             (1955)
Smooth and serious. Start at a groove to the right of the tree-filled chimney, about 20 feet right of the edge of the buttress.
**1** 45 feet. Climb the groove and traverse right under the overhang to an awkward move, which leads to a ledge on the corner of the buttress. Alternatively, climb the less prominent groove just to the right.
**2** 50 feet. Step up and left to a ledge. Make a few thin moves left and climb the right wall of a groove to a large ledge and tree belay.
**3** 50 feet. Climb easily to the top.

# Moel Ddu

These are a collection of small crags, on the flanks of Moel Ddu, directly above Craig y Gelli. The first climbs were made in the 50s, these routes were left to wallow in obscurity and lack of interest until guidebook work led to a visit. Although much of the rock on this hillside is broken and heathery it is far more continuous than it appears from below. It is also steeper than it looks. The main climbing is found on the East Face, much of which faces south with views over the former estuary and it stays in the sun until mid afternoon. The South Face also has steep rock, stays in the sun for longer, but is rather scrappy.

The climbing is in an area of stunning scenery, on a fine day one can look out over the patchwork of fields known as Traeth Mawr, the reclaimed estuary of the Glaslyn, towards the ruddy heather strewn slopes of the Rhinogau. Even the views of the mountain fastness of Cnicht and Moelwyn Mawr seem different from this angle. On this hillside, there are many areas where one can while away a few hours bouldering or picnicking near cool mountain streams.

# Access

On the A498 Beddgelert to Tremadog road about half a mile north of Craig y Gelli, at OS Ref 593 445, a little track leads up through the woods of Parc y Llys to reach Llys at 589 445. Parking is possible on the grassy verge on the side nearest to the river but please ensure that no gates are blocked. The crags can be reached from the road in about half an hour.

The first area of rock, with its obvious capping overhang, is seen up and left from the track leading to Llys, this crag is Craig y Llys. Follow the public footpath left, heading south, to reach the crag.

## Craig y Llys                                OS Ref 587 442

This slabby little cliff is easily seen from the track. The obvious feature is a prominent capping overhang, slanting up from left to right. Descent is by means of an easy gully on the left.

**Perthi Gwyn**   90 feet   Severe 3a                        (1998)
A slight route which starts at the bottom of the rib just right of the base of the descent gully. Climb the rib and step right to the continuation rib and follow this past a rowan tree to reach a crack leading up a rounded slab; finish up this crack.

**Llys y Mynydd**   100 feet   Hard Severe 3c                 (1998)
A reasonable little route which starts directly below the overhang at the toe of the main slab, about 10 feet left of the arête. Climb up past a flake to reach slabs. Go up these to a short right-facing

groove which allows one to gain the right-hand end of the overhang. Step up and right to finish easily.

**Gelli'r Haul**   100 feet   Hard Severe 4a                    (1998)
The best on this craglet; start at the base of the arête or climb the block below first. Go steeply up the arête, hidden pockets reduce apprehensions, then follow the very edge of the slabs to steeper ground. Continue delicately to reach a wide crack and easier climbing above.

From Craig y Llys, head towards the main mass of Moel Ddu. However, before reaching the upper cliffs, a clean buttress with a prominent cleft or chimney can be seen just above the stone wall. This is:

# Craig Glaslyn                         OS Ref 586 441

The huge block at the foot, and the prominent cleft to its right, are the easiest locators. The crag can be reached by heading towards the main mass of Moel Ddu from Craig y Llys. This particular cliff is also slabby in the main, but has some steeper rock to start; indeed the arête to the right is undercut. Descent is by means of the slope on the right.

**Llygad yr Haul**   130 feet   Very Severe 4b              (1999)
A bold pull through the overlap provides the meat of the route, though a sling round the chockstone will calm the nerves. Start at the base of the chimney, just right of the huge block. Ascend the slab to the initial steepening , some flakes then lead to the upper slab below the overlap. Move right to the arête and surmount the overlap by means of a high step up onto the top slab; finish easily.

**Simddau Fawr**   140 feet   Severe 3b                      (1953)
A route where one has an interesting choice of attack. Start at the base of the chimney, just right of the huge block. Either, succumb to fear and the challenge of the traditional ethos to squirm your way up the chimney or, in a modernist manner layback and footbar an ascent. A pull out onto slabs after 40 feet allows one to head up easily for the top.

**Cleddyf**   140 feet   Very Severe 4b                       (1998)
A reasonable route; start at the very base of the buttress about 15 feet right of the chimney. Go up rightwards to the steepening and gain a horizontal crack. Big holds allow one to gain the slab above. Head towards a massive downward pointing flake, pinch this on either side and move right to gain easy slabs; head for the top.

**Cnwc**   130 feet   Very Severe 5a                              (1998)
The interest is in the first 30 feet. Start directly below the right-
hand arête. A high step followed by a strenuous pull allows one
to gain the easier angled arête, some delicate moves up this gain
a wide crack; easy slabs to finish.
Variation
**Gorwedd Nol a Meddwl**   Very Severe 5a           (1998)
The corner to the right is taken by a layback sequence to the
wide crack mentioned above.

The upper cliffs of Moel Ddu are, as one would expect, slightly
higher.

# Clogwyn y Celyn                          OS Ref 586 441

The lower tiers of crags run along the top of steep heathery and
scree slopes, well above the stone wall, and forming corners at the
south and north ends of the East Face. The south corner is a ridge
providing an easy scrambling route to the upper mountain — a
useful way of descent after a climb. The north corner turns back
westward along the base of tiers of small crags.

The crags of the East Face begin immediately north of the easy
Corner Ridge. There are some obvious opportunities for new routes
in this area, but only to those with the necessary dedication, not to
mention determination, to hack up the hillside to savour their delights. A slight track runs close under the cliffs, above scree. About
halfway along, and easily identified, is a small grey buttress split in
two by a cleft in which there is a large holly tree; the two halves of
this 60-foot buttress give the Left and Right Starts of *Holly Buttress*.

**Holly Buttress**   240 feet   Very Difficult              (1956)
The Right Start takes the steep wall on the right of the holly
beginning a little left of its centre.
**1** 85 feet. Climb the wall by traversing a few feet right where it
becomes nearly vertical and gaining the arête; it can be made
easier. Go easily up the short cleft on the left and up a heathery
glacis to the foot of an orange wall.
**2** 60 feet. Climb directly up the steep orange wall to below
another steep wall; climb directly up this.
**3** 70 feet. The short heathery wall is climbed to a belay on a
large heather shelf; easy ground on the right. The last of the
walls, easier but with some loose stuff on top, ends at a belay
and the finish of the climb.

If the faint track skirting the bases of the crags is followed north-
ward, the cliffs begin to lie back and become more broken. Just
before the north corner is reached a short easy gully with steep
back walls is seen above on the left. Passing through this gut and

out over grassy slopes above, one can walk across to the right to the edge of the north corner. Above on the left is a fairly wide expanse of slab with a steeper wall above.

**North Edge Route**   160 feet   Difficult          (1956)
Takes a line up the slabs directly below the reddish wall.
**1** 100 feet. The slabs give pleasant moderate climbing to a big heather ledge below the wall.
**2** 60 feet. On the left, beyond a small cleft, is a reddish-hued wall; the red wall is climbed straight up.

By scrambling straight up from the gut mentioned above, or by walking 100 yards left from the top of *North Edge Route* a prominent little cliff is seen, dropping vertically on the east in a narrow nose. This nose is split by a crack with a juniper bush growing in it 20 feet up. It gives:

**Juniper Crack**   85 feet   Very Difficult          (1956)
A strenuous and interesting little climb in two sections. Start at the foot of the crack. Go up on the left of the crack until it is possible to claw into the crack through or over the juniper, which turns out to be an essential hold. Fight the very narrow crack that follows, until it breaks out unexpectedly overlooking the right wall. Haul out up to the left of the slabby crest and go straight up and over to belay.

Walking 60 yards right (north) from the foot of *Juniper Crack* brings one to a 60-foot wall giving a variety of routes of Difficult and Moderate standard. There is a lot of juniper growing at its right-hand end.

Back down at the lower tier of cliffs, but further to the right of the gully or gut mentioned above, is a final area of rock. This has some very steep bits and is just waiting for those with the time and patience to go up and clean them.

## South Face                                OS Ref 585 437
The path along the base of the East Face, if followed southward, crosses the Corner Ridge and turns west along the South Face. Here the face consists roughly of a very steep lower tier, a chaotic glacis above it and steep broken crags above that. About 100 yards west of the Corner, is a prominent little crag sticking out right of the foot, slightly overhanging. On the left side (west) of it is a steep narrow cleft.

**South Face Route**   175 feet   Difficult          (1956)
A rather artificial route; start at the toe of the prominent little crag.

**1** 65 feet. The cleft to the left is climbed by stepping into it from the left, go past a chockstone and up the continuation cleft but finish by stepping out on the right. A belay can be found by going 35 feet higher up the grass. This is the glacis and the face steepens again above it in a clean slab.

**2** 110 feet. An easy route scrambles up on the left of the slab, but the slab itself gives good climbing straight up its centre with an awkward finishing move. The ridge above is climbed to finish off.

# Aberglaslyn and Nantmor

This fascinating area has been little frequented by the climber up until now. With the relatively recent interest in the short technical pitch, away from popular honeypots, the crags and bluffs around Nantmor have increased in popularity especially for bouldering. The area described runs from Beddgelert south to Carreg Hylldrem, still the most important crag hereabouts. Except for Carreg Hylldrem, which has always been fairly popular, the other crags offer the seeker of solitude a marvellous opportunity to escape from the crowds at Tremadog and involve oneself in a more relaxed climbing experience.

## Access and environment

These valleys are some of the most scenically beautiful in Snowdonia, with lakes dotting the valley bottoms and relatively well wooded lower slopes rising to ruggedly impressive mountain summits. Despite the extensive invasion of Rhododendron in this area, the woodlands in these valleys are important in that they represent the remnants of a once much more widespread cover throughout Snowdonia, reduced by centuries of felling for timber and heavy grazing by sheep and cattle, and more recently goats. These upland woods are generally in a poor condition with little regeneration and little in the way of a shrub or ground flora, but they can be magical places with a luxuriant coating of mosses and lichens on the ground, on boulders and on rotting trees. Many of them are part of larger upland NNRs or SSSIs and, due to their small size and to the lack of regeneration within the existing boundaries, management agreements are currently being discussed between the landowners and conservation bodies such as the Countryside Council for Wales, Snowdonia National Park Authority and the National Trust. The aim of these agreements is to remove or reduce grazing in and adjacent to the woodlands to allow them to regenerate and spread laterally as well as up the mountainsides. Without this intervention, these woodlands would disappear in a number of years as the dying trees are not replaced due to the heavy grazing of seedlings and saplings.

Many of the climbing crags in these valleys are located in or adjacent to these woodlands, some of which are on private land. The above management measures may result in the necessary erection of a few fences to prevent grazing animals from gaining access to the woodland. The fences are not necessarily to keep people out and stiles or gates will be erected where any fences cross rights of way or recognised paths. It is hoped that climbers will co-operate by using these and not climbing over fences as this damages the fence, causes additional expense and may allow the animals to gain access, so destroying the agreement and the future of the woodland. The fences are hopefully temporary until enough regeneration has taken place to ensure the future of the woodlands and the re-establishment of controlled grazing. Keeping to the paths and not damaging vegetation will also help conserve the woodland flora and speed the regeneration process.

## Aberglaslyn Gorge
OS Ref 596 463

The east side of Aberglaslyn Pass becomes very steep where it narrows to a gorge. Most of the rock is poor, but by no means all of it. Of the climbs recorded *Canyon Rib* is easily the best and deserves its popularity. At the time of writing a currently disused railway line follows the gorge and is a popular tourist jaunt in the summer, this situation may change. It is best to leave one's car in the car park on the A4085 just before Nantmor. Follow the old railway track through a long tunnel to emerge into the gorge.

Directly above the tunnel entrance is a steep heather slope with a high rocky bay above. **Tunnel Rib** V Diff, uses the rocks on the right of this bay. **Gam Bay** Severe (11.6.54) takes the next mass of rock to the north beyond the bay. Right again is **Pineways** Difficult (20.5.52). All three climbs are poor and included for the historical record only. The next climb, however, is much better and well worth seeking out. Park as for the tunnel but walk back down the road to the Aberglaslyn bridge. From the kissing gate walk 170 paces taking a higher fork where the path rises, passing two vertical larches, and stopping in a dip before the path crosses a tumble of boulders. Go up right through the gap in the undergrowth to the rocks and along right to a clean rib in the trees with distinctive strata dipping down to the left.

**Canyon Rib**   235 feet   Severe                                    (3.9.51)
A very good, traditional sort of climb in dramatic surroundings. The pitches can be run together. Start well above the path at a small oak tree.
**1** 35 feet. The clean, sharp rib is climbed to a stance below a large block.
**2** 15 feet. Pull up onto the block and walk back to the base of a fine wall with an edge on the right.
**3** 35 feet. Climb the wall to a stance on the right edge.
**4** 45 feet. Cross to the right and gain the edge of the next rib. Follow the sharp edge steeply to a small stance.
**5** 30 feet. Easy rocks lead to a stance and belay below the final wall.
**6** 75 feet. The wall above is vertical and forms the left side of the rib. Climb up right into a groove with a sapling from which an airy move left onto the hanging arête leads to the top.

A few hundred yards upstream of the Aberglaslyn bridge is a lay-by and opposite a steep red wall on the other side of the river. The next route takes this wall and is best approached by walking along the old railway line and bushwhacking up the hillside.

**The Bear of Tralee**   70 feet   E2 5c   †                    (6.93)
A route to delight the connoisseur. Shy, esoteric and perhaps a little dirty. After an awkward approach the base of the red wall can be reached. Climb the obvious cleaned line up the centre of the orange-coloured wall. The traverse right brings the crux before the easier finishing crack is reached.

## Craig y Llan (Crag of the Church)        OS Ref 594 477

The ridge bounding the Aberglaslyn Pass on the east gives a pleasant walk. On its west flank is Gravestone Buttress, the main buttress of the crag nearest to Beddgelert and facing Gelert's Grave. It may be reached from the village by the Fisherman's Path which is followed to a point just beyond the last barn. The crag is then directly above. A bushwhacking approach leads up to the routes, both of which are very overgrown and hardly worth the effort.

**The Ordinary Route**   250 feet   Difficult   ‡        (8.1.50)
Start below a steep pillar capped by a small cannon stone and take the easiest line up the front of the slabs and traverse left onto the main rib and go up this and the final wall.

**The Direct Route**   245 feet   Very Difficult   ‡     (15.1.50)
Start at the toe of the buttress and take a direct line to the top, crossing *The Ordinary Route*.

# Moel y Dyniewyd

The hills surrounding the valley of Nantmor have very large areas of exposed rock, some of which have provided excellent bouldering venues for enthusiastic locals. A more substantial crag, Craig y Dyniewyd, lies on the south side of Moel y Dyniewyd, not far below the top. There is an escarpment of about half a mile running north-east which is dotted with short rock buttresses. Most of these are of no interest to the climber, but Craig y Dyniewyd itself and another crag on the eastern end of the escarpment provide good climbing with grand views down the Glaslyn estuary.

Craig y Dyniewyd is about 140 feet high with short gullies on either side. A loose wall, with an interesting pinnacle at its foot lies beyond the right-hand gully. The crag is south-facing so it gets the sun all day and provides nice climbing with the odd loose flake here and there. A rectangular sheep fold with a subsidiary pen directly

Adam Wainwright on the well-trodden ochre-coloured slab of *Vector* E2, Craig Bwlch y Moch.
Photo: Ray Wood

George Smith pioneering *Swift Undercut* E7,
Craig Bwlch y Moch.
Photo: Ray Wood

Robert Mulley on *Meshach* HVS, Craig Bwlch y Moch.
Photo: Carl Ryan

Meirion Jones on *Grim Wall Direct* E1, Craig Bwlch y Moch. Photo: Carl Ryan

# MOEL DYNIEWYD & ABERGLASLYN

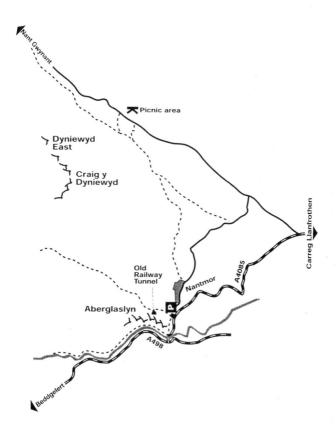

below the crag is an obvious distinguishing feature. A smooth, white wall about 150 yards to the east provides a couple of steep routes. The escarpment continues northeast and comprises two small rocky bluffs. There is a small lake behind the first one. The crag of Dyniewyd East lies directly below the summit of the second bluff which is marked as spot height 343 on the OS map.

The crags may be approached from Buarthau, park at a lay-by on the road running parallel to the river Nantmor (OS Ref 625 477). Cross the bridge and follow the path in front of the house until it bears up the hill. Zigzag up the steep slope to an area of marsh and continue until the escarpment come into view. Dyniewyd East is on the right looking in. For Craig y Dyniewyd contour round to the left (southwest) until a rocky pinnacle comes into view, the crag is just around the corner from this; the approach time is about 30 minutes. It is also possible to approach from either Clogwyn Farm in Nantmor itself, or from a lay-by on the road running parallel to the river Nantmor at OS Ref 620467 but these approaches take longer. It should be stressed that there are no rights of way to the crag and the crossing of stone walls should be avoided.

## Craig y Dyniewyd (Crag of the Steer)     OS Ref 612 475
**Christmas Climb**   110 feet   Severe                    (25.12.47)
A nice little climb, well worth the walk. It goes up the front face making for the right-hand end of the overhang, traverses left under it to a crack on the left and follows a short wall to finish. Start at the toe of the buttress.
**1** 60 feet. Step onto the wall and climb the groove which slants to the right, to a bollard. Climb the steep rib above to another bollard under the roof. Now traverse left across the wall to the far side of a hanging slab.
**2** 50 feet. Follow the steep cracks above for 30 feet, climb the vertical side wall with difficulty and pull over the crest to finish.

**Christmas Climb Direct**   120 feet   Very Severe 4c   (2.6.97)
Quite eliminate but good fun. Start below the left edge of the buttress. Climb directly up the left edge of the rib sharing a few moves with *Gash Wall*. Keep on the extreme left edge and join *Christmas Climb* to finish up this.

**Christmas Cracker**   120 feet   E1   †                (19.10.97)
Start at the right toe of the buttress taken by *Christmas Climb*.
**1** 30 feet. 4b. Climb straight up to the bollard on the first stance of *Christmas Climb*.
**2** 90 feet. 5b. Step left and climb the wall to the middle of 'the gash'. Step right onto the upper wall and continue straight up past a finger and toe ledge to finish by a little goove on the left.

Small wires and some ingenuity are required to protect this difficult top section.

**Gash Wall**   150 feet   Hard Very Severe         (26.5.50)
Rather a meandering line, but good climbing nevertheless. Start left of *Christmas Climb* below the left edge of the buttress.
**1** 95 feet 5a. Climb straight up the edge of the buttress to the overhang. Pull up and cross to a ledge on the right. Make a hard move over the overhang and climb the groove above to a mantelshelf on the right. Continue more easily for a few feet to the second stance of *Christmas Climb*; possible belay. Now make a descending traverse right to the bollard under the steep wall.
**2** 55 feet 4c. Climb diagonally right across the steep and rather rotten wall. Follow the crackline for a few feet and make a short traverse left to finish.

**Skyline**   140 feet   E1 5b         (11.11.90)
The line of the buttress, which follows a steep crack before climbing the obvious groove in the headwall. A good sustained pitch. Start up and right of the toe of the buttress, below a crack running up through a small overhang. Climb the crack and bulge above to the bollard on *Christmas Climb*. Step left and climb the steep slab to the groove. Move up this (crux) and finish out to the left.

**Chimney and Face Climb**   120 feet   Severe         (5.48)
A minor route, loose in places. Follow the gully on the right of the buttress until it overhangs. Move onto the loose right wall and climb it to the top.

Further east (right) of Craig y Dyniewyd is a steep white wall. The next two routes climb this feature.

**Mezzanine**   60 feet   E1 5b         (1998)
Short but sustained; start on the left and climb a short slab until the wall steepens just right of the arête. Climb up first right, then left, and move up to a crack. Climb this, using the arête on the left for a couple of moves, to a steep finish.

**End of an Era**   70 feet   E4 6a         (1990)
The next climb offers a more technical challenge; bold climbing on good rock. Climb the left side of the wall to an obvious crack, move up this to a horizontal crack and traverse right to a flat hold. Stand on this and step up left to another horizontal break and make a steep move to gain the top.

# Dyniewyd East                                   OS Ref 618 479

Approach as for Craig y Dyniewyd but head straight up the scree
to the crag. It is quite broken on the left but is more substantial on
the right where a band of overhangs at half height is an obvious
feature. Right again is a slab with two overlaps at half and three
quarters height. The first route starts in the centre of the crag and
follows a continuous rib to exit through an overhanging quartz block.

**Second Death**   80 feet   Hard Very Severe 5a      (30.4.98)
A disjointed route giving straightforward slab climbing up the rib
to an exciting finish through the 'quartz forehead'. Start just left of
an overhanging groove at the base of the rib. Climb up to the left
to avoid the overhangs and follow the slab up the rib until it
steepens. Strenuous moves up through the capping quartz block
provide the entertainment.

**Tao of Stone**   90 feet   Very Severe 4c      (22.6.98)
A loose start leads to a grand finish. Start at a slabby wall just
left of a vegetated gully with a holly tree at half-height. Climb the
slabs and enter the shattered groove, continue up this to the
heather bay and a possible belay. Gain the blunt arête on the left
and climb directly and airily up this to the top.

**Reservoir Frogs**   75 feet   E1 5b      (30.4.98)
A good route on sometimes hidden holds which takes a steep
groove and crack up the arête right of the obvious band of
overhangs. Start about 30 yards right of the previous route.
Climb the slab below the overhangs and move right to the arête.
Steep moves up lead to a crack. Follow the crack strenuously just
right of the arête to a pull left onto it near the top. Finish more
easily.

**Llyndy Groove**   60 feet   Very Difficult   ‡      (5.48)
The vegetated groove just to the right. Follow the groove, passing
much heather.

**Camel Whip**   60 feet   Very Severe 4c      (30.4.98)
A pleasant climb which takes the slab to the right with an overlap
at half height. Start in the centre of the slab. Climb up to a thin
crack and follow it to the overlap. Pull through on good holds to
step right and finish up an open groove. A variation finish can be
made by traversing left under the second overhang to finish up
the right-hand side of the gully wall, no change in grade.

**Llyndy Arête**   50 feet   Very Difficult      (5.48)
This minor route follows the arête just to the right. Climb the arête
direct with an awkward move near the top.

## Craig y Mwynwr (Crag of the Miner)

Left of the main area of rock is an independent buttress contained by two blind gullies. There is an old copper mine just right of this below the scree fan. The next two routes described climb the left and right edges respectively.

**Orbita**  90 feet   Very Difficult                    (22.6.98)
Start at the lowest point on the left and climb directly up the slabby rib pasing through an overlap near the top.

**Vasco**  100 feet   Very Severe 4b                    (22.6.98)
Awkward initial moves lead to much easier climbing above.
**1** 70 feet. 4b. Climb across the lower slabs and make a committing move left to a small ledge beneath the main arête. Continue to a pinnacle and belay.
**2** 30 feet. Move down slightly and climb the slabby wall to the top.

**Stonecrop**  80 feet   Very Severe 4b                 (7.7.98)
Right of the main buttress is a knife-edge arête with a holly tree and pinnacle at its base.Start in the groove behind the holly and gain the main arête from the right, continue to a ledge on the left. Move around the arête on the right and enter a steep, shallow groove. Move up and gain the arête via a hidden flake and continue more easily to the top.
Variation E1 5a                                          (1998)
The original finish goes left from the ledge on the arête and feels bold. From the ledge enter the shallow groove just left of the arête and make some thin moves left towards a good hold. Swing steeply left to better holds and continue more easily to the top.

## Clogwyn Coch (Red Crag)                    OS Ref 636 479

A pleasant south-facing crag; the routes are short but the rock is excellent. Park in a lay-by on the minor road running beside the river Nantmor at OS Ref 633 485. Follow the track past the club hut at Gelli lago and follow the path up the valley for half a mile. Cross the stream and follow the stone wall which runs up to meet the crag.

**Mary King of Scots**  90 feet   E1 5b                 (15.7.98)
Start beneath the rib leading to the overhang and hanging slab at the left side of the crag. Climb the rib (bold) to a detached block beneath the overhang. Step left and pull through the overhang at a steep crack and onto the hanging slab. Climb the poorly protected but easier slab direct up its centre to the top and nut belays well back.

**Left Groove**   45 feet   Very Severe 4b                (17.8.86)
Straightforward and on good rock. Follow the groove 20 left of
the stone wall.

**Cat Woman**   50 feet   E2 5c   †                (17.8.86)
A good route which feels quite bold. Climb the centre of the facet
(past an old peg) with fingery moves on very good rock.

**29 Not Out**   45 feet   E1 5b                (17.8.86)
A pleasant route. Start just right of the stone wall at some cracks.
Follow the cracks and a shallow groove to the top.

**Right Groove**   40 feet   Very Severe 4b                (17.8.86)
Not quite as good as its partner to the left. Follow the groove 15
feet right of the stone wall.

Approximately 150 yards left of Clogwyn Coch is a small gully
bounded on its left side by a short overhanging cliff where is one
route.

**Burnt Carp**   50 feet   E3 5c                (15.7.98)
Climb the steep dog-leg crack near the base of the gully;
strenuous but well-protected.

## Castell Clogwyn Coch                OS Ref 639 478

A small southeast-facing cliff with a slabby base and an overhang
across its right half. The approach follows the route to Clogwyn
Coch and continues past this crag to turn left up the valley, Castell
Clogwyn Coch is up on the left flank about a quarter of a mile from
the river.

**Office Rocker**   30 feet   Severe 4a   †                (6.3.99)
Start at the left end of the crag and climb directly to an obvious
left-facing corner, follow this to the top.

**Sais is Nice**   50 feet   E1 5c   †                (30.8.99)
Climb the wall to a ledge beneath the left end of the overhang.
Bridge up and leftwards to pass the overhang at the obvious
weakness. Slabby moves lead to the top.

**Cockney Cranker**   50 feet   E1 5b   †                (30.8.99)
Follow the cracked slab and strenuous overhang directly to the
top.

## Carreg Bengam (Round-topped Rock)        OS Ref 620 453

This location consists of two crags; a traditional slab and a recently
developed series of walls. The latter is a particularly fine little out-

crop of compact rock offering a number of short fingery climbs in the middle E grades. The cliffs are reached in about 15 minutes from the junction on the minor road from Nantmor to Nantgwynant, marked as Bwlchgwernog on the map. There is parking space for only one car. Follow the track up the hill for half a mile to a boggy plateau. Alternatively, walk up the path from Fronwen a little to the north which has more parking space to the same plateau area. The larger slabby crag can now be seen a little to the east.

The large slab offers a traditional route of Very Difficult standard with an easy initial section, leading to a high step towards the top. Just right the rock steepens and offers one short groove pitch.

**Irene Handel**   25 feet   Very Severe 4c              (17.2.98)
Short but sweet, start at the foot of the short white groove just off the path. Climb this to the top.

The back of Carreg Bengam gives another short pitch up an obvious flake crack. Go through the gate and follow the stone wall up the hill for a few yards. The route is on the left.

**Dark and Bim**   30 feet   Hard Very Severe 5a        (17.2.98)
Climb the finger-flake and corner using holds on the side wall past a heather bush to the top; steep.

## Carreg Bengam Bach

The main crag comes into view on the left as one follows the track through the gate. Strike up the hillside from the sheepfold to the base of the crag. The routes are short but the rock is excellent. A crevasse formed by boulders is an obvious feature of the right-hand side of the crag. The cliff is south-facing and in a delightful position with fine views down to the Glaslyn Estuary. The first two routes are on the extreme left of the crag on a short gully wall.

**Hong**   25 feet   Very Severe 4b                      (1.89)
Enter and climb the wide crack on the left; it turns out to be a bit of a thrutch.

**Kong**   30 feet   Very Severe 4c                       (1.89)
A fine little pitch. Follow the cracked groove right of *Hong*.

**Kennedy's Mile**   30 feet   E1 5b                      (1.89)
The first route on the main crag follows the leftward-slanting overhanging crack. A steep route on good holds. Step off the boulder and climb the crack with increasing difficulty to an awkward finish. Purists will start via the crack in the boulder below; also 5b.

# Carreg Bengham Bach

1. Kennedy's Mile E1
2. My Dear Holmes E3
3. Wild Orchid E3
4. The Pig Elf E3
5. Crocodile Goose E4
6. Zeitgeist E1
7. Hong VS
8. Kong VS

# YR ARDDU

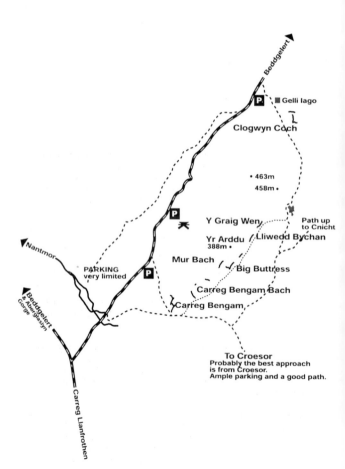

Beddgelert

Gelli Iago

Clogwyn Coch

• 463m

458m •

Y Graig Wen

Path up
to Cnicht

Yr Arddu
388m •

Lliwedd Bychan

Mur Bach

Big Buttress

Carreg Bengam Bach

Nantmor

PARKING
very limited

Carreg Bengam

Beddgelert
& Aberglaslyn
Gorge

To Croesor
Probably the best approach
is from Croesor.
Ample parking and a good path.

Carreg Llanfrothen

**My Dear Holmes**   40 feet   E3 6a                              (6.89)
Technical, but the hard moves are well-protected. Start from the
right side of the large boulder. Climb steeply to a peg runner and
make difficult moves over the bulge above to a final cracked
groove.

**Wild Orchid**   40 feet   E3 6a                              (6.89)
Just to the right is a hanging crack in the arête. A very good
route, the classic of the crag. Make a bouldery start and climb
the crack direct to the top.

The corner in the centre of the crag has been climbed but has been
reclaimed by an expanse of ivy, and rightly so.

**Little Towse on the Prairie**   45 feet   E6 6b          (5.99)
The wall to the right of the corner past a peg runner gives a fierce,
technical problem.

**The Pig Elf**   50 feet   E3 5c                              (6.89)
Nice climbing with a gripping start. To the right of the central
corner is a blank wall with a white streak descending from a
nose of rock on its right side. Start below this nose and above a
crevasse in the rock. Make a difficult pull onto the steep wall
above the crevasse and go steeply up to a rest in a V-groove.
Move right and then go straight up to a steep juggy finish.

**Crocodile Goose**   40 feet   E4 6a                         (2.89)
A bold, steep route which takes the white groove right of *The Pig
Elf* to climb a final short wall. Step into and climb the overhang-
ing groove to a sloping exit. Follow the short wall to the top.

**Zeitgeist**   35 feet   E1 5b                               (2.89)
An excellent route with good protection. Start just right of the
preceding route at a flake. Pull into the flake above the crevasse
and follow it directly to the top.

The hillside either side of the crag is scattered with excellent boulders so that when wandering up towards Yr Arddu many fierce
problems can be found. However, behind and slightly left of the
crag is a prominent hanging slab which contains the only other
route at the moment.

**Honcho Foot Path**   60 feet   E4 5c   †                    (6.89)
A fine, hanging slab is the largest feature and certainly the best.
Start by a tree on the left-hand side of the slab. A very good
route taking the centre of the fine slab direct. Fingery moves past
a faint overlap lead to slightly easier but bold climbing to the top.

The area of hillside behind the preceding route has many rocky ribs and walls and has recently become *the* alternative bouldering venue in North Wales. Superb rough rock, grassy landings and excellent views across the Glaslyn Estuary combine to give a crimp-pullers paradise.

# Yr Arddu (The Height)

The mountain of Yr Arddu forms a sort of table, not as impressive as its South African counterpart but with rock on all sides. Half a mile northeast of Carreg Bengam lies a rocky hillside with four main outcrops. The rock is superb and similar to that found on the crags above Tanygrisiau. The views across the Glaslyn Estuary more than compensate for the walk. Awaiting full development this area has been climbed upon for years, many routes having been rediscovered and named recently as first ascent details were hard to come by.

The crags are best reached via the Carreg Bengam approach. Continue along the track to where it crosses the stream and follow the stone wall by the side of the stream for half a mile until the outcrops appear. Strike directly up the hillside to another stone wall with two stiles crossing it. The left-hand (western) stile lies directly below a broad gully which contains Mur Bach. The eastern stile lies below Big Buttress. Alternatively a shorter but steeper approach starts from OS Ref 621 469; much more parking space. Follow the path up through the woods, difficult to find at times, until the open hillside is reached. Contour round right to hit the stone wall and follow it round to the stile. One can also approach from Croesor.

## Mur Bach                                    OS Ref 626 459

Above the western stile lies the broad gully, the best descent route. On the left-hand gully wall is a steeper area of rock with good incut holds. The first route starts at a massive block perched on a platform 40 feet from the beginning of the wall.

**Jam Chimney**   30 feet   Very Difficult
Climb the crack behind the block to its summit. Step right into a chimney and ascend a further 10 feet by jamming and cursing.

One hundred and twenty feet further up the gully a little rock wall contains a worthy route.

**Marmalade Wall**   50 feet   Very Difficult
Start below the right-hand end of a long ledge 10 feet up on the wall. Gain the ledge, step up to another ledge above on the right and finish by trending slightly left to the skyline.

The next route takes a shallow groove in the middle of the wall.

**Punky's Dilemma**  50 feet  Hard Very Severe 5a  (26.1.98)
The crack forms a very shallow corner. Climb this to a ledge and continue up to an overlap. Make an awkward move over this to a ledge. A hard move left into the final crack leads to the top.

Nearing the top of the gully the next route makes the most of the more broken face where a block with a small overhang is seen 40 feet up.

**Potted Precipice**  70 feet  Very Difficult
Start directly below the little overhanging block, stepping off from a low detached flake in the gully bed. Climb up to the left and step right to a ledge. Climb the wall above; harder on the right, easier on the left.

**Route 66**  40 feet  Hard Severe  (26.1.98)
Near the top of the gully is a wide crack with a green slab to the right. Climb the crack, pulling out on to the slab at 20 feet. Finish directly through the overhang on good holds.

## Big Buttress
OS Ref 627 458
Rising above the stone wall is a huge mass of rock, slabby on its right-hand side but with a steeper face running round in a band to the left above an area of heathery slabs. The right-hand side of the slabs is also denoted by a large patch of quartz. A blunt arête running down towards the stile forms the most recognizable line, *Shani's Climb*. Most of the routes here, although the longest in the area, degenerate somewhat towards the top.

**Steelworker**  150 feet  Hard Severe  (5.3.98)
Nice climbing on good rock.
**1** 60 feet. 4a. Begin on the lower left wall of the buttress at an unusual conglomerate wall. Start on the right and make a rising traverse left to the edge of the wall. Climb directly up to a heather bay.
**2** 90 feet. 4b. Move right to a rib with an old peg *in-situ*. Follow the narrow crack directly up the slab, moving slightly left near the top; a good pitch.

**Joy Division**  170 feet  Severe  (31.1.98)
Another pleasant route which starts 12 feet left of a rowan tree on the lower wall
**1** 30 feet. Climb up to the small sentry-box and move left to a spike. Go directly up to the stone terrace to belay.
**2** 40 feet. Climb directly over large blocks and traverse left across the hanging slab to the edge of the buttress.

**3** 30 feet. Climb the steep rib directly to a heather bay.
**4** 70 feet. Move left and climb the rib which borders the *Steelworker* slab to finish.

**Obscurer**   160 feet   Hard Severe                    (26.1.98)
A more direct line. Start at the twisting groove 30 feet right of the rowan tree.
**1** 30 feet. 4a. Climb the groove to belay.
**2** 50 feet. 4b. Move easily left, then climb the awkward slab to gain the hanging slab of *Joy Division*; belay as for that route.
**3** 80 feet. 4b. Move back right and climb the short, steep wall with a dirty crack to a ledge. Move right and climb another short, steep wall to easier slabby climbing which leads to the top.

**Shani's Climb**   190 feet   Severe                    (1950s)
A steep start leads to much easier climbing above. Start directly below the blunt arête at the lowest central part of the buttress.
**1** 100 feet. Climb a steep wall with a crack on the right to a step right onto the arête. Follow this to a good stance but poor belays.
**2** 90 feet. Continue up the much easier rib to the top.

To the right is a steeper area of rock set back above easy slabs.

**Twister**   150 feet   Severe                    (31.1.98)
Enjoyable steep climbing with an easy finish. Climb the steep, broad, twisting groove which begins from the bay just left of the wall to a break. Easier slabby climbing now leads to the top.

**Artifex**   190 feet   Very Difficult
A wandering route which starts just left of the 8-foot block.
**1** 90 feet. Climb the slab to a ramp which is followed, smooth at first, trending rightwards to a ledge.
**2** 100 feet. Go steeply up above the boulder via a heathery crack to a ledge. Six feet left of a large boulder move right and follow the left-hand of two cracks.

**Stone the Crows**   110 feet   Hard Severe                    (14.2.98)
Start on the left-hand side of the wall at a block.
**1** 40 feet. 4a. Step off the block and climb the steep wall moving left to gain the edge. Continue steeply but more easily to a ledge.
**2** 70 feet. 4b. Climb the steep crack directly behind the first pitch to the top.

**King Crimson**   120 feet   Severe                    (14.2.98)
**1** 60 feet. Gain the prominent, deep crack on the right of the wall by climbing a groove on the left and then hand-traverse across to the base of the crack. Climb this to a terrace.
**2** 60 feet. Climb the right-hand crack above the terrace to the top.

# Lliwedd Bychan
OS Ref 628 459

Not such a large crag but the rock is at a more consistent angle and the extensive views over Cwm Dylif are magnificent. (Perfect for a family day out in the easier grades; a large expanse of grass at the base of the cliff provides an idyllic picnic spot.) It is situated 100 yards east past the stone wall towards a perched block. A pyramidal boulder lies near the base towards the centre of the cliff. On the left-hand side, the first obvious feature is a heathery gully. An old peg marks the top of *Central Route*; belays can usually be found well back from the edge. The name came from its apparaent resemblance to a one tenth scale model of Lliwedd on Snowdon.

### Left Gully Rim   100 feet   Difficult
Start 15 feet left of the heather-choked crack. Move up left and then right to a ledge, step left again onto the wall and up to a ledge. The pillar on the right leads to the top.

### Heather Gully   100 feet   Difficult                    (1950s)
A good introduction though a bit blocky towards the top. Start 10 feet right of the heathery gully below a crack. Climb the steep lower section to reach the heathery cleft. Follow this past blocks to follow a vague groove and so to the top.

### Right Gully Rim   100 feet   Difficult                 (1950s)
A good, varied route on excellent rock. Start as for the preceding route, 30 feet left of the pyramidal block. Climb up and right to gain a niche, climb up to a wide crack and go past some heather. Continue up the crack to the top.

### Central Route   100 feet   Very Difficult              (1950s)
Once again good climbing on good rock. Start about 10 feet left of the pyramidal boulder, below a crack. Climb up steeply at first and follow the crack until it fizzles out. Continue up the vague arête and follow the continuation seam to the top.

### Orthin   110 feet   Hard Severe 4b                     (1950s)
Start behind the pyramidal boulder at the base of a slight tower of rock. Move up the wall and climb through a slight bulge. Follow the crack above until easier climbing leads to the top.

### Eastern Route   110 feet   Severe                      (1950s)
Another good and varied climb on fine rock. Start behind and just right of the pyramidal boulder, at the base of an obvious crack. The crack leads to a groove system slanting slightly right at its top; head directly up to easier slabs.

### Battel   120 feet   Severe                             (1950s)
Fine climbing at the grade. Start right of the boulder at a short

wall. Move steeply up the wall and follow a slab to a short crack. Climb this to a slight rib and follow it on superb holds to the top.

**Croesor**   120 feet   Hard Severe                               (1950s)
Start right again and just left of a short green corner. Climb the wall, crux, and continue in the same line up slabs and shallow cracks to the top.

**Chimney Corner**   100 feet   Difficult
A poor route up the chimney on the right-hand side of the crag. Climb the chimney and the corner above; a bit dirty.

# Y Graig Wen                                    OS Ref 629 460

The next crag is a squarish block of rock 100 yards to the north-east. It is smaller than the previous crag but provides a very steep wall of compact white rock with a square ledge system at two-thirds height and a more broken, but still steep, area to the right.

**Lurking Libido**   50 feet   E3 6a                               (16.5.98)
Technical climbing which takes the groove immediately left of the white wall. A hard start leads steeply to a jammed flake. Pass this rightwards following a fault line to a spike; finish direct.

**Test on Your Own**   60 feet   E2 5b                             (16.5.98)
Climb the thin leftward-slanting line trending to the left edge of the big ledge at three-quarters height. A microwire protects the line until the ledge is reached. Take a few steps rightwards on the ledge to finish more easily up the short wall direct.

**Teaching Organon**   60 feet   E3 5c                             (16.5.98)
The right edge of the white wall leading to the leftward-facing groove. Climb the edge, past a few good runners, before committing yourself to good but spaced holds above (microwires in the groove on the right). Gain the big ledge and finish as for the preceding route.

**Chairman's Folly**   90 feet   Hard Severe 4b                    (1950s)
Steep, but with good holds, starting directly beneath the overhang and gaining the ledge by climbing the steep wall direct. Step right and make a steep move up which is followed by easier climbing to the top. The original route started further left and followed the sloping ramp to start.

The narrow, northern end of the plateau overlooks Cwm Gelli Iago, from which it rises in marshy steeps to a rocky rim where a few quality boulder problems can be found. The long, west flank drops steeply into the Nantmor valley. At its northern end there is loose rock and looser scree with nothing of interest. Going south along this flank sounder crags and slabs obtrude themselves above a long, grassy shelf. There are short buttresses and walls here which offer a blinkered scrambler much entertainment. There is one excellent chimney (Cantilever Chimney) with a wedged pinnacle in it, just above the stone wall that separates the grassy ledge from steeper things above.

North of Yr Arddu several scrappy, scrambling type routes at Moderate standard have been described in the past. These tend to follow ridge lines but are hopelessly broken by ledges and heather. The area is worth a wander, however, for the seeker of esoteric boulder problems.

# Craig Nant y Fedw (Birch Vale Crag)    OS Ref 617 444

This excellent little outcrop is to be found in a secluded valley which runs northeast from the road. It is best to park at a large lay-by (OS Ref 612 433) just before Carreg Hylldrem when approaching from Beddgelert. Walk back up the road towards Nantmor for 400 yards to a red gate. Go through this past a stone cottage on the left and follow the valley for half a mile until the crag becomes visible on the right. Alternatively, follow the ridge up and right of the path to descend on the far left of the cliff. The setting is idyllic with good views up to Cnicht and the rock dries quickly after rain although some routes are a bit mossy. The crag is northwest-facing and therefore only gets the sun in the evening. The crag offers everything from delicate slab climbs to super steep desperates.

The first buttress encountered on the left-hand side is an area of steep slabs with a vegetated crack slanting up left. The routes offer poorly protected, technical climbing on good rock; the friction is marvellous.

**Phuddi Crack**   60 feet   Hard Severe 4b   ‡          (4.91)
Follow the obvious left-trending ramp-line to where the heather becomes impenetrable. Climb the crack above, the top part of which is particularly vegetated.

**Wagtail**   50 feet   E3 5b                              (2.7.90)
A fine bold route with virtually no worthwhile protection. Start 5 feet left of the central crackline. Move up the ramp for a few feet and follow the clean, ripply slab via the cleaned central line. Belays may be found in the bluff of rock behind.

The central crackline has been climbed at Very Severe but is rapidly being overtaken by nature.

# Craig Nant y Fedw

1. Wagtail E3
2. Caleb E2
3. Stub HVS

**Caleb**  50 feet  E2 5b                                                (5.90)
An equally good route, bold but with just enough protection.
Balance up the slab just right of the central crackline to a peg
runner at 30 feet. Compose oneself and continue to the top.

**Stub**  50 feet  Hard Very Severe 5a                         (30.8.91)
Another good route with better protection than its neighbours.
Start right again at the cleaned line. Ascend the slab to the right
by delicate and enjoyable climbing with the crux towards the top.

The second buttress contains one route which is possible in most
conditions because of its sheltered nature. The buttress is short but

has an overhang running across it at half height slanting up to the left. A grassy ramp below and a tree on the left-hand side are obvious features.

## No Sheep Till Buxton   80 feet   Hard Very Severe 5b
(3.91)

A good route which traverses below the overhangs. Climb up from the right-hand corner to gain the traverse line. Follow this leftwards, always interesting, to the crux finishing move.

## Ymosodiad Gwybed   50 feet   E4 6b                (6.99)
Start as for *No Sheep...* to the traverse line but breach the overhang above at its first weakness.

The main crag is to the right and, although short, offers those who relish steep, technical testpieces a welcome choice of routes to go at.

## Chute Up or Chute Off   50 feet   E5 6a          (26.9.90)
A surprisingly awkward route which takes the obvious black chute running left-to-right. A hard and friable move low down leads into the chute. This provides a really steep, balancy problem with protection being conspicuous by its absence, until easier ground leads to the top.

## Cracking Up   50 feet   E7 6c                     (31.3.91)
The obvious 'mega' layback flake in the centre of the overhanging main facet. Climb up very strenuously to an *in-situ* wire. Move left to a large hole and then make some mean moves up to an obvious ramp sloping up to the right to finish.

## Sad Cow   50 feet   E7 6c                         (6.91)
A direct finish to *Cracking Up* and even more of a beast; the hardest route on the crag. Follow *Cracking Up* to the *in-situ* wire but continue straight up past it by desperate moves to a peg. Another hard move above leads to a direct finish.

## Cookie Munster   50 feet   E6 6b                  (31.3.91)
A very sustained route taking the groove and crack right of *Cracking Up*. Climb up, via a peculiar contorted start, into the groove and eventually gain some better holds. Move up and left (crux) to top out with a bit of a pump.

## The Hayward Slot   60 feet   E5 6a                (7.90)
On the right-hand side of the crag is an obvious overhanging slot. Move up to the slot and enter it via some awkward and tiring moves. The exit above calls for persistence and will only be overcome by the strong.

# Craig Nant y Fedw

**Ripcurl**   50 feet   E6 6c                                   (5.93)
Right of *The Hayward Slot* is a short overhanging wall. Climb up
the easy slab to where the rock starts to overhang alarmingly.
Attack the horribly steep wall, passing two tied-off knifeblades
and two good pegs; good luck.

## Craig Creua (Enclosures Crag)          OS Ref 614 438
This minor crag which can be reached from the next gate on the
road heading towards Carreg Hylldrem. Leave the road and scramble up past a cave, follow a shallow valley for 200 yards to a steep
bulbous cliff (southeast-facing).

**Steep for 5 Minutes**   30 feet   E6 6b              (2.93)
A route to be blasted, otherwise gravity will intervene all too
quickly. Follow the obvious central crack/groove past two
worrying pegs to a further peg. Haul up on enormous holds with
difficulty and breathe a sigh of relief. Belay well back on a
boulder.

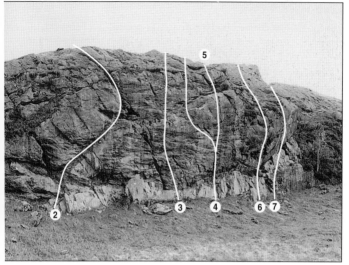

1. No Sheep till Buxton HVS
2. Chute Up or Chute Off E5
3. Project
4. Cracking Up E7
5. Sad Cow E7
6. Cookie Munster E6
7. Ripcurl E6

# **Carreg Hylldrem** (Forbidding Crag)

OS Ref 614 432

Carreg Hylldrem is situated immediately above the Aberglaslyn-Penrhyndeudraeth road, about 1 mile north of the village of Carreg. When approaching the cliff from Tremadog it is clearly seen across the fields as a rocky dome terminating a small spur of Cnicht. Closer inspection reveals a crag of awe-inspiring steepness, composed of smooth compact rock and giving a number of impressive climbs, which require strength and boldness as much as good technique. Many of the routes follow grooves which overhang viciously and give dramatic situations. The steepness of the crag means that it stays dry for most of the year and the girdle traverses together with several other routes can be climbed in a downpour; particularly useful given the vagaries of North Wales's weather. The bouldering wall right of the crag is always dry but suffers from a surplus of chalk.

The crag is quite complex on first acquaintance. Starting from the left side of the main crag the most obvious feature is a large overhang near the foot climbed by *King Kong* (via a prominent flake). Above and to the right a series of overhanging grooves gives the lines of *Primus*, *The Burner* and *Samurai Groove*. The right side of the crag is characterised by a rightward-sloping gangway, from which *Hardd* traverses into the concave centre of the main face. *Poker* starts at the same point and takes a direct line up the steep rock above the gangway. The best descent is well to the right of the crag.

At the extreme left end of the cliffs a short overhanging bluff gives worthwhile bouldering. Forty yards right of this the cliff begins as a wide bay of rock some 40 feet high. There are several pitches here, the most substantial being **Lone Wolf** E1 5b, which takes the curving scoop towards its left side. Thirty yards right of the bay, beyond an ivy-covered section which should on no account be stripped, clean rock reappears as a smooth impending wall with a projecting spur of rock at its base.

**Big Fin Reef Squid**   40 feet   E5 6b                    (4.91)
Short but very strenuous. Climb the fine rightward-facing flake directly above the spur; 2 peg runners.

**Fin Bar**   45 feet   E6 6c                                     (4.92)
Takes the cleaned wall right of the previous route. Swarm up through brambles to a steep ramp; peg. Make a desperate move up right for a huge jug. Complicated climbing leads up to ledges and a slab to finish.

After a further 30 yards of jungle-infested rock the main crag proper begins. Its base is guarded by a 45-degree roof.

**Troubador**   130 feet   E3                               ( 25.3.73)
A messy and devious approach to a spectacular overhang. Start by scrambling up vegetation on the left-hand side of the crag to a small slab.
**1** 90 feet. 5c. Go across the small slab and step down right onto a ramp about 30 feet above the ground. Follow this to beneath the obvious flake in the roof above. Climb the detached flake and the chimney above to a poor stance.
**2** 40 feet. 4b. Climb the groove to finish on easy slabs.

**Compromising Positions**   40 feet   E4 6b         (2.6.83)
A bold start leads to very strenuous climbing. Start just left of *King Kong* at a weakness in the roof. Climb the line of least resistance through the roof (2 pegs) to reach a stance and belay on *Troubador*, bold and pumpy. Finish either as for *Troubador* or, more in keeping, *The Chimp In Me*.

**King Kong**   120 feet   E3                                    (6.74)
A spectacular roof pitch, powering up a flake which is beginning
to show signs of wear; cams useful. Start at the left side of the
main crag, below an obvious flake-crack splitting the lower roof.
**1** 30 feet. 5c. Climb the flake-crack quickly, to reach good
finishing holds over the lip of the overhang, where there is a
cramped stance and peg belay.
**2** 50 feet. Traverse right for 20 feet to reach a slab, which leads
back left to a stance and peg belay where the angle eases.
**3** 40 feet. 5a. Walk to the right for 10 feet and climb the
overhanging chimney to the top.

**King Kong-Troubador Connection**   135 feet   E3
The best climb on this area of the cliff is this combination which
features two impressive roof sections. Start as for *King Kong*.
**1** 30 feet. 5c. Climb the flake-crack in the roof to the stance and
peg belay (as for *King Kong*).
**2** 25 feet. 5b. Traverse left along the hanging slab, with one
awkward move, and belay beneath the detached flake in the roof
of *Troubador*.
**3** 40 feet. 5c. Climb the detached flake and chimney above to a
poor stance (as for *Troubador*).
**4** 40 feet. 4b. Climb the groove to finish on easy slabs.

**The Chimp in Me**   50 feet   E6 6c                            (10.91)
A highly enjoyable but butch exercise taking the roof directly
above *King Kong*; high in its grade. First pummel up *King Kong*
and place some cams in a good break. A desperate series of
moves gain flat jugs in the middle of the roof, this sequence
passes 3 pegs and culminates in a mantelshelf. Finish up left.

Right of *King Kong* is an obvious crack containing a peg and leading to a deep V-niche. It has probably not been climbed.

**Primus**   180 feet   E2                                      (26.2.60)
The lower section of the crag is split by a prominent groove. The
route takes this groove and a steeper groove in the upper section
reached by a hard traverse across an overhanging wall. A steep
and impressive climb; the main difficulties are short. Start at a
slabby rock, just to the left of the prominent groove.
**1** 75 feet. 4c. Climb up onto the slabby block and make an
awkward traverse rightwards into the groove. Climb this easily to
a peg stance beneath the overhangs (junction with *The Girdle*).
**2** 55 feet. 5c. Traverse across the slab on the left to the rib and
climb this for a few feet. Move back right across the very steep
wall until it is possible to gain the overhanging groove (peg
runner). Continue awkwardly up the groove to easier rock and a
good spike with an impressive but comfortable stance on the
right.

# Carreg Hylldrem

1. Troubador E3
2. King Kong E3
3. Primus E2
4. The Burner E2
5. Samurai Groove E3
6. The Wildebeest E4
7. Hardd E2
8. Poker E3

**3** 50 feet. 4c. Climb up above the spike and move left to finish. Directly above the initial groove of *Primus* is an overhanging tower taken on the left by *Spooks* and head-on by *Of All the Bars...* and *Flare-Up*. All start from the first stance of *Primus*.

**Spooks**   80 feet   E4 5c                                        (1.6.88)
Move up and left from the sharp rib to reach a short crack. Continue straight up to a detached pinnacle and finish up the groove above.

**Of All the Bars in All the World**   80 feet   E6 6b   (4.91)
Climbs directly up the buttress using various fins and scoops. Essentially a sport climb with all-fixed protection. Launch straight up the steep groove (peg runner) to slopers and a knee-bar rest. Lunge right into the recess and grab the fins to follow them direct by some very strenuous moves to easier ground.

**Flare Up**   90 feet   E6 6c                                     (6.88)
Strenuous and impressive, a traditional route up the buttress but encroached on by the fixed gear of *Of All the Bars...* The slab on the right is followed for a few feet until it is possible to launch boldly up the overhanging wall above an undercut to reach a hidden peg runner in a niche. Hard moves past the peg lead to a good jug. An even bigger jug above leads to a swing up left into a slanting chimney; continue up easier rocks to the top.

**Sunset Traverse**   200 feet   Hard Very Severe        (1977)
A low-level girdle following slabs between the jutting overhangs on the left-hand side of the crag. Start below twin grooves about 30 feet right of the prominent groove of *Primus*. The bold start can be unsettling.
**1** 50 feet. 5b. Start up the right-hand groove, but then traverse left with difficulty onto the slab. Continue leftwards to a stance in the groove of *Primus*.
**2** 50 feet. 5a. Step down and traverse left across the slab to a tree belay (junction with *The Girdle*).
**3** 100 feet. 5a. Continue easily leftwards to the end of the slab and climb up steeply to  finish.

**The Burner**   180 feet   E2                              (21.8.66)
A good climb, crossing the overhangs right of *Primus* in a very exposed position. Start below the twin grooves as for *Sunset Traverse*.
**1** 80 feet. 5a. Climb the right-hand groove to its top and a junction with *The Girdle*. Follow this leftwards to a stance and peg belay on a rib.
**2** 70 feet. 5b. Climb the rib on the left to a small platform. Move left across the overhanging wall to a large spike and pull up into

a small niche. Move left round the arête to reach the stance on *Primus*, with a good spike on the left.
**3** 30 feet. 4c. Climb up above the spike and move left to finish as for *Primus*.

**Flatulence**   110 feet   E3 6a                                    (6.86)
The direct finish to *The Burner*; the hard section is short but the climbing very powerful. Start at the first stance of *The Burner*. Follow the second pitch until it escapes left. Blast up and onwards to reach better holds and the top, beware of a loose flake that has to be used.

**Raving Lunatic**   160 feet   E5                            (5.84)
The obvious gash right of *The Burner*. A technical first pitch followed by outrageous climbing through a massive roof on the second. Start as for *The Burner*.
**1** 60 feet. 6c. Climb up left on to a slab and make hard moves straight up to reach holds above the overhang. Continue to the belay of *The Burner*.
**2** 100 feet. 6a. Move up right to a ledge, step down and left to the start of the jagged roof crack. Follow this, moving left at the lip to bring sanctuary within reach.

**Raging Bull**   110 feet   E5 6b              (24.3.67/25.5.83)
An equally stunning and challenging line up the shallow, coffin-like chimney which slices through the roof. Originally aided this beast of a route now goes totally free. Yard Dogs need not apply. Start at the first stance of *The Burner*. Ascend a short groove to an obvious traverse line leading rightwards beneath the overhangs; follow this to a saddle below the overhanging chimney. Climb this (3 rusty peg runners, wires to back up) using arm bars, knee locks, back-and-footing etc. until the lip is reached. Continue up steep rock to easier ground; belay.

**Samurai Groove**   180 feet   E3              (25.4.71)
A superb route giving very steep climbing in a position of incredible exposure. Great care is needed on the main pitch to avoid rope drag. Start as for *The Burner*.
**1** 60 feet. 5a. Climb the right-hand groove to the traverse line which leads leftwards to the stance and peg belay on the rib (as for *The Burner*).
**2** 80 feet. 5c. Climb the short groove behind the belay to an obvious traverse line leading rightwards beneath the overhangs. Follow this to a saddle beneath an overhanging chimney (*Raging Bull*). Make a sensational move down and right around the overhanging nose to gain a steep groove. Follow this to an overhung niche and exit leftwards out of this to a belay on easier ground.

**3** 40 feet. Climb up broken rocks to finish.
Variation
**Direct Finish — Total Bull**  110 feet  E4 6a        (8.9.87)
Steep climbing in an awesome position. From the 'saddle'
beneath the overhanging chimney, swing right and go up an
exposed scoop until the angle eases. Finish up easier rock.

**Going for Gold**  130 feet  E6 6c                (26.5.88)
A direct and sustained line taking the blank, overhanging groove
right of the top of *Samurai Groove*. Start as for *Samurai Groove*.
Move up and right onto a steep wall next to some ivy. Move up
left to an easier groove leading to a short chimney. Climb this to
a smooth overhanging wall where hard moves up past a roof
lead to a slab below the overhanging groove. Go up past a poor
peg to clip a much better one and blast the groove above to gain
a ledge above it. Finish as for *Samurai Groove*.

**Gwyddbwyll**  100 feet  E5 6b                (1.8.87)
The name means 'chess', an accurate description of the subtleties
required to beat this fine route. Go 15 feet along *The Girdle
Traverse* to an obvious crack (cams). Ascend the crack to a peg
runner and traverse right for 10 feet to another peg. Move
straight up to 2 pegs together and go left and up a groove to join
*Hardd* at the stance. Finish via *The Wildebeest* pitch 2.

**One Fine Day**  150 feet  E5                (20.4.88)
Start 6 feet left of the arête of *The Wildebeest*, below a line of
thin cracks leading to a downward-pointing flake.
**1** 80 feet. 6a. Gain the thin cracks from the left and move up to
the flake. Pull up leftwards over the bulge to a small ledge just
right of *Gwyddbwyll*. Step up and right and climb up past an
obvious undercut to reach some sloping ledges. Continue up a
steep groove immediately left of *Hardd* to its slab. Go up the
continuation right of the overhang to the stance of the original
route.
**2** 70 feet. 5c. A sensational pitch. Climb the short corner above
the stance to the obvious rising traverse line. Follow this for 30
feet past a large spike, then, keeping low round a bulge continue
to an obvious exit and easy ground.

**The Wildebeest**  150 feet  E4                (1.81)
An excellent climb which takes the direct start to *Hardd* to the first
belay and finishes up the *Direct Finish*. Start by scrambling up
behind the large oak tree to reach the start of the gangway
leading rightwards, at the foot of a sharp rib.
**1** 100 feet. 6a. Climb the rib to the obvious large undercut. From
there move left and up to the block roof. Climb over this rightwards to join *Hardd* at the foot of the short crack. Climb this to a

bulge and make a delicate traverse left to a good resting place. Climb straight up over the bulges to reach the small stance (as for *Hardd*).

**2** 50 feet 5c. Step right from the stance into a short groove (peg runner). Step right onto the smooth little wall and make a difficult move up to gain an awkward position on the left side of an overhanging groove. Climb straight up on very steep rock to a niche beneath an overhang. Escape left to easy ground and the top.

The impressive central section of the cliff is crossed by two excellent traverses which stay dry in almost all weathers.

**Dion**   100 feet   E4 6b                                          (29.5.88)
Start as for *Hardd*. Climb up to and clip a peg runner on *Hardd*, step down and left to a point above *The Wildebeest*. Make hard moves left to a peg on *Gwyddbwyll*. Reverse this past its first peg runner to a good ledge before the obvious ramp. Traverse this to below *Raging Bull*. Step down to *The Girdle* stance to finish.

**Welsh Water Subversion**   120 feet   E5 6b      (26.5.88)
A spectacular line having some bold and technical climbing. From the start of *Hardd* move left to the flakes above the over-hang of *The Wildebeest* and traverse left with these at foot level until thin climbing up and across the slab gains the break of *Gwyddbwyll*. Continue leftwards past the pegs below the top groove of that route to a bay beside an overhanging nose. Climb round the nose with difficulty into *Samurai Groove*. Go up this for a few feet and break left along a crack in a fantastic position.

**Hardd**   160 feet   E2                                          (Easter 60)
The classic of the crag — a must on a rainy day. This is a superb and very exposed climb with an atmosphere out of all proportion to its size. Start by scrambling up behind the large oak tree to reach a good ledge some way up the obvious rightward-sloping gangway.

**1** 80 feet. 5c. Step left onto the steep wall and climb leftwards to the foot of a short crack. Climb this to the bulge and make a delicate traverse left to a good resting place. Step onto the smooth slab on the left and continue in the same line over some bulges to reach a small stance in a very exposed position. A superb pitch.

**2** 40 feet. 4b. Climb down the steep groove below the stance until it is possible to escape left on good holds to reach easier ground. Climb this to a good stance.

**3** 40 feet. Climb broken rocks easily to the top.

Variations

**The Original Way**   80 feet   E2
**1a** 60 feet. 5c. Climb to the good resting place as for pitch 1,

but instead of stepping left climb straight up bulges to reach a small stance.

**2a** 20 feet. 4b. Traverse left into a groove and climb this for a few feet until it is possible to step left to the small stance at the end of pitch 1.

**Hardd Direct Finish** is now included as the second pitch of *The Wildebeest*. It can be followed from the top of pitch 1 to make the route an excellent E3.

**Poker**  140 feet  E3                                          (10.9.66)
A strenuous and poorly-protected climb with some doubtful rock. Start as for *Hardd* at the stance on the gangway.

**1** 70 feet. 5c. Climb the broken overhanging groove above the stance (peg runner). Move right and climb straight up into an overhung niche and peg belay.

**2** 70 feet. 5c. Climb the smooth groove on the left to an obvious spike runner. Continue awkwardly onto a slab and move right and then back left round a bulge. Traverse diagonally left across the steep wall to finish.

**The Spook**  140 feet  E2                                      (6.66)
A poor route up the broken rock at the end of the gangway, which utilises the niche of *Poker* as a stance. Start as for *Hardd*.

**1** 70 feet. 5a. Climb up the gangway and step left onto the wall; climb up this trending left to belay in the niche of *Poker*.

**2** 70 feet. 5c. Climb with difficulty out of the right-hand side of the niche and then trend left across the upper wall to reach the top.

**Biggles**  140 feet  Hard Very Severe 5a                       (30.8.79)
A pleasant pitch. Start as for *Hardd*. Climb up right of *The Spook* and eventually gain a rightward-sloping ramp. Climb this delicately to finish.

**The Girdle Traverse**  220 feet  Hard Very Severe  (27.3.60)
A very good outing, especially suitable for a wet day because it is sheltered by big overhangs. Start by the large oak at the foot of the gangway.

**1** 65 feet. 4c. Climb leftwards along the obvious break to reach a short groove. Climb this and make an awkward move onto the slabby rib on the left; peg belay.

**2** 35 feet. 4b. Traverse awkwardly left across a short slab to another rib and descend the groove on the other side for 20 feet to a small stance.

**3** 40 feet. 4b. Cross the slab on the left and descend a broken groove to a good ledge below the obvious slab. (Many parties abseil from this point.)

**4** 80 feet. 4c. Climb the slab to a tree belay. Alternatively, climb

the groove until forced onto the slab.
Variation
**Maybelline Finish**   100 feet   Hard Very Severe 5a   (8.6.65)
**2a** Climb the groove to the overhang and pull over it into a
rightward-slanting groove, which leads to the top.

**A Nightmare of Black Donkeys** 350 feet E3 is a high-level
girdle of the crag and covers little independent ground. The route
follows *Primus* to the junction with *The Burner*, where a rising
traverse to the right leads to the last stance on *Hardd*. Pitch 2 of
*Hardd* is followed in reverse to the exposed stance, when a very
exposed traverse right gives a difficult finish.

At the right-hand side of the crag, just past a small fence, is a
sharply overhanging wall flanked on both sides by ivy. This wall
is a popular bouldering venue and provides several short
ferocious routes, all of which stay bone dry in wet weather.

**The Big Six Fun Box**   35 feet   E5 6b                    (13.3.88)
Takes the overhanging wall some 20 feet left of the central niche.
Good climbing (3 peg runners).

**Bay of Pigs**   40 feet   E5 6b                           (11.5.88)
The overhanging pod left of *The Weirpig* is particularly testing.
Boulder to the base of the pod (small *Friend*) and climb it past a
poor peg, using holds on the right arête. Lower off the belay of
*The Weirpig*.

**The Weirpig**   40 feet   E5 6b                           (3.81)
A worthwhile challenge — high in its grade. Start below the
obvious niche in the middle of the wall. Climb up and make hard
moves (*Friend 3*) to attain a standing position in the base of the
niche. Exit leftwards and continue to a lower-off sling.

**First Blood**   40 feet   E4 6a                           (4.83)
Start 3 yards right of *The Weirpig*. A pokey start leads to a sling,
make a difficult move past it and continue more easily to reach
fixed slings, abseil off.

**Tarzan** 40 feet E3 5c started from the boulder just to the right
and climbed up to a groove via a peg and a thread. It is now
overgrown with ivy and should be left that way.

**Ryan's Son**   50 feet   E4 6b   ‡                        (7.83)
Climb up to and through the obvious large roof right of *Tarzan*, (2
peg runners). A good route but one that is rapidly being reclaimed by the ivy.

# Nant Gwynant

This beautiful valley presents the climber with a variety of objectives, from traditional routes offering a good honest thrutch to technical single pitch lines on very steep rock. The area stretches from Beddgelert northwards to the Pen y Gwryd and takes in all the recorded routes on both sides of the valley. As with the Nantmor area this district also presents limitless bouldering opportunities for those with a nose for a line.

The valley is in no way as popular as some of the venues in the nearby Llanberis Pass or Tremadog. Only Clogwyn y Wenallt and a couple of routes on Clogwyn y Bustach receive much traffic. The advantages are solitude, beautiful surroundings and sheltered climbing on low-lying crags often facing away from the prevailing winds. Disadvantages are that some of the routes are returning to their vegetated pre-first ascent states and that loose rock may occur on some of the less frequented climbs. Not everyone, however, wants cleaned, prepared rock with a line of chalk to follow. The Gwynant Valley will provide those who climb for more aesthetic reasons with a wonderful playground.

## Craig Bwlch Derw (Crag of the Oak Pas)

OS Ref 616 494

A small crag set in a delightful position on the shore of Llyn Dinas. It can be seen well from the road. Park near the outflow of the lake, cross the foot-bridge and follow the path around the side of the lake to the foot of the crag. The rock is a little shattered and loose blocks at the top make both routes a serious proposition.

**Qualen**   50 feet   Very Severe 4b                    (3.5.98)
Follows the slab on the left side of the buttress. Start near the left-hand edge. Scramble up and step left at a grass ledge to gain a crack. Follow this past an overlap to reach some perched blocks. Clamber over these with some trepidation.

**Brewer's Troupe**   50 feet   E1 5a                    (3.5.98)
A serious route which takes the shallow corner on the right-hand side of the crag. Climb the right-facing corner system on large holds via a series of lock-offs. Pulling on the large flakes near the top is worrying.

The following route can be found a little bit southwest of Craig y Llyn. Park in the first small lay-by on the left when driving towards Beddgelert. Go up the hillside opposite until above the tree line whence, out of the blue, a two body-length roof is found.

Will Nazarian climbing *Geireagle* E3,
Craig Bwlch y Moch.
Photo: Ian Smith

John Keightley on
*Chwys* E1, Craig
Bwlch y Moch.
Photo: Alan Leary

Gill Round on Canyon Rib
Severe, Aberglaslyn
Gorge.
Photo: Terry Gifford

Martin Crook on the first ascent of The *Bear of Tralee* E2, Aberglaslyn Gorge. Photo: Glenn Robbins

**Manta Ray Hone Hang**   Hard Very Severe 5c      (4.97)
Obscure but quite good fun. Thug out along the roof; if the Hone
Hang bouldering start is used it is 6a.

# Craig y Llyn (Crag of the Lake)   OS Ref 619 502

Rising above the woods and close to the A498 at the head of Llyn
Dinas is this southeast-facing and easily accessible cliff. Although
close to the road, it is not easy to view the crag and it is best seen
from the spur to the right of the crag. A smaller cliff, with a rounded
top, can be seen poking its head out of the trees about 80 yards
down and to the left of the main cliff, the line of *Honorary Grit* is
situated there. Park at the large lay-by near the lake and walk back
up the valley to the old bend in the road. Go through the gate and
scramble over mossy boulders through the woods to reach the base
of the rocks.

The climbing can be characterised as being bold and precarious
especially on the harder slab routes. A long neck, a good pair of
boots and a certain ingenuity with protection will be found to be
the prerequisites for this unique cliff.

The crag can be divided into five main areas, the first and lowest
section of rock is rather poor, with a downward pointing fang an
obvious feature. A short wall of excellent rock further right gives the
line of *Honorary Grit*. Up and to the right is the second section, a
diamond-shaped wall, *Perdido Street* and *The Moon* are two of the
climbs there. This wall is topped on the right by a diagonal gangway leading up from left to right, the line of *Terra Nova*. The gangway separates the lower wall from an upper diamond-shaped wall,
the location of *Wailing Wall* and *Chance Encounter* to name just
two routes. Once again, up and to the right after the *Wailing Wall*
area, is an impressive tower with overhangs at about half height,
cleft by the obvious crack of *Sybilla the Pun*.

The right-hand side of the crag forms a wall gradually degenerat-
ing into the hillside. The Sanctuary, a large grass ledge beneath the
upper section of the crag, provides the starting point for *Aquila* and
*Thirty-Nine Steps*, and is reached by climbing an awkward wall
near the foot of the grassy gangway in the left wall. Some of the
lines may seem very eliminate in style from the descriptions, however, once on the routes this notion will quickly become an illusion.
It should be stressed that Craig y Llyn is no longer a popular cliff,
the bold nature of the climbing probably putting off many climbers.
This unfortunately means that many routes have fallen into disuse
with moss being a major problem on the less frequented offerings.
A good clean from an abseil rope would see many routes back to

# NANT GWYNANT

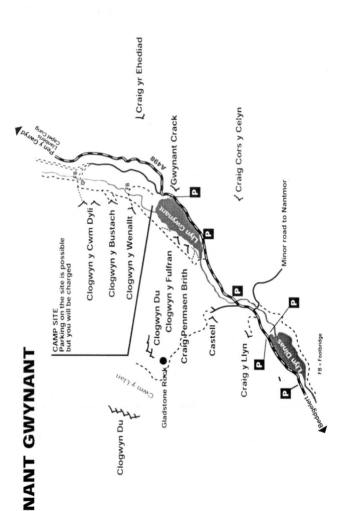

their initial state. So for those of you who enjoy bold, run out headgames Craig y Llyn could provide excellent sport.

One hundred yards left of the left-hand wall there is the open gully which is the best means of descent for all the routes on the main cliff.

**Erotickos**   140 feet   Hard Very Severe 5a   †   (c1979)
Ascend slabs on a small overhanging buttress to the left of the first main area of rock, just right of the downward-pointing fin of rock.

The next routes are situated on a small, round-topped cliff which is directly above the second lay-by after the bend heading for Tremadog. However, it is best reached by gaining Craig y Llyn itself, then contouring around the hillside from the lowest area of rock on the main crag.

**Beyond the Cosmos**   70 feet   E2 5b   (22.11.83)
A fine bold pitch, quite high in the grade. Start at a faint arête in the centre of the crag, just left of a tree. Strike diagonally right till beneath an overlap. Take this leftwards and climb onto a ledge reached from the left to finish up an obvious slim crack.

**Honorary Grit**   20 feet   E5 6c   (8.8.86)
A superb problem with the most technical of sequences. Start at the ledge below the top crack of *Beyond the Cosmos*. A thin crack left of that route is climbed with subtle moves on directional holds to a final dyno (one peg runner low down in the crack).

The first route on the main cliff is:

**Honeysuckle Wall**   160 feet   Severe   ‡   (12.6.53)
The left edge of the left-hand wall gives a steep little climb, which leads to a tedious heathery scramble. Start at the crack on the left of the large flake leaning against the wall.
**1** 80 feet. Climb the flake and step left onto the wall. Work up slightly left, step right, and go on straight up to ledges. Move up right under the wall above, pass round the corner onto the right-hand face of the buttress and go diagonally up right to an ash tree below a rake.
**2** 40 feet. Move obliquely left across the exposed wall left of the rake, passing a ledge, to two wedged flakes at the top of the rake.
**3** 40 feet. Step left for a few feet, then go directly up to a good flake belay; scrambling remains.

**Clonus**  120 feet  Very Severe  ‡                    (5.69)
Start above and to the left of a dead tree lying near the foot of
the crag.
**1** 60 feet. 4b. Climb steeply to a small ledge at 20 feet. Step left
and climb vegetation rightwards to a sloping heathery ledge.
**2** 60 feet. 4b. Go left for a few feet and climb the obvious
groove.

**Split Finger**  150 feet  Very Severe                    (5.69)
Start at a large perched block above and to the right of the dead
tree.
**1** 30 feet. Climb the easy, diagonal crackline to the top of a
large pinnacle.
**2** 120 feet. 4b. Step onto the slabby wall with difficulty and
move up to a good spike near a ledge. Step left from the ledge
and climb a groove to a small overhang. Step right and into
another groove, which is climbed to easy ground.

The next routes lies on the steep slab to the right.

**Perdido Street**  150 feet  E3                    (29.9.79)
A good route; delicate and bold. Start at a large block as for *The
Moon*.
**1** 40 feet. Scramble up left to a tree below the steep wall.
**2** 110 feet. 5c. Climb the rib directly behind the belay to reach a
spike. Move right to a small V-slot and from this gain the wall
above. Traverse right to a large spike. Move up and follow flakes
to a ramp and open corner. Finish up the corner.

**Death Can Be Fatal**  120 feet  E5 6a                    (20.11.82)
A serious pitch, although technically low in the grade ascending the
wall to the left of *The Moon*. Start at a pointed flake left of the start of
*The Moon*. Step right off the block and go straight up for 30 feet to
sharp holds below a very steep wall. A technical traverse leads left
for 10 feet to a V-slot and a good wire. Pull straight up on large
flakes to a long horizontal flake. Move up and rightwards until better
holds lead up leftwards to the base of a thin crack. Gain this and
follow it directly to the top. The good holds leading to the base of
the thin crack can be attained direct, eliminating the rectangular
excursion into *Perdido Street*, at no change in grade.

**Eclipse**  120 feet  E4 6a                    (1996)
A splendid, bold climb taking a line between *The Moon* and
*Death Can Be Fatal*. Start at the block, as for *The Moon*. Climb
*The Moon* to just past a peg and move left below the hanging
arête onto the wall. Move up a blind flake/groove and boldly
layback this to a rest and good protection where the crack is at
its widest. Move up a little left and traverse horizontally leftwards

with difficulty to reach the vague, thin crack leading to the highest point of the compass. Climb the crack to reach the top just to the right of *Perdido Street's* final groove.

**The Moon**   200 feet   E4                          (4.77)
A delightful and sustained initial pitch leads to a hideous green corner, which although short is very hard in normal conditions. Start at a square-cut block below a big steep wall with a slim groove in its upper half.
**1** 120 feet. 6a. Climb the steep wall to reach the slim groove, which is followed to a difficult finish on the right. Belay on the big grass ledge above.
**2** 80 feet. 6a. Go up an easy-angled slab to a fierce overhanging crack. Usually verdant and sludge-covered; climb this and the groove above to easy ground.

**Get Weaving**   120 feet   E5 6a                    (1989)
Takes the serious slab just to the right to give a committing lead. Climb the first 20 feet of *The Moon* and traverse right above the overlap to climb the slab just right of the water streak. Finish as for pitch 2 of *The Moon*, or up the slab on the left.

**Terra Nova**   200 feet   Hard Very Severe   ‡    (14.4.66)
The good groove is little compensation for the unpleasant approach. Start at a tree below a groove which leads up to the grassy gangway leading up left and forming the bottom left edge of the *Wailing Wall* area.
**1** 150 feet. 5a. Climb the wall behind the tree to a vegetated ledge. Step left and climb the mossy crack, with difficulty, until it is possible to step left onto the grassy gangway. Go straight up the grass to belay at the foot of the obvious groove.
**2** 50 feet. 5a. Climb the fine groove to easy ground on the ridge

The next five routes can be gained by ascending the grassy wall to reach the gangway as for *Terra Nova* pitch 1. A better method of approach would be to ascend *Perdido Street* and descend the gangway rightwards to reach the routes.

**Marshall Hearts**   145 feet   E3                    (17.4.81)
A good introduction to the style of climbing found on this wall. Start 15 feet below and right of the groove on pitch 2 of *Terra Nova*.
**1** 75 feet. 5c. Climb diagonally rightwards to a spike on the right. Hand-traverse left on the slab below the ramp of *Wailing Wall* to a small niche. Climb up to a peg belay in the corner.
**2** 70 feet. 5b. Traverse right below the blunt arête and move up rightwards under the square overhang into the corner. Follow this, moving left at the top.

# Craig y Llyn

1. Perdido Street E3
2. Death Can be Fatal E5
3. Eclipse E4

4. The Moon E4
5. Get Weaving E5
6. The Thing of Shapes to Come E6

7. Danger Days E4
8. Marshall Hearts E3
9. Wailing Wall E4
10. The Killing Fields E5

**The Thing of Shapes to Come**   60 feet   E6 6c       (1989)
The desperate groove left of the top pitch of *Marshall Hearts*
starts from the first stance of that route. Climb out left to enter the
very technical groove which is climbed past 3 peg runners with
excruciating bridging.

**Danger Days**   120 feet   E4 5c                    (5.81)
Good climbing; the moves over the overhangs are easier than
they look. Start as for *Marshall Hearts*. Follow *Marshall Hearts* to
an old peg stump and continue upwards to join the ramp of
*Wailing Wall*. Follow this rightwards for a few feet and then
make bold moves left across a steep slabby wall to the foot of a
corner. Climb over the square overhang and follow the crack
(peg runner) and wall to the top.

**Wailing Wall**   160 feet   E4 6a                  (25.8.78)
Superb climbing, both thin and bold, up the slabby wall above
the grassy gangway. Start on the gangway of *Terra Nova* at a
crack forming what is the left-hand side of a large flake. Step
right onto the wall and the flake, continue straight up to gain the
foot of a groove (part of *The Deceiver* utilises this groove).
Traverse left to gain a ramp and follow this for 40 feet to where it
gets wider. Climb another ramp leading up rightwards until it
merges with a steep rib. Ascend the rib, sustained and difficult,
to gain better holds. Easier climbing leads to the top.

**The Killing Fields**   160 feet   E5              (1985)
Start as for *Wailing Wall*.
**1** 80 feet. 6a. From 40 feet up *Wailing Wall*, continue up the
groove above until a shallow groove leads left to the middle of
the slab. Move up and trend right to a poor nut belay.
**2** 80 feet. 6a. Follow the obvious line back left to join and finish
as for *Wailing Wall*.

**Chance Encounter**   155 feet   E2 5b              (6.78)
Excellent, but poorly protected climbing to the right of *Wailing
Wall* at an easier standard. Start as for *Wailing Wall*. Step right
onto the wall to a flake and continue straight up for 40 feet to
gain the foot of a groove (part of *The Deceiver*). Climb the
groove and then move left to a flake-crack, which leads to a
ledge. Climb straight up the wall above, via flakes, to the foot of
a giant flake and take the face of this to the top.

**Peachpla**   230 feet   Very Severe               (1962)
An interesting climb taking a more or less direct line up the
middle of the crag. An obvious feature is the ramp of pitch 2.
Start at the left-hand end of the wall guarding entry to the
Sanctuary and below the grassy gangway.

**1** 30 feet Climb the wall to a grass ledge below a slabby ramp, trending rightwards.
**2** 80 feet 4c. Step right and climb delicately up the ramp until it is possible to move left and climb a crack forming the right side of a large flake. From the flake climb a short wall to a small ledge and belay.
**3** 120 feet. 4c. Climb the wall behind the stance and continue up a steep, awkward crack to some shattered blocks. Step left onto a ledge and go up to a niche. Move awkwardly left and climb directly to the top.

**The Deceiver**   240 feet   E2                              (6.8.71)
A serious route taking the obvious line of grooves in the middle of the wall left of *Peachpla*. Start at the left-hand end of the wall guarding entry to the Sanctuary, as for *Peachpla*.
**1** 30 feet. Climb the wall to a grass ledge below the ramp of *Peachpla*.
**2** 70 feet. 5c. Step right and climb the ramp until it is possible to move left with difficulty onto the steep wall under a roof. Move up to a fang and climb round it into a groove, which leads to a poor ledge and peg belays.
**3** 100 feet. 5b. Traverse left delicately for 10 feet to reach the obvious groove and follow this to a large hanging flake. Climb the flake and then move left into another groove, which leads to a belay on the gangway above.
**4** 40 feet. 5a. Climb the corner and cracks above.

**Aquila**   200 feet   Hard Very Severe                   (27.8.55)
This quite enjoyable route follows a rib and a crack to the steep section, which it avoids by a traverse right to finish near the gully on the right. Start from the Sanctuary, at a rib left of a shallow wet corner.
**1** 100 feet. 5a. Climb the rib to the upper reaches of the shallow corner. Go up an easy crack in the left-hand part of this to a block belay below the steep wall. The stance is round to the left behind the block.
**2** 35 feet. 4b. Traverse right on grass ledges, awkward at first, under the steep wall to a huge block overlooking the gully.
**3** 25 feet. 5a. Climb a short wall to the foot of a shallow groove and move right round the corner, where a crack leads to a good ledge .
**4** 40 feet. 4c. Climb a corner to another good ledge and then the crack on the left to finish.
Variation
**The Beakin**   90 feet   Hard Very Severe 5a        (Easter 69)
**1a** Climb the shallow corner, usually wet, for a few feet and then climb the left wall until it is possible to regain the corner by a small bulge. Climb the bulge and step left to join the easy crack of pitch 1.

**Sybilla the Pun**   150 feet   E4                    (6.78)
Very bold climbing on the first pitch gives access to the superb
crack splitting the tower. Start at the foot of a diamond-shaped
wall 30 feet higher up the Sanctuary from *Aquila*.
**1** 70 feet. 5c. Climb the faint grooves, moving left halfway up the
wall into a better defined groove. Continue up this to the block
stance at the end of *Aquila* pitch 2. A poorly protected pitch.
**2** 80 feet. 5c. Traverse down left on a quartzy break into a
groove. Climb this to a square-cut roof. Pull round to the right to
enter the straight crack, which leads in an impressive situation to
the top.

The right-hand side of the large recess right of *Aquila* has been
climbed by a poor route.

**Bychan**   135 feet   E3 6a                    (7.83)
A technical but well-protected route taking a steep groove in the
arête left of *Thirty-Nine Steps*, opposite to and similar to *Sybilla
the Pun*.
**1** 35 feet. Climb a corner and step right onto a ledge and belay.
**2** 100 feet. 6a. Follow a crack in a groove in the arête snaking
up and leftwards to gain the top.

**Cunnyson**   E4 6b   †   (1987) is the groove left of *Thirty-Nine
Steps* and probably has some very long reaches.

**Thirty-Nine Steps**   130 feet   E1                    (6.69)
A serious and impressive pitch up the grooved arête right of the
large recess. Start by scrambling up to the foot of twin cracks
beneath the right-hand wall of the crag.
**1** 20 feet. Climb the left-hand crack to a stance and belay.
**2** 110 feet. 5a. Go diagonally left, stepping round to a flake at
the foot of a corner-crack. Climb the crack and move awkwardly
right to the foot of a very shallow chimney. At the top of the
chimney traverse right to a leftward-trending crack, which leads
to a niche. Step up and right to finish.

In 1955 two routes were climbed on the far right-hand side of the
crag. Both are now completely overgrown and hence best forgotten. Just above and to the right of the gate giving access to Crag y
Llyn is an obvious orange groove, the location of the following
route.

**Power Snob**   30 feet   E4 6b                    (4.97)
A short technical offering. Climb the groove via a boulder
problem start past 2 peg runners.

The next four crags lie on the flanks of Snowdon and are approached via the Watkin path. Various routes have been claimed over the years but few merit detailed description.

# Castell (Castle)                                O S Ref 625 513

A steep little cliff of good compact rock just 5 minutes walk up the Watkin Path beside the old tramway incline. The obvious central crack is taken by *Saeth*.

**Bwa**    80 feet    E2 5b                                (29.6.98)
The steep face left of the crack of *Saeth*. Start 10 feet from the left end of the initial wall. Climb rightwards then straight up via a shallow niche to some ledges. The harmless-looking wall above proves to be the crux.

**Saeth**    90 feet    Very Severe 4c                       (31.5.98)
Interesting climbing with a thought-provoking finish which takes the central crack. Gain it via a short steep wall, pull out left at its top to a ledge and continue to a ledge with a small oak. The tantalising ledges up to the left can be reached in several ways, all of them tricky. Finish leftwards to belays well back on the left.

**Oakum**    100 feet    Hard Severe 4a                      (29.6.98)
Arboreal, but with character. Start at the lowest point of the crag beneath the great oak. Climb a steep rib and groove to the tree and continue up beside this for 15 feet. Continue by making a rising leftwards traverse around the buttress to finish via a crack system.

# Cwm y Llan                                    OS Ref 615 525

The Gladstone Slab lies to the right of the Watkin Path at the Adwy Bwlch Du, just beyond the Gladstone Rock. It gives some moderate routes of 200 feet on a fine slab and is popular with outdoor centres.

# Craig Ddu (Black Crag)                          OS Ref 618 526

This large, rambling cliff lies higher up the hillside on the back of Lliwedd, above the Gladstone Slab. The crag is broken and vegetated.

# Clogwyn Du (Dark Cliff)                         OS Ref 605 530

This lies on the extensive line of broken cliffs on the flank of the south ridge of Snowdon, which forms the head of the cwm. It is the least broken and highest of these cliffs, about half a mile north of Bwlch Cwm Llan and above the disused reservoirs in the cwm. The cliff is loose and broken but offers long mountaineering routes which unfortunately degenerate into loose scrambling towards the top. Routes have only been described in outline, their quality not deserving of detailed description.

The crag is situated to the right of *Shadow Gully* (a good winter excursion) which can be reached by slogging up the hillside from the ruined buildings. An old stone wall stops directly below the foot of *Shadow Gully*. To the right of *Shadow Gully* the rocks are fairly steep at the base. A little way along there is a prominent hanging gully about 100 feet up.

**Crystal Rib**   600 feet (including scrambling)   Hard Severe
                                                                      (3.3.56)
This climb takes the buttress immediately left of the hanging gully followed by a sharp quartzy ridge. Scrambling remains.

**Mistrust**   500 feet   Very Difficult                               (3.3.56)
This follows the prominent ridge between *Crystal Rib* and *Shadow Gully*. It is reached by climbing several bands of rock on the tongue thrown down to the cwm. It has three pitches of interest before the scrambling takes over.

**Shadow Ridge**   600 feet   Difficult                               (1950s)
A poor route. Start immediately left of *Shadow Gully* and follow the discontinuous arête, which includes some gendarmes. The only steep section can be avoided on the right if so desired.

**Rancour**   500 feet   Difficult                                    (2.4.56)
The main face of the crag offers slightly better rock, although this deteriorates the higher one ascends. Two thirds of the way along the face is a prominent gully leading up to a nick in the skyline. This route follows the curving ridge between this gully and the large open gully on the left bounding the main face. Pleasant climbing up the ridge on good rough rock leads to loose scrambling.

**Contempt**   300 feet   Severe                                      (2.4.56)
This route follows a long, deep chimney rising out of a little scree amphitheatre in the prominent gully. Above the initial wall, which is rather loose, interest can be prolonged by keeping right towards the top.

# Craig Cors y Celyn (Crag of the Holly Marsh)

OS Ref 649 509

This innocuous-looking crag is actually steeper than appearances suggest and the slopey nature of the rock makes the routes harder than one would expect. The crag can be reached in about half an hour from a parking space by the side of Llyn Gwynant; OS Ref 645 516. Follow the footpath for 500 yards to a stone wall. Follow the track on the left for 100 yards and strike up the now open hillside to the foot of the crag. It faces northwest and so catches the late afternoon sun. Heavy drainage from the hillside above means it should be left to dry out for a couple of days.

**Last Knight**   50 feet   E2 5b                                        (5.96)
Awkward but well-protected climbing. Start just right of a deep groove at the left-hand side of the main section of crag. Follow the 'barn door' layback cracks up the arête which gradually ease towards the top.

**First Night**   50 feet   E1 5c                                        (5.96)
Start 10 feet right of the preceding route below a square block in the overhangs. Climb easily up to the block. Hard moves past this and the overhang above lead to the top slab.

**Braveheart**   50 feet   E3 6a                                        (5.96)
A fine route. Start 10 feet right of the preceding route and to the left of a deep crack. Move up to the right-hand side of the overhangs. Pull through leftwards via a short slanting groove before trending slightly leftwards up the excellent technical slab to the top.

**Not Tonight Dear I've Got Sore Elbows**   50 feet   E3 5c
(5.96)
Steeper and quite sustained. Climb the crackline at the right-hand side of the crag. Step left near the top and finish up the left-hand crack.

# Craig Penmaen Brith (Crag of the Mottled Promontory)

OS Ref 640 518

This crag is best reached from a lay-by on the right (when travelling towards Pen y Gwryd) just before the Gwynant Youth Hostel. Cross the road and walk towards the Youth Hostel, find a gap in the wall which allows access to a path leading to a small bridge over the Afon Glaslyn at the western end of Llyn Gwynant. Walk around beside the lake for 10 minutes to a large boulder-field just past a wall. The left-hand section of the crag is reached by ascending the boulder field until a hidden 80-foot high needle detached from the main crag comes into view. This is the Gwynant Needle. The delightful setting combined with the shelter given by the trees makes this crag well worth a visit.

High on the left side of the crag is a steep, compact wall reached from the first belay of *Red Star Belgrade*. **Twister** Hard Very Severe 5a (5.3.98) takes the steep cracks on the left side and the arête above. **Magnum** E2 5b (31.1.98) is a little gem taking the shallow groove on the right-hand side.

**Red Star Belgrade**   120 feet   Very Severe          (7.8.96)
An execrable route but the first pitch is useful. Forty feet left of the Gwynant Needle are some deep cracks near the base of the buttress.
**1** 50 feet  4b. Climb the cracks, exit left up a ramp and climb an easy rib to a narrow cave stance.
**2** 30 feet  4a. Traverse right across the wall above to reach a grass terrace.
**3** 40 feet  4c. Move up right and gain a holly tree ledge on the wall above. Step left and climb the steep wall to exit at a small overhang.

Left of the Gwynant Needle is a wide bay defined on the left by a narrow tower. **Tower Groove** 80 feet Hard Severe (1983) takes the deep groove beside this but is now somewhat vegetated. The next groove to the right (Severe) is even more overgrown.

**Pink Wall**   80 feet   Severe                      (1983)
Links various short walls and ledges in the middle of the bay to finish up the corner right of the big, blocky nose on the skyline.

**The Gwynant Needle**   90 feet   Very Difficult      (1965)
The classic ascent of the Needle, good fun. Start in the bay and climb the chimney behind the Needle to the gap behind the final pinnacle; stance possible. Work up left and around on to the front face where exposed moves gain the top. From there, leap to the actual cliff top (terrifying) or climb/abseil back down to the gap and descend easily to the right (east).

**Priapic Worship**   80 feet   E2 5b                 (4.94)
This good little route climbs the front face of the Needle in a fine position. Climb the smooth, blunt arête at the base of the pillar to better holds at 20 feet; bold. (An easier start is to climb the left arête.) Continue up the steep little groove in the front face followed by easier climbing to the summit. The jump across to *terra firma* follows and will be found to be the crux.

**Needle Cracks**   80 feet   Hard Severe             (1983)
Start at the obvious corner cracks on the front face of the Needle. Climb on good jams to reach wider, more broken cracks leading to the gap behind the pinnacle. Two short steep cracks above lead to the big Scots Pine.

Approximately 200 yards from the Needle in the direction of Elephant Rock (Clogwyn y Fulfran) is the right-hand section of the crag. This has its share of interesting routes with a traditional flavour and a nice setting beside the lake. The first route is located where a stone wall meets the cliff at a prominent buttress.

**Taylor-Made**   45 feet   E1 5b   (1972)
The obvious crack running up the left side of the buttress. A fierce start gains a ledge and ancient peg on the right. Reach back left to the crack and follow it to the top.

**Eloquence**   50 feet   E3 6a   (24.1.98)
Delightful climbing up the nose of the buttress. Follow the rib until a bold move gains good jams and camming device placements at the break. Overcome the bulge (*Friend 0*) to good finishing holds.

**Tronsience**   50 feet   E2 5c   (4.95)
Nice face climbing followed by a good old-fashioned thrutch. Climb the obvious thin crack in the slab towards a short chimney formed by a massive perched block. Enter and squirm through the chimney if slim enough, otherwise finish up the outside.

**The Hangman's Favourite Daughter**   50 feet   E1 5a
(5.5.96)
The wide, heavily gardened crack just to the right. Those expecting an energetic thrutch are in for a surprise as the crack provides little in the way of holds or protection and is climbed via its edge except for the very top.

At the right-hand end of the cliff, and clearly visible from the other side of the lake, is a great cleft running up from right-to-left. This gives the line of *Excalibur*. On its left is a smooth slab.

**Cat's Paw**   80 feet   E2   (31.3.98)
The centre of the slab gives some nice moves. Start below the middle of the narrow ledge 10 feet up.
**1**  45 feet. 5c. Gain the ledge, step up from its right end, trend left and follow the weakness to the big ledge.
**2**  35 feet. 4c. Climb the wide crack for a few feet, pull out left onto the nose and finish easily.

**Heddwch**   120 feet   Hard Very Severe   (24.1.98)
A good route taking the 'tramlines' on the right-hand side of the slab. Start at a shallow groove just left of *Excalibur*.
**1**  45 feet. 5a. Climb the groove for 15 feet and step left to a large foothold. Follow the parallel seams to the ledge above the slab.

**2** 35 feet. 4b. Follow the wide crack slanting right to the oak belay of *Excalibur*.

**3** 40 feet. Climb pitch 2 of *Excalibur*, or escape down to the right via a chimney formed by a massive flake (Moderate).

**Excalibur**   120 feet   Very Difficult                    (1965)
The big slanting fault — an excellent climb which can be tackled in most weather conditions. Watch for tawny owls.

**1** 80 feet. Enter and climb the obvious chimney running up towards a massive oak tree growing out of the crag. A troglodytic passage for the emaciated; those of normal girth will gain the final rib from the oak branch. Continue up the groove above to a good tree belay.

**2** 40 feet. Climb the rib behind the tree and finish via a crack on the left.

**Trout Fishing in America**   60 feet   Severe 4a   (11.4.96)
At the extreme right-hand end of the crag is a wide crack with another smaller oak growing out of it. An awkward start leads to a pull around the tree on 'wooden jugs'. Ascend the crack above and, again, beware of tawny owls who maybe nesting within its confines.

# Clogwyn y Fulfran (Cormorant Rock)      OS Ref 644 521

Famed for its lake-level traverse this idyllic setting offers a few short routes on its 'suntrap' flanks. It is best approached from the camp site at the northern end of Llyn Gwynant in about 10 minutes. It was known in previous guides as 'Elephant Rock', from its shape when viewed from the other side of the lake. The crag faces generally east and catches the early morning sun.

The first routes take the steep slabby face on the left (west) side of the Rock.

**Liposuchfun**   50 feet   E3 6a                          (1995)
Start on the drystone wall beneath the obvious groove. Lasso a spike on the right arête of the groove to protect a hard starting move into the groove. At its top, step left and follow vague cracks up and right to a tree belay.

**Rise and Fall**   50 feet   E2 6a                        (1991)
Start as for *Liposuchfun*. Pull onto the undercut right arête of the groove and climb straight up to a blank section at 25 feet. Thin moves gain better holds leading straight to the top.

**Early Riser**   70 feet   Very Severe 4c                 (1990)
Start from the foot of the grassy ramp running up right beneath

the wall. Go straight up for 15 feet, step right and climb to below a grassy niche. Step left and climb to the upper ramp; belay. The rock above this gives another reasonable pitch, or descend the ramp carefully to the base.

**Sunrise**   80 feet   Hard Very Severe 5a        (1990)
The rightward-trending line leading to a shallow rake on the right-hand side of the face. A nice open pitch starting 10 feet up the rake from *Early Riser*.

The ledgy central area of the Rock can be climbed by a number of ways but is used more for jumping or diving into the 90-foot deep water at its base. The right flank of the Rock consists of a steep wall crossed by overhangs at half height.

**Personal Problems**   100 feet   E5 6c        (11.93)
A unique feature giving a technical challenge. Climb the groove in the lower wall, step left and go up to the overhangs, peg runner (back up wire). Climb the obvious shallow recess above the roof, somewhat baffling, to easier ground with belays well back.

The low-level traverse of the Rock in either direction offers a fine problem for a hot summer's day; deep water soloing at its best. The easiest line is Very Severe but it can be spiced up by many variations. At the west end it is necessary to go higher onto the grassy ramp or take to the water. To climb along the base here will be at least E7 and it remains unconquered.

# Clogwyn y Wenallt (Cliff of the Bright Bluff)

OS Ref 647 528

Clogwyn y Wenallt is the dome-shaped crag, about 200 feet high, set on the hillside just to the northeast of Llyn Gwynant. It can be reached in about 10 minutes from the gate by the side of Hafod y Rhisgl on the old road (50 yards from the main A498 road). If you park on the camp site you may be charged a fee, especially in summer. Please do not block access around Hafod y Rhisgl. Cross the river by the foot-bridge about 300 yards above the lake and walk steeply up to the crag, crossing a stile at the top of the stone wall.

The rock is usually sound with the odd loose flake here and there and runs to good holds giving steep, enjoyable climbing. A stone wall and a large boulder meet the foot of the cliff in its middle. A broad grassy ledge cuts into the cliff on the left at one third height getting smaller towards the right. The second pitch of *Ferdinand* is

# Clogwyn y Fulfran

located at the far end of this ledge. The first three routes described start from this terrace reached by walking up left of the main crag and traversing right onto the ledge.

**The Gamekeeper**   80 feet   Hard Very Severe 5a   ‡   (9.79)
A line up the steep left edge of the buttress at the beginning of the terrace containing the top pitch of *Ferdinand*. Climb a left-slanting V-groove to a small ledge and some flakes. Bridge up slightly and swing out right to finish directly up the wall.

1. Liposuchfun E3
2. Rise and Fall E2
3. Early Riser VS

4. Sunrise HVS
5. Personal Problems E5

**Caligula**  90 feet  E1                                    (31.8.79)
Quite a nice climb with a short sharp crux. Start 40 feet left of the
second pitch of *Ferdinand*, beneath an arête.
**1** 50 feet. 5a. Climb the arête, passing a large tree, and move
slightly right and up a groove right of the arête to a stance.
**2** 40 feet. 5b. Move left and, passing a spike, climb strenuously
up an overhanging groove to a delicate mantelshelf. Finish up the
arête.

**Alt Stazione**   70 feet   E5 6b                    (10.10.93)
A very hard route at the top end of its grade, but safe on the crux
moves. Start about 20 feet left of *Ferdinand* pitch 2 below an
arête obscured by trees. Climb a crack and pull onto the scoop.
Climb easily up to the arête and from the top of a flaky spike clip
2 peg runners. Slap up the arête to the top; all a bit frantic.

**Bovril**   100 feet   Very Severe                    (1.8.54)
Quite a good route despite its vegetated surroundings, with a
delicate fingery second pitch and a strenuous crack to finish.
Start at the first corner on the left-hand side of the lower tier.
**1** 25 feet. 4b. Climb diagonally left until it is possible to traverse
right to a tree. Go up to the large terrace and belay at a tree in
the corner.
**2** 45 feet. 4c. Climb the wall immediately left of the tree, move
left above a small holly into a niche. Traverse delicately to the left
to a small tree at the foot of a steep crack.
**3** 30 feet. 4c. Climb the difficult crack to finish.

**Ferdinand**   140 feet   E2                    (7.2.59)
The second pitch follows a steep, strenuous and sustained crack
which still stops a few leaders. The classic route of the crag and
a must in any crack climber's itinerary. The first pitch is scrappy
and can be avoided by walking round onto the terrace. Start at a
shallow corner about 6 yards right of *Bovril*.
**1** 60 feet. 5a. Climb a short wall into an overhanging niche.
Move right on good holds to a tree and continue across the grass
ledge to an easy sloping crack. Climb this to belay at the foot of
a corner.
**2** 80 feet. 5b. Climb the corner for 20 feet until it is possible to
pull into an overhanging crack in the right wall. Climb this to the
overhang, turning it on the left to finish up another crack; belay
well back. It is possible to climb the crack direct from its base but
this is harder.

**Picador**   150 feet   Hard Very Severe                    (31.8.79)
An awkward final pitch. Start as for *Carol Crack*.
**1** 50 feet. 4b. As for *Carol Crack*.
**2** 40 feet. 5b. Climb up the leftward-slanting crack to reach a
series of ledges. Follow these rightwards to reach a belay below
the final pitch of *Carol Crack*.

# Clogwyn y Wenallt

1. Caligula E1
2. Toreador E1
3. Oxo VS
4. Poacher E5
5. Bovine HVS
6. The Death Wisher E2
7. Shake VS

**3** 60 feet. 5a. Climb the wide and slightly overhanging crack and then a rib on the right to finish.

**Carol Crack**   140 feet   Hard Very Severe          (11.53)
A rather disjointed climb with a poorly protected last pitch. Start at a corner-crack containing a tree, about 10 yards right of *Ferdinand*.
**1** 50 feet. 4b. Climb up and into the corner, this leads to a battle with a holly tree and a steep pull out onto the grassy terrace.
**2** 40 feet. 4b. Go up the easy sloping crack in the middle of the wall and climb an awkward little wall to a niche below the final wall.
**3** 50 feet. 4c. Climb the wall above the niche, trending right to the top.

**Torero**   140 feet   E1                          (5.59)
Hard and bold on the second pitch, but with good climbing. Start to the left of a prominent corner about 7 yards right of *Carol Crack*.
**1** 50 feet. 5a. Traverse into the corner and climb up onto a small ledge. Traverse diagonally right across the short wall to reach the grassy ledge below an easy groove.
**2** 90 feet. 5b. Stand on the flake and pull into the scoop. Move up and step back right onto a flake. Step left into a corner to finish.

**Don't Look Now**   160 feet   E6          (15.11.93)
Good climbing throughout, building up to a memorable crux in the final groove, which is both hard and serious. Start as for *Torero*.
**1** 50 feet. 6a. Climb the shallow groove left of the corner of *Torero*, undercut left at the bulge and up the continuation groove (peg runner) to a grassy ledge.
**2** 20 feet. 6b. The obvious weakness in the wall behind is climbed with considerable interest.
**3** 90 feet. 6c. Climb the corner as for *Ferdinand/Toreador* to the nose where the cracks end. Sustained bridging up the blind groove above (eventual small *RP* placement) gains the top and a tree belay a little higher.

**Toreador**   150 feet   E1                          (4.64)
An enjoyable climb with a technical final pitch. Start below the prominent corner of *Torero*.
**1** 70 feet. 5a. Climb the corner more or less direct and cross the grass ledge to the foot of an easy groove on the right.
**2** 25 feet. Climb the easy groove to belay at the foot of a corner.
**3** 55 feet. 5c. Climb the corner up which the final pitch of *Ferdinand* starts and continue until the right-hand wall starts to

overhang. Make a difficult move right onto a slab and climb this
to the top.

**Oxo** 220 feet   Very Severe                                    (12.4.53)
The easiest climb on the crag, interesting and enjoyable. The
route wanders first right and then left seeking the easiest line.
Start at the left end of the lowest bulge by a black recess about
10 yards left of the stone wall.
**1** 100 feet. 4b. Climb up and traverse horizontally right to a
black ledge. Continue right past a detached pinnacle to a small
wall. Ascend this and go up to a gangway. Follow the gangway
to the grass ledge on the right.
**2** 30 feet. Climb the easy slab on the left to a tall tree at the foot
of a crack.
**3** 90 feet. 4c. Climb the crack and step round the rib to a ledge
on the right. Continue across the wall on the right, crossing a
small groove, to finish straight up on good holds. Alternatively,
instead of crossing the wall climb the difficult corner above the
ledge and swing right to finish.

**Fishbox**   45 feet   E5 6b                                    (2.5.84)
A very sustained piece of climbing; the gear is reasonable for
those with strength to put it in. Start from the first stance of *Oxo*.
Climb the obvious thin overhanging crack just left of *The Death
Wisher*. At 35 feet, where the crack steepens, move out right onto
the arête and easy ground. The direct finish has only been
climbed with 2 points of aid.

**Sharky**   160 feet   E4                                       (10.90)
Gains and climbs the obvious pod in the middle of the wall
between *Fishbox* and *The Death Wisher*. Start right of *Oxo* below
an orange patch in the steep lower wall.
**1** 90 feet. 5b. Climb past the patch then trend left easily via a
groove on *Oxo* to a ledge beneath the second corner of *Bovine*.
Climb a steep layback edge right of the corner to a grass ledge
and continue to the second tree of *Oxo*.
**2** 70 feet. 6a. Fix a runner 8 feet up *Fishbox*, step right onto a
small spike and pull rightwards across the wall to gain the base
of the pod. Climb the pod to a ledge and continue directly up the
wall to the top.

**The Death Wisher**   170 feet   E2                             (6.77)
The last pitch takes the crack to the left of *Bovine's* top pitch. A
scary route but with fine, steep climbing on positive holds. Start a
few feet left of *Bovine*.
**1** 80 feet. 4c. Climb up to the traverse of *Oxo* (the line can be
varied at will) and follow that climb to the stance and tree belay.
**2** 90 feet. 5b. Follow *Bovine* for 10 feet and then traverse left

into the steep crack. Climb this, passing a wafer-thin flake (very precarious), and continue up the crack to the top. It is possible to climb directly into the crack instead of starting up *Bovine*, but this is much harder.

**Poacher**   180 feet   E5                                    (4.78)
A direct line up the centre of the cliff. The last pitch takes the overhanging groove in the headwall to give a very hard pitch. Start a few feet left of *Bovine*.
**1** 90 feet. 5c. Pull over a bulge and go up to join the traverse of *Oxo*. Move left and climb the wall left of the corner on the first pitch of *Bovine* (bold) to reach a ledge. Move slightly right and climb a shallow groove to the terrace.
**2** 45 feet. 5b. Move right into a groove and follow this to a good ledge and belay (junction with *Oxo*).
**3** 45 feet. 6b. Climb directly up the overhanging groove above, passing 2 peg runners. Bold, technical and spectacular.

**The Matador**   180 feet   Hard Very Severe                  (6.77)
A good way up the crag, but covering little new ground.
**1** 90 feet. 5a. Follow *Bovine* to the terrace.
**2** 50 feet. 5a. Climb the first few feet of *Oxo* before moving left onto the wall to reach a scoop. Climb the wall above to a stance and peg belay on *Torero*.
**3** 40 feet. 4c. Climb the crack on the left as for *Torero*.

**Bovine**   200 feet   Hard Very Severe                       (19.5.57)
One of the classics of the valley giving excellent but disjointed climbing, although the top pitch up the overhanging wall is ample compensation for the wandering nature of the route. Start midway between *Oxo* and the stone wall.
**1** 90 feet. 5a. Climb the impending wall, first right and then back left, to the detached flake on the *Oxo* traverse. Continue up the corner above (peg runner) to a gangway and climb the right-hand corner (awkward) to the terrace.
**2** 20 feet. Move down the slab on the right to a tree belay at the foot of a steep wall (*Oxo* pitch 2 in reverse).
**3** 90 feet. 4c. Climb a groove for a few feet and then swing right onto the wall, which is climbed on excellent holds to the top. A superb pitch.

**Oxine**   190 feet   Very Severe
The first pitch of *Oxo* followed by the top pitch of *Bovine* gives a very good climb, probably the best Very Severe in the area.

**Shake**   170 feet   Very Severe                             (12.3.54)
The line of steep cracks in the front of the buttress above and to the right of the stone wall. Quite steep, but the difficulty is short.

Start about 20 feet right of the stone wall.
**1** 90 feet. 4b. Scramble up to a stout ash tree. Climb the steep wall, traverse left, and go up to a small slab. Move back right to a crack and climb it to a large ledge.
**2** 30 feet. 4a. Continue up the fault to a tree.
**3** 50 feet. 4b. Climb onto and up the rib on the right, stepping left into the groove for a few feet until it is possible to move back right across the rib to reach a slab which is climbed to the top.

**The Fugitive**   170 feet   E3                               (6.80)
An interesting eliminate taking the obvious corner left of *Shake*.
**1** 50 feet. Scramble up to a tree belay on the first pitch of *Shake*.
**2** 40 feet. 6a. Climb the corner on the left of the stance to a belay on the big grass ledge.
**3** 20 feet. Walk right along the ledge to a tree below the final pitch of *Shake*.
**4** 60 feet. 5c. Climb the overhanging groove on the left (care needed with some flakes) until it is possible to move right to a tree. Finish up the arête behind the tree.

**Rattle and Roll**   160 feet   Hard Very Severe           (8.92)
A scrappy line, but with some good moves. Start at the wall right of the cracks of *Shake*.
**1** 60 feet. 4b. Climb the wall to a corner and traverse right to a tree belay on the arête.
**2** 100 feet. 5a. Ascend the arête to a ramp, climb this and the final wall to the top.

**The Hanging Tree**   190 feet   E4                          (10.90)
Two good pitches, the second improving on *The Fugitive*. Start beneath the prominent right-angled arête 25 feet right of the huge boulder above the stone wall.
**1** 80 feet. 6a. Climb the initial wall to a grass ledge at 40 feet. Move left and climb the arête to a small ledge, harder climbing up the upper arête gains a stance.
**2** 20 feet. Go easily left to belay at a wide crack with a holly in it (on *Shake*).
**3** 90 feet. 5c. Climb the steep groove on the left as for *The Fugitive*, but instead of moving right as for that route continue straight up the buttress, keeping just left of the arête to reach easy ground.

**Foxy**   160 feet   E1                                       (c.1984)
A worthwhile route which starts as for *The Hanging Tree*.
**1** 80 feet. 5b. Climb to the grass ledge and go up the corner behind the tree to a peg runner below the overhang. Move left across the wall past another peg to a ledge.
**2** 80 feet 5b. Climb the rib above and move up right to beneath

the smooth final wall (peg runner). Climb slightly leftwards through the bulge to reach the easy upper slabs.

**The Wolf**   100 feet   E2 5c                                    (31.4.84)
A direct on *Foxy* up the 'mini-*Vulture*' crack through the overhang. Start from the grass ledge 40 feet up *Foxy*. Climb the corner and follow the crack rightwards to reach better holds on the wall above. Continue to the smooth final wall (peg) and take this slightly leftwards to easy upper slabs.

**Psychedelic Cult**   250 feet   E2                            (28.4.84)
A right-to-left high girdle of the crag. Contrived but with good situations.
**1** 90 feet. 5a. Scramble up to ledges at the right-hand side of the crag, below a small overhang. Go up the corner to an overhang and traverse left, passing some old aid remnants, to the arête. Go diagonally up to the tree belay at the end of *Shake* pitch 2.
**2** 90 feet. 5b. Step down and traverse left into *Bovine*. Move across into *The Death Wisher* above the crux and trend left to belay just before the last groove of *Poacher*.
**3** 70 feet. 4c. Continue left to finish up the last crack of *Torero*.
The fin up and left of the main crag is reached by a steep flog up the hillside.

**Hugh Walton's Legendary Flying Arête**   30 feet   E4 6a †
                                                                      (4.93)
A connoisseur's pitch. Climb the fin with *RP* protection, the last move being the crux.

## The Gwynant Crack                      OS Ref 648 518
This lies on a small vertical wall on the east side of the main road, just before the bank of Llyn Gwynant when approaching from the Pen y Gwryd.

**The Gwynant Crack**   25 feet   Severe 4b              (1900s)
A fine traditional problem. Struggle as elegantly as possible up the wide fissure using all your power and a variety of techniques.

**Bleed for the Dancer**   25 feet   E5 6a                    (1987)
A short route but a big commitment. The wall left of the crack is climbed by technical moves on small holds; no protection. A top rope inspection may pay dividends.

## Craig yr Ehediad (Crag of the Birds)      OS Ref 663 520
This collection of little craglets can be reached by parking at a small lay-by on the Gwynant Valley road directly above the farm of Hafod Rhisgl (OS Ref 657 527). Follow a path up through the woods

until a fence line is reached. Follow this to the right (southeast) for 300 yards before cutting over rightwards into a strange area of flat marshy ground with many craglets on the uphill sides of the valleys. The approach is very boggy, take your wellies.

**The Caretaker**  70 feet  E3 5c  †                    (23.9.96)
A good route in a lovely situation. It climbs the arête and the white face of the obvious tower. Protection is provided by a couple of pegs and some ingenuity with *RPs*. Start just right of a vegetated crack. Move up to a blocky ledge. Gingerly step off the block and climb up left off the arête for a few moves until able to delicately swing right onto the white face. At the second peg runner step back left and finish up a groove.

**Urban Cookie Collective**  40 feet  Hard Very Severe 5c  †
                                                          (23.9.96)
Isolated but fun. Start left of *The Caretaker* at a small crag with a diagonal crack running right-to-left. A boulder problem start past a small overhang gains the diagonal crack. Follow this, much easier now, past a flake to the top.

Continuing along the fence for a couple of minutes beyond *The Caretaker*, another rock valley feature can be found. The sharp-edged slabby arête at the right-hand end is Hard Severe 4a. The whole area is dotted with craglets which give generally slabby, none-too-desperate bouldering in a remote and scenic environment. Following the fence line further for about 20 minutes a big slabby crag is reached. It can be climbed almost anywhere at Difficult standard. The short pocketed crack in the steep gully wall at the top right-hand side is Severe.

A couple of minutes walk diagonally down right is a short but impressive pocketed slab, which provides the next route (OS Ref 664 516).

**To Pick a Pocket or Two**  40 feet  E2 5b  †    (23.10.96)
An exciting route which is poorly protected (don't fluff the last move). Climb the centre of the gritstone-like pocketed slab to a long reach at the top.

# Clogwyn y Bustach (Cliff of the Ox)

OS Ref 625 535

Comparatively unfrequented this extensive cliff does contain some very good adventures, the best-known being the classic *Lockwood's Chimney*. Although the rock demands caution in places, some of the steep pocketed walls give very good climbing reminiscent of Dinas Cromlech.

The cliff is best approached from a parking space on the Cwm Dyli road at OS Ref 657 539. Cross the stream and go through a small gate to follow a path down the hill to the river. Cross this via a footbridge and walk up to a stile. A track now runs along the side of the river to a point where the crag suddenly appears. A path runs up to the crag; bear left for Marble Arch and the start of *Lockwood's Chimney*; bear right for the North Buttress and *Gallop Step*.

There are four distinct walls or buttresses. High on the left is a sheer, light-coloured wall taken centrally by *Kellogg Crack*. Right of this, beyond a steep vegetated area, is the impressive black-streaked wall taken by *The Maelstrom*. To the right again and roughly in the centre of the cliff is an obvious natural arch — The Marble Arch — an important landmark. Directly above this lies The Shield, a steep, clean wall guarded by big overhangs, while the broken buttress above and to the right of Marble Arch contains *Lockwood's Chimney*. On the far right, beyond the broad, vegetated North Gully, is the clean impressive sweep of the North Buttress with its distinctive overhangs at half height.

The first route is actually found on a huge overhanging boulder down by the river, a little further south than the path running up to the crag.

### The Tawg: In Homage to a Hound   30 feet   E4 6a

(6.86)

On the steep side of the boulder the crack-cum-layaway in the roof is climbed. It overhangs by 45 degrees in the first 25 feet and is, naturally, more than a little sustained.

The first routes on the crag proper take the steep white wall high up on the left. This is best reached by bearing left up the path and ascending the descent gully on the south side of the crag. A short traverse along a grass ledge leads to the base of the wall.

### Peak Frean   100 feet   Hard Very Severe 5a          (1973)

Gripping climbing in a good position which starts beneath the arête on the left-hand side of the wall. Climb up the arête and into a groove. Follow the shallow groove to a step right towards the top. The holds are large but the rock is frightening.

### Prince of Darkness   100 feet   E3 5b          (5.6.83)

A serious route with its share of dubious rock. Start beneath the obvious groove near the left edge of the wall. Follow the groove for 30 feet then climb the wall on the right until a traverse back left leads to better holds on the finishing wall.
Variation

**Enlightenment**   100 feet   E2 5b                          (1.5.98)
Slightly more amenable than the parent route. Climb the groove
then continue up and leftwards to some small spikes. Climb
directly up the buttress on improving holds and rock to the top.

**Kellogg Crack**   100 feet   E1 5a   ‡                    (15.10.61)
The central weakness of the wall, a fine steep route despite a
short bushy bit. Start at the rightward-trending crack. Follow the
crack to a dead tree at the base of a deep groove. Climb the
groove until it bulges and swing right on a horizontal break and
climb more or less straight up the wall to the top.
Variation
**Original Finish**   ‡
After swinging right at the bulge, move back left and climb the
vegetated groove to a ledge and belay. The corner at the left end
of the ledge leads to the top (4b).

The next few routes are based on the black-streaked wall located
above and to the left of Marble Arch. The corner bounding the wall
on the left has been climbed but is now dense jungle, as is the route
which took the rib to its left **The Tenth Rib** 220 feet Very Difficult
(28.8.52). Both are best left to nature. At the base of the wall are
two substantial ash trees.

**Femaelstrom**   200 feet   E2                           (15.5.66)
A good pitch taking the wall towards its left side and making for
the obvious bottomless corner. Start 10 feet left of the left-hand
ash.
**1** 120 feet. 5b. Climb the wall, trending right, until after a steep
section it is possible to move left to the bottomless corner.
Continue straight over a bulge and move left to a rib leading to
the large, tree-covered ledge at the top of the wall.
**2** 80 feet. Move right along the ledge and climb to the left-
slanting break which is followed to the top. Alternatively, abseil
from the large ledge.

**Paranoia**   200 feet   E1                              (27.9.70)
A steep and serious route which crosses *The Maelstrom*. Start at
the left-hand ash tree.
**1** 120 feet. 5a. Go straight up for 30 feet and then traverse right
with difficulty to a small ledge in the centre of the wall. Climb
diagonally right to cross *The Maelstrom* and continue straight up
to a small holly tree. Climb the wall above, moving right to an
arête and peg belay; junction with *Side Entry*.
**2** 80 feet. 4c. Climb the arête and step off the top of a pinnacle
onto a steep wall. Climb the wall, passing a small tree on the left,
continue to easy ground.

**The Maelstrom**   205 feet   Hard Very Severe   (5.58)
An enjoyable but serious route; the rock requires care and the
protection is poor. It remains a worthwhile objective. The climb
takes a rising right-to-left traverse across the black-streaked wall.
Start at the right-hand end of the wall.
**1** 60 feet. 4c. Climb a corner for 10 feet to a big tree. Traverse
left with difficulty and go steeply up the wall until it is possible to
traverse horizontally left to a shallow scoop and belay.
**2** 90 feet. 4c. Traverse left for a few feet and move up onto the
upper traverse. Go across left to a small tree, climb the wall to
another tree on the right and continue up steep vegetation to a
large tree.
**3** 55 feet. 4b. Ascend the little wall on the right to a big flake
and finish up the wall above.

**Side Entry**   220 feet   Severe   (31.8.52)
Devious and not really worthwhile. Start as for *The Maelstrom* at
the overgrown corner.
**1** 40 feet. Jungle bash the corner past a tree and continue to a
stance on the broad rib above Marble Arch.
**2** 60 feet. Climb a short crack to a left-trending gangway. Climb
this and continue easily to belay at the highest of a group of
trees.
**3** 60 feet. Climb the slab above until it is possible to traverse
horizontally left around the corner to gain the long grassy ledge
above *The Maelstrom* wall. Large tree belay in the centre.
**4** 60 feet. Move right and climb the slabby wall trending
rightwards to the big holly tree; exit right.

**Marble Rib**   200 feet   Difficult   (early 1900s)
A pleasant preamble to *Lockwood's Chimney*, *New Slant* or
*Forest Wall*, taking the spur immediately below Marble Arch and
then over the Arch itself. Having located the Arch, scramble down
on its southwest side to the base of the rib.
**1** 70 feet. Climb the rib past a tree to belay at a small pinnacle.
**2** 70 feet. Climb the front face of the pinnacle until ribs on the left
lead into Marble Arch. Quit here for *Lockwood's Chimney*.
**3** 60 feet. Climb the steep wall on the right to the top of the Arch,
continue along the ridge to the blocks at the start of *New Slant/
Forest Wall*.

**New Slant**   190 feet   Severe   (1950s)
A more logical version of *Side Entry* taking the leftward-slanting
break which runs the full height of the cliff above Marble Arch.
Combined with *Marble Rib* it gives the longest easier climb in the
valley. Start by going through and scrambling up above Marble
Arch till the rocks steepen at some blocks.
**1** 60 feet. Climb the short crack and left-trending gangway to

reach easy ground. Belay at the highest of a group of ash trees (as for *Side Entry* pitch 2).
**2** 40 feet. Climb the slab above to a small pinnacle and stance to its left.
**3** 90 feet. Continue in the same line past a small oak until a stepped wall leads to a big holly tree. Trend left up the airy final wall to the top. Belays back on the left.
Variation
**Direct Finish**   Very Severe
Steep and exhilarating.
**3a** 80 feet. 4b. Step off the pinnacle and trend up right to a good flake beside a holly sapling in a niche. A steep rib gains easier ground; finish rightwards.

The following routes take The Shield and give the some of the best-positioned climbing on the cliff.

**Forest Wall**   160 feet   Severe                              (1934)
The second pitch takes the left edge of The Shield and is steep and exposed with splendid holds. Start as for *New Slant*.
**1** 60 feet. As for *New Slant* or, more energetic, pitch 2 of *The Precipice Walk*.
**2** 60 feet. Climb the slabs for 20 feet and move out right onto the wall and continue till beneath the big holly, which is passed on the right to the large flake belay of *Lockwood's Chimney*.
**3** 40 feet. The final pitch of *Lockwood's Chimney*.
Variation
**The Direct Finish**   Hard Severe                             (1952)
**2a** 60 feet. After climbing the slab, rather than moving right onto the wall follow the wide crack to a cave below the overhang and traverse right awkwardly to the holly tree.

**The Precipice Walk**   240 feet   Hard Severe           (18.4.98)
Steep lower walls lead to an airy excursion across The Shield which, fortunately, has the comfort of good holds all the way. Start at the short buttress immediately left of Marble Arch, 5 feet left of a hawthorn tree.
**1** 60 feet. 4b. Climb the wall to a ledge and tree on the right. Swing back left and up on pockets to a flake and rib leading to the blocks at the start of *New Slant*.
**2** 60 feet. 4a. Climb the crack and continue up the steep wall directly above which leads to easy slabs. Scramble up left to belay at the highest of the ash trees.
**3** 80 feet. 4a. Climb the slab for 20 feet until a traverse right to a sizeable shelf. Continue traversing into a shallow depression, break right again and finish diagonally rightwards to belay on the crest of the huge flake forming *Lockwood's Chimney*.
**4** 40 feet. The slabby face above.

**Stampede**   90 feet   E5 6b                                    (1993)
The centrepiece of The Shield; a fine sustained route. The odd
loose flake should be treated with caution. Start at the first belay
of *Forte Strapiombo*. Climb to the right-hand corner of the roof
and move left (peg runner) with one's feet on the lip, into the
middle of the hanging wall (peg runner). Climb directly up the
wall, moving slightly right to finish.

**Forte Strapiombo**   130 feet   Hard Very Severe   (17.9.61)
A steep and exciting main pitch which skirts the overhang
guarding the base of The Shield to gain a big crack in the
headwall. *Friends* useful (2½ to 3½). Start 25 feet right of *New
Slant*, below a steepish wall.
**1** 50 feet. 4a. Climb the wall to gain the slab below the overhangs. Either belay near the corner or over to the left on some
small trees.
**2** 80 feet. 5a Climb rightwards across the steep wall to the right-
hand end of the overhang. Move up into the wide crack above
and follow it, gradually easing, to belays on the crest of the huge
flake that forms *Lockwood's Chimney*.

**Wizard**   100 feet   E3 5c                                    (3.5.98)
Intricate, open climbing up the rib and buttress right of *Forte
Strapiombo*. Climb the initial wall of *Forte Strapiombo* to move
right on to the arête and follow it (good microwires for the eagle-
eyed) to small ledges level with the roof. Climb rightwards for 10
feet and go straight up the centre of the narrow face, using the
crack on the left for the last few moves. Belay and finish easily on
the left.

**Lockwood's Chimney**   200 feet   Difficult           (1908)
A unique and most traditional route. It used to be customary to
do this climb by moonlight in the worst possible conditions, a
practice that should not be discontinued. The party should
preferably be large and of greater than average girth. The
pitches should be kept short for maximum entertainment and
belays can be taken at will. From the Marble Arch, descend a
few feet and traverse right along ledges to belay at the foot of a
short wall split by a crack.
**1** 30 feet. Climb the crack and scramble up to belay at a larger,
steeper crack.
**2** 30 feet. Climb the crack awkwardly and exit left to ledges,
move right to a tree belay below a chimney formed by a massive
flake. (In wet conditions this pitch can be avoided by an easier
line 20 feet further left.)
**3** 100 feet. The chimney may be entered from the front or by
walking round the rib to the right. Once inside, climb 20 feet to a
chockstone (the crux). Wriggle along the base of the cleft (harder

Harold Drasdo on the traverse
on pitch 1 of *Christmas Climb*
Severe, Craig y Dyniewyd.
Photo: Terry Gifford

Emma Alsford climbing *First Knight* E1, Craig Cors y Celyn.
Photo: Alan Leary

Martyn Eade on *Braveheart* E3,
Craig Cors y Celyn.
Photo: Alan Leary

Graham Frost on the strenuous, jamming testpiece of *Ferdinand* E2, Clogwyn y Wenallt. Photo: Ray Wood

for the corpulent) and climb up at the end to make a sudden exit onto ledges. Belay on the trees or to the top of the great flake.
**4** 40 feet. Climb to the cliff-top on polished flaky holds; stake and spike belay.
Variations
Severe
**3a** Back-and-foot upwards between the walls in the middle of the cleft to reach an outer window. Unprotected and requiring steadiness
**3b** Above the chockstone, move to the outside edge of the chimney and climb this in a dramatic position to the top of the flake.

**Great Chimney Wall**   80 feet   Very Severe        (17.4.51)
Could not be identified from the description in the old guide which said 'Climb the wall left of the ordinary route more or less direct'. It may be variation **3a** above.

## North Buttress

The next routes are on the North Buttress, which is characterised by the large overhangs running first up and then down the cliff to form a broad arch. This unique feature gives the line of the next route.

**Gallop Step**   165 feet   Hard Very Severe         (8.1.56)
A sort-of-girdle taking the fault-line going from left to right below the big overhang. Unusual, in that it starts and finishes at the foot of the crag. A good climb that is now relatively solid, it can be done in poor weather although the easier second pitch does get wet. Start from a block beneath the left-hand end of the over-hang.
**1** 65 feet. 5a. Climb up and traverse diagonally right under the overhang. At 50 feet pull strenuously round the arête into a niche and belay (old pegs, good wire backups).
**2** 100 feet. 4c. Follow the same line of weakness across the face, passing a large block and a tree, to a vegetated section. Continue easily right until it is possible to step off the cliff onto the ground.

**False Destiny**   170 feet   E4          (16.10.96)
Traverses the lip of the overhang above *Gallop Step* in a very exposed position, some fragile holds and the close proximity to vegetated areas detract little from the spectacular situations.
**1** 100 feet. 5c. Climb directly up the wall to a narrow footledge, move right on pockets to a recessed ledge. A committing series of moves leads onto the arête and up to a break-line. Continue traversing right above the lip, rising slightly to flat handholds just left of a short crack. A hard move gains the crack which leads to ledges. Belay by the huge block of *Anniversary Waltz*.

# Clogwyn y Bustach

1. False Destiny E4
2. Gallop Step HVS
3. Anniversary Waltz E2
4. The Ox Bow Incident E4

**2** 70 feet. 5b. Traverse awkwardly under the roof to a groove with a small sapling. Pull through the bulge onto the upper wall and continue along the lip to a stride across the apex of the roof. A cleaned finish leads rightwards to a tree.

To the right a line of pegs runs up the overhanging wall below the roof and gives the line of the following route.

**The Prowler**   80ft   E5 6a   †                              (23.6.99)
Excellent climbing up the steep pocketed wall left of *Lost Tango* then the impressive prow above. Start below the line of *in-situ* pegs in the wall (placed by persons unknown several years ago). Climb past the 5 pegs then trend rightwards and up a rib to the break of *Gallop Step*. Step right to fix protection at its stance, move back left and climb the steep wall (peg) until it is possible to pull leftwards to gain the crack in the prow; belay on the pinnacle. Either continue via pitch 2 of *False Destiny* or abseil.

**Lost Tango**   45 feet   E3 6a                              (10.70)
The slim groove leading directly to the stance of *Gallop Step* gives a steep and sustained pitch. Abseil off or finish up pitch 2 of *Anniversary Waltz*.

**Anniversary Waltz**   120 feet   E2                        (28.5.56)
An enjoyable route as far as pitch 3 with a serious start and a hard but well-protected second pitch through the overhang above the belay of *Gallop Step*. Start directly under the very large overhangs in the lowest part of the North Buttress, about 10 feet right of a detached flake.
**1** 45 feet. 5b. Climb the smooth wall, on small holds, to an open groove; poor protection. An easy slab leads to a small stance and peg belay, wire back-ups.
**2** 40 feet. 5c. Follow the corner, on large holds, to the overhang. Traverse left very strenuously in an exposed position to reach a comfortable stance at a tree.
**3** 35 feet. Traverse 10 feet left and climb the wall to a tree at the top, very vegetated.

**The Ox Bow Incident**   200 feet   E4                      (1972)
A difficult and serious climb taking the white wall right of *Anniversary Waltz* and avoiding the overhangs on the right. The last pitch is hopelessly overgrown. Start below a shallow groove in the white wall.
**1** 90 feet. 5c. Climb up to the groove and follow it to a poor peg runner. Make a hard move left on small holds and move up to a hollow flake. Move left again and up to join *Gallop Step*. Traverse right along this to a tree belay.
**2** 90 feet. 4c. Go right for 15 feet to the top of a black pinnacle.

Climb steeply up to two small trees and then move left onto a narrow gangway, which leads awkwardly onto a steep slab below the final roof. Belay at a poor tree.
**3** 20 feet. 5b. Finish up and to the right over the final overhang to battle with brambles and the herbaceous border.

**Foxtrot**   180 feet   E3   ‡                                    (14.4.71)
A good route, unfortunately now very overgrown with brambles on pitch 2. Start at a block 15 yards right of *Anniversary Waltz*.
**1** 70 feet. 5b. Climb a leftward-sloping ramp, usually wet, and go up tentatively to a spike on *Gallop Step*. Climb the overhang to two small trees.
**2** 110 feet. 5c. Traverse left and take the left-slanting groove to the apex of the slab. Hard moves up through the overlap gain the jungle on the top of the crag.

Below and to the right of the main crag is a small isolated buttress about 30 yards above the river. This provides a fine and spectacular route.

**Sleeping Beauty**   120 feet   E4 6a                        (20.8.81)
Bold and exciting climbing which may have become harder due to the loss of a crucial hold. Start at a layback flake on the right-hand side of the cliff. Climb the flake for 15 feet and then hand-traverse leftwards to a peg runner. Climb the overhanging wall on improving holds to a roof, go over this on the right using enormous holds. Climb up a slab for 20 feet to a tree belay. The best descent is to abseil from the tree. A direct start has been made up the wall direct to the peg, **The Witching Stick** 6b.

# Craig Cwm Dyli                              OS Ref 650 538

This is the large, very broken crag high up the hillside above the Cwm Dyli Power Station. It is about 350 yards further up the valley from the North Buttress of Clogwyn y Bustach and is considerably higher up the hillside. The front face consists of two long, very broken ribs with a gully between. Round the edge to the left is a smaller but more satisfactory face. A number of routes have been recorded, the best of which are described here. The crag can be reached directly from the Power Station but a much less arduous approach is to traverse up and right from the North Buttress of Clogwyn y Bustach. The best descent is to zigzag steeply down from the north end of the crag.

**Willy Wobbles But She Don't Fall Off**   100 feet   Very Severe †
                                                                      (9.4.97)
An exposed route taking the sparsely-protected gangway running left-to-right up the left-hand side of the crag. Climb the gangway

to an airy step rightwards over the bulge. Continue in the same line to finish up easier slabs.

**Irn Bru**   130 feet   E4 6a   †                          (19.5.97)
A fine steep route which takes the overhanging red wall direct. Start to the left of a small tree at a short leaning corner. Climb the corner to a ledge on the left. Step back right and climb the wall just right of the arête. A steep pull leads to a sloping shelf. Move right to ledges above the initial corner of *Gwastadanas* (peg runner). Bold moves diagonally left lead to hollow spikes in the middle of the face. The bulge above is climbed on pockets first right and back left (peg runner) to better holds. Continue directly up the wall to finish up a slab.

**Cymru Heb Geidwadwyr**   130 feet   E4 5c   †   (2.5.97)
A steep and impressive variation on *Irn Bru* but not as good. Follow *Irn Bru* to the hollow spikes in the middle of the face. Step up and make a long move left for the base of a flake, big camming device. Climb this to its top and make a hard move up to a sprint up the final wall on improving holds. Finish up the slab.

**Gwastadanas**   260 feet   Very Severe                 (4.68)
This route takes an area of reasonably clean rock. Start below the open, vegetated corner running up to the overhanging reddish wall.
**1** 90 feet. 4c. Climb to the small rowan tree, step right into the corner crack and continue to a strenuous exit onto a good ledge. Move right to a rowan tree belay.
**2** 80 feet. 4c. Move right below a vegetated chimney and climb a short rock rib before going back left (awkward) into a cleaner chimney. Climb this to a broad ledge.
**3** 90 feet. 4b. Climb steep slabs to a grassy section and a way off to the left.
**Direct Finish**   Hard Very Severe 5a                  (27.4.98)
**2a** Rather than traversing left into the chimney climb the rib above direct.

**Goebbels**   145 feet   Very Difficult                 (9.9.56)
Further to the right there is a large tree-filled niche and right of this a long broken rib. The route takes this rib which is better than it looks, although care should be taken with the rock.
**1** 100 feet. Pull onto the left-hand side of the rib and go up to a small tree. Continue over easier ground for 40 feet to a pinnacle where the wall steepens. Climb up the steep juggy wall to pull over into the left side of the tree-filled niche.
**2** 45 feet. Go up for a few feet and traverse right to a tree. Struggle up the dirty corner behind the tree to finish.

# First Ascents

## Tremadog Area

| | |
|---|---|
| 1940s-50s | Moel y Gest routes |

'First ascents are not given in detail, but most of the Difficults and Moderates were first done solo by myself during the last five years. In making the harder routes, leaders and seconds from the Midland Association of Mountaineers have taken part, including A C Waine, John Scott, F H Restall and Hester Norris. Young climbers from Portmadoc pioneered some of the later climbs — Bob Davies, Glanfor Williams and Harold Morris'.
Showell Styles, MAM Journal 1951.

**1950 June 11**    **Pen y Ci** G Williams
The first ascent of Pen y Ci (translation: hound's head) but also known as Tremadog Pinnacle was made by Glanfor Williams up the short inside route (solo). The line taken by Tony Moulam was climbed on a top rope by Glanfor Williams and friends on 25th December 1950 and christened Christmas Crack but later became the following route.

**1951 Mar 28**    **Hound's Head Buttress** A J J Moulam, G J Sutton
The buttress was blown up in 1963 as it posed a danger to passing traffic due to the unstable nature of the rock. It has since been replaced by the route R.I.P.

**1951 May 13**    **Shadrach** A J J Moulam, G W S Pigott, D Thomas
'A splendid climb, probably the best at Tremadog or indeed anywhere in the area.'
Snowdon South 1960.
The rotten oak tree next to the perched block has long since gone.

**1951 July 12**    **Creagh Dhu Wall** J Cunningham, W Smith, P Vaughan
Now acknowledged as one of the best Severes in Wales. First climbed by a visiting party from the infamous Scottish climbing club. They dismissed the route as being insignificant. How

times change. 'The route proper finishes up a
groove over to the left, a little awkward,
polished, nasty, hard groove where once I was
stuck for half an hour, standing on my laces,
unable to move.'
Jim Perrin, Classic Rock.
'I could not resist putting a peg in, although I
nearly lost my false teeth in the effort of
threading the rope through the krab'. Glanfor
Williams's personal log.
The variation finish was ascended by D T
Roscoe, A J J Moulam on Jun 2 1957. Variation
pitch 1 by A Beanland, C T Jones in November
1957.

| | |
|---|---|
| 1951 July 12 | **Valerie's Rib** P Vaughan, W Smith, J Cunningham |

"Boring, trivial little climbs" John Cunningham's
comment on his routes at Tremadog.
Valerie's Rib Direct D Yates, D H Jones 1964.

| | |
|---|---|
| 1951 July 23 | **Belshazzar** P Vaughan, K V Ingold |

Quite a hard lead; by 1956 the route had
been graded Extremely Severe.
Belshazzar Variation J Proctor, R Crisfield
18 April 1965.

| | |
|---|---|
| 1951 Sep 5 | **Ham Route** J N Mather, J B Lawton, M Hartley |

Provided the meat of what is now the second
pitch of Grim Wall.

| | |
|---|---|
| 1952 Sep | **Wardroom Hatch** S Styles, G Williams |
| | **Wardroom Deckhead** S Styles, G Williams |
| | **The Chains** G Williams, S Styles |

Glanfor Williams had forgotten that he'd taken
part in these little climbs.

| | |
|---|---|
| 1952 | **Monkey's Island Superdirect** R Davies, G Williams |
| | **Jacob's Ladder** R Davies, G Williams |

The latter route was originally named Kestrel
Crack.

| | |
|---|---|
| 1952 Mar 8 | **Rienetta** (1 pt aid) A J J Moulam, D Thomas |

This climb has suffered from several large
rockfalls. It was cleaned up and reascended by
C J Phillips on a number of occasions.

| | |
|---|---|
| 1953 Jan 3 | **Simddau Fawr** G Williams and party |

'I aimed for the eastern side of Moel Ddu,
Dewi had said that there were 400-foot slabs
here, mentally I had halved the estimate and

|             |                                                                 |
|-------------|-----------------------------------------------------------------|
|             | *therefore was not unduly disappointed'.*                       |
| 1953 Sep 5  | **Yggdrasil** D R Fisher, E A Wrangham, A Tissieres, R R E Chorley |

*'A feeble climb, except for the crack at the top of the rake on Shadrach Buttress'. The top crack at the top of the rake is now the top pitch of Nifl Heim.*

|              |                                            |
|--------------|--------------------------------------------|
| 1953 Dec 13  | **Backstairs** M J Harris, J Neill         |
| 1953 Dec 13  | **Bramble Buttress** M J Harris, J Neill   |

*'The next pitch consisted of an ivy-covered and quite exposed pinnacle. There were no rock holds but I found that my tricounis bit into the ivy stalks quite well'. Glanfor Williams, 6 August 1956.*

|              |                                            |
|--------------|--------------------------------------------|
| 1953 Dec 19  | **Princess** M J Harris, J Neill           |
| 1953 Dec 19  | **Scratch** A J J Moulam, W R Craster      |

*'Only the crux is hard but it is inescapeable. The aid of pitons may be needed if the rocks are greasy'.*

| 1953 Dec 20 | **Poor Man's Peuterey** G J Sutton, J Gaukroger |
|-------------|-------------------------------------------------|

*Originally this started up what is now the lower part of* Borchgrevinck *and was known as* Curving Slab.

| 1953 Dec 20 | **Clutch** (4 pts) A J J Moulam, W R Craster, J F Mawe |
|-------------|--------------------------------------------------------|

| 1953 Dec 20 | **Sheerline** D R Bell, D Thomas |
|-------------|----------------------------------|

*Right-hand start by M J Harris on December 13 of the same year.*

| 1953 Dec 25 | **Christmas Curry** A J J Moulam, J M Barr |
|-------------|--------------------------------------------|

*A fine Christmas present for Moulam and one of the most popular routes on the cliff. The upper part of the* Micah Eliminate *was climbed in 1954 by M J Harris, and the lower part was added later by A Strapcans, R Brown.*
*The* Treemudrock Finish *was climbed in 1968 by C T Jones and the* Lleolwyr Finish *by Mike Lewis in the same year.*
*The* Finish of Moments *was added by G Gibson in 1978.*

| 1953 Dec | **Gamma**, **Beta**, and **Alpha** (Craig y Gesail) |
|----------|-----------------------------------------------------|

*were all climbed by a Cambridge University Mountaineering Club party.*
*All three routes took easy vegetated lines on the lower slabs of Princess Buttress. The same party also ascended what they called the*

*Gallt Wen Pinnacle, a short tower at the right-hand end of the crag, now taken by Puki.*

1953    *Clwb Dringo, a local climbing club based in Porthmadog was founded. Officers elected were: Chairman, Showell Styles; Vice-Chairman, E Lloyd-Evans; Secretary, G E Owen and Treasurer, G Jones. The club made many early repeats at Tremadog as well as prospecting new routes at Borth y Gest, Yr Arddu and the Moelwyn crags.*

1954 Jan 1    **The Lamp that Failed** G J Sutton, J H Longland

1954 Jan 1    **The Link that Failed** G C Band, P Denton
*Both of the above routes were graded Difficult and are located on Verdant Buttress, an area of rock to the right of Two Face Buttress on Pant Ifan.*

1954 Jan 2    **Hogmanay Hangover** M J Harris, J Neill
*Pitches 1 and 2 were added six months later by S G Moore. C T Jones, G A P Knapp, K J Clark
Direct Finish M Lewis, H G Davies 29 June 1966.*

1954 Jan 3    **Badger's Buttress** G J Sutton, G C Band

1954 Jan 4    **Olympic Slab** J K Disley, S Cheeseman
*Pitch 1 was added in October 1958 by B D Hogan and C T Jones.*

1954 Mar 28    **Has Beens' Holiday** A J J Moulam, B Hilton-Jones
*A long lost Diff on Verdant Buttress, Pant Ifan.*

1954 Mar 28    **Hail Bebe** A J J Moulam, J M Barr
*'It is difficult to find and care should be taken not to wander into the steep bramble slabs.' Snowdon South 1960.
It is now much easier to follow.*

1954 Apr 4    **Ave atque Vale** M J Harris, J Neill
*In Latin 'Hail and Farewell'. A vegetated route up the left-hand side of Peuterey Buttress.*

1954 Aug 8    **Bulging Wall** T J Baugh, P Baugh, D J Williams

1954 Aug 8    **Central Arête** D Thomas and party
*Right-hand and usual start climbed by T J Baugh, P Baugh and D J Williams.*

1954 Aug 18    **Falling Block Crack** C T Jones, S G Moore

**1954 Aug 25**   **Quatre Fois** C T Jones, F Davies
*Variation start added 10 December 1955 by
P R C Steele, T A K Wright.
'During the summer of 1954 Pant Ifan
farmhouse was taken over by the Cave and
Crag Club. H Smith of this group discovered
climbing at Tremadog after his years of caving
and soon started with his own inventions.'*
Snowdon South 1960.

**1954 Sep 4**   **The Castle** M J Harris, J Neill
*'The crags are for the most part small, steep, at
low altitude and not infrequently rising from a
jungle.'* N J Soper, Geological Notes Snowdon
South 1966.

**1954 Oct 10**   **Dotheboys** M J Harris, J Neill
*The original route on what was later known as
the Neb Buttress. In the contents page of the
1955 Climbers' Club Interim Guide the route
was given an 'Ugh' standard. 'Severe
vegetation — hardly a climb. Dotheboys
Buttress is festooned with creepers and
brambles... A route to be avoided until a forest
fire can be arranged'.* J Neill.

**1955 Jan 30**   **Mimsy** G D Roberts, J Neill

**1955 Feb 6**   **Lucretia** (4 pts/A2) R R E Chorley, M J
Harris, D C Bull
*An early aid route on Avalanche Buttress. Three
pitons and one etrier were used on the
traverse.
'He tried a peg in the vertical crack and at this
crucial point his piton (on which he was
dangling) came out. Somehow and without
apparent effort he landed back on the
foothold'.* Glanfor Williams 1958.

**1955 Apr 17**   **Much ado About Nothing**
*A variation finish to Hound's Head Buttress.
Ascended on a top rope by C T Jones and
party.*

**1955 May 7**   **Workers Playtime** W H Little, S Bodsworth,
B Boughton
*This was about 20 feet right of Hound's Head
Pinnacle.*

**1955 May 14**   **Tumbleweed** D H Briggs, E W Dance
*'A catastrophe was narrowly averted when I
dropped my pipe and Dewi managed to catch*

it for me, not a very good climb'. Glanfor
Williams's personal log.

1955 May 14   **Pothook** G W S Pigott, Hon. R R E Chorley

1955 May 21   **Strapiombo** D D Whillans, G J Sutton
'One of the most exhausting climbs in the
district. After the first ascent it was
acknowledged to be both impressive and
strenuous'. Snowdon South
'I think ascents of Strapiombo should be
rewarded with free cups of tea at Eric's'. Mike
Lewis.

1955 June 5   **Oakover** A J J Moulam, G W S Pigott
'Moulam was one of the leading explorers of
the comparatively little known cliffs above
Tremadog. Many of these are very good routes
that deserve to become more widely known,
and have lifted the cliffs they adorn straight
from the embryonic state into maturity.'
Snowdon Biography, 1957.

1955 June 5   **Knell for a Jackdaw** G R Robson, J Neill,
G W S Pigott

1955 June 5   **Glade Way** G W S Pigot, A J J Moulam, G
R Robson, J Neill
On Ivy Buttress, Craig Bwlch y Moch, which fell
down in the 1970s.

1955 June 11   **Whittington** J Disley, J Neill
'From below the big corner a traverse right not
far above the ground (from which it could be
reached at many points, but only by painful
penetration of thorny jungle) looking for and
finding the easy way up the face but only at
the right-hand end' CC Journal 1956.

1955 June 26   **Niobe** (2 pts) G R Robson, D H Briggs,
J Neill
'... but it is surely much better to have a climb
of Hard VS with no pegs than a VS with two
pegs. If people go around sticking pegs in any
old climb, the crags will soon become like the
Alps where nothing is hard and the only thing
that matters is getting to the top'. Pete Crew,
Rocksport, August 1970.

1955 July 3   **Tantalus** H I Banner, J Neill (or was it A T
Griffith)
The route originally finished up Niobe. The
independent finish was added in 1964 by D
Yates, G Simpkin (1 pt).

1955 Aug 13    **Marath** C T Jones, R Moseley
1955 Sep 24    **Rammer's Route** G F Williams, A H Vereker
1955 Sep 27    **Nifl Heim** H I Banner, E M Baldwin
*The final crack, the best part of an earlier route
called* Yggdrasil *was added by D R Fisher and
party in 1963.*
*The Bastion Variation was added by C E
Davies, B D Wright in 1959. This is now part
of* Venom.

1955 Sep 27    **Helsinki Wall** (1 pt) J H Longland, B E H
Maden
*'Climb the slab behind the stance for 15 feet
with aid from a piton on the way to a large
clump of heather, then traverse left to small
footholds and a small ledge (hand inserted
piton). Then climb a series of cracks to 6 feet
from the top, step right and mantelshelf into or
round a thorn bush'. First ascent description.*

1955 Nov       **Oberon** A J J Moulam, J Neill, J B Glass, P D
Chapman
*The route originally went out left to join the top
section of* Merlin.

1955 Dec 25    **Pear Tree Variation** H Smith, H Drasdo, F
Davies
*So-called because of the difficulty in the
pronunciation of Peuterey.*
*Lower section first climbed by Bramfitt and
Neill in 1954.*

1955 Dec 27    **Breeze Buttress** J H Longland, A J J Moulam
*A climb on the right-hand side of Bwlch y
Moch. 'Much vegetation. Start; penetrate the
vegetation to where this steepens'. CC Journal.*

1955 Dec 28    **Strangeways** H Smith, H Drasdo
*'Unfortunately the brambles are tenacious and
painful and a prospective party must ponder
whether the suffering is worthwhile. Once the
rock is reached the climbing is delightful'.*

1955 Dec 31    **Nos Calan Rib** J H Longland, P Gordon
*On the buttress to the right of Hound's Head
Pinnacle. 'Moss, gorse, oaks etc'.*

1956 Jan 4     **Limpopo** J H Longland, H B Carslake, P
Gordon, R E Kendall
*'Very vegetated. Not advised, a variety of
undergrowth, rockeries and trees'.*

1956 Apr 15    **Merlin** A J J Moulam, B A Jillot
*Pitch 2 was climbed by C E Davies, A Cowburn*

*in 1958.*
*The Direct Finish by H Smith and party in*
*1959.*
*'The starting pinnacle on Merlin fell down in*
*Oct 1986; or rather was pulled down by a 15*
*and a half stone climber 'Captain Carjack'*
*laybacking up it.'*
*P Williams, Mountain Magazine.*
*Reclimbed direct by A Newton. Alternative left-*
*hand start at Very Severe by P Williams,*
*C Whitehead.*

| | |
|---|---|
| 1956 May 6 | **Holly Buttress**, **North Edge Route**, **Juniper Crack**, **South Face Route** |
| | J Trumper, S Styles |
| 1956 July 8 | **W.O.B.** D H Briggs, A J J Moulam |

*While Others Bathed. The route described is a*
*more difficult version of the climb. The Pagoda*
*Finish up the groove was so called because a*
*film; 'Inn of the Sixth Hapiness' was being*
*made in the area.*

| | |
|---|---|
| 1956 Aug 7 | **Stromboli** H Smith, C T Jones |

*Variation by F E R Cannings, M A Toole in*
*1966.*
*The Creature Variation by M Griffiths, M Crook*
*on 18 March 1981 takes the top overhang a*
*little further to the left.*

| | |
|---|---|
| 1956 Sep 16 | **Javelin** D P Davis, D Thomas, J Neill, M J Harris |

*The final pitch was climbed by D Yates,*
*G Simpkin in 1964.*

| | |
|---|---|
| 1956 Oct 6 | **Raven's Nest Wall** G W S Pigott, A Birtwistle |

*A number of pitons were used, mainly for*
*protection. The finish described was climbed*
*by D Yates in 1967.*

| | |
|---|---|
| 1956 Oct 6 | **Pincushion** (16 pts) D P Davies, M J Harris, R R E Chorley |

*Numerous attempts were made over the years*
*to free this route. By 1958 the aid had been*
*reduced to 6 points and by 1966 to 3 points.*
*Finally freed by H Barber in 1973.*
*A local team of climbers often climbed in the*
*evenings. An early repeat of this route was*
*thwarted by benightment over the roof.*
*Thankfully, an abseil was rigged by*
*candlelight, the candles being stuck in the*

*crack system. When they got down to the road they could still see the flame flickering high up on the cliff.*

1956 Oct 7    **Krakatoa** C T Jones, G Eveson
*'There were very few people on the cliffs then, but the views over Tremadog were just as beautiful. The Porthmadog soccer club dashed about like multi-coloured ants and whenever they scored the faintest of cheers drifted up to the crag.'* Trevor Jones, Welsh Rock 1986.

1956 Oct 13    **Two Face Girdle** C T Jones, G Eveson
*The abseil was caused by the leader slipping off whilst indulging in rope antics.*

1956 Oct 27    **The Arctic Circle** C T Jones, H Smith, C Pryke, M G Hanson
*A long-lost girdle on Pant Ifan.*

1956 Oct 28    **Seven League Chimney** C T Jones, M G Hanson
*On the right of Hound's Head Pinnacle.*

1956 Nov 10    **Next of Kin** (1 pt) C T Jones, M G Hanson

1956 Nov 18    **K.M.A.** C T Jones

1956 Dec 8    **Rock 'n' Roll** C Pryke, N Knight

1956 Dec 24    **Eifionydd Wall** C T Jones, G Eveson, M J Hanson, K J Clarke

1956    **Via Gellia** M J Harris, J Neill, R F Jones

1956    **Orodruin** (3 pts) C T Jones and party
*Rediscovered, climbed with 1 point of aid and named by F E R Cannings, M A Toole in March 1966.*

1957 Jan 19    **Great Western** C T Jones, M J Hanson

1957 Mar    **Grim Wall** C T Jones, H Fox (AL) H Smith
Grim Wall Direct — *first ascent unknown.*

1957 Mar    **Triangulum** H Smith, H Fox, J R Sims, C T Jones

1957 Apr 22    **Borchgrevinck** C T Jones, J R Sims
*Originally this started up what is now the lower part of Poor Man's Peuterey.*
*'By exchanging the original starts you end up with one superb Severe, possibly the best anywhere, and one mediocre V Diff.'* Pete Crew, Rocksport Aug 1970.

1957 June 9    **Oakway** C E Davies, B D Wright, E Millington

1957 June 9    **The Brothers** C T Jones, B A F Jones
*The Independent Finish was climbed by*

|            | *D Yates, T Parker in September 1964.*<br>*The Direct Finish was added later in 1968.* |
|------------|---|
| 1957 Oct   | **Oak Tree Wall** C Pryke, A Fisher |
| 1957 Nov   | **Touch and Go** R James, P Benson<br>*The crack above the V-groove was climbed by*<br>*M Crook, H Walton in 1976* |
| 1957 Nov   | **Foul Touch** R James, P Benson, M Connelly |
| 1957 Nov   | **Rombold** (1 shoulder aid) A Beanland, C T<br>Jones |
| 1957 Nov   | **Right Touch** R James, A Marshall<br>*A direct finish was added in 1963 by*<br>*D Wilson.* |
| 1958 Mar 20 | **Cottage Buttress** (A2) C J Mortlock, J Cole<br>*An assualt on the jungle left of Hound's Head*<br>*Gully, now called Fear Buttress.* |
| 1958 May 11 | **One Step in the Clouds** C T Jones,<br>R Moseley<br>*One of the best routes of its grade at*<br>*Tremadog.* |
| 1958 May 25 | **Lakeland Gem** C T Jones, C E Davies, B D<br>Wright |
| 1958 Aug 16 | **Barbarian** (A2) C T Jones, C E Davies,<br>E Millington, M King<br>*'The corner was very grassy and the party took*<br>*10 hours and 10 pitons'. It was climbed free*<br>*sometime later by J Brown.* |
| 1958 Aug 23 | **Tiercel** (1 pt aid) C E Davies, W A Trench |
| 1958 Nov 16 | **Castell Lower Girdle Traverse** C T Jones,<br>C E Davies |
| 1959 Apr 4 | **Agrippa** H Smith, S Thomas<br>*Took a line between W.O.B. and Raven's Nest*<br>*Wall.* |
| 1960 Mar 13 | **Leg Slip** J Brown, C E Davies<br>*Leg Slip Direct Start by C J Mortlock in 1961,*<br>*became part of Venom.*<br>*Alternative Finish by J Pasquill, R Evans, 1967,*<br>*became part of Certain Slip.* |
| 1960 Mar 13 | **First Slip** (1 pt aid) J Brown, C E Davies<br>*Leg Break Finish by E Ward–Drummond, S*<br>*Brown March1968. It had previously been*<br>*credited to J Pasquill, R Evans but they had*<br>*failed below the overhang.* |
| 1960 Mar 26 | **Vector** (2 pts aid) J Brown, C E Davies<br>*A tremendous masterpiece of route finding.*<br>*One piton was used on the Ochre Slab and*<br>*another to exit from the groove on the top pitch* |

Gavin Foster in *The Gwynant Crack* Severe.
Photo: Ray Wood

Martin Crook on *Priapic Worship*
E2 on the Gwynant Needle.
Photo: Ray Wood

Glenda Huxter on the first
pitch of her own route
*False Destiny* E4, Clogwyn
y Bustach.
Photo: Alan Leary

prior to the excavation of good holds.
'Climbed by Brown in 1960, Vector rapidly
acquired a huge reputation. Trevor Jones,
attempting to second the first ascent, found
himself dangling ten feet away from the rock,
and was lowered down to spread his ample
gospel amoungst the climbers of Wales. Leader
after leader plummeted from the crack of the
top pitch; an inscrutable, smiling crack slipping
across the lip of the overhangs, it established
for the climb a devastating psychological
advantage; of having a strenuous crux right at
the top after a great deal of hard and technical
climbing.'
J Perrin, Hard Rock.

1960 Apr     **Avalon** C T Jones, E Siddall
'While pointing out that the true mountain
atmosphere is almost wholly absent, enthusiasts
cite the low rainfall and the nearness of Black
Rock Sands bathing beach as compensating
attractions.' E C Pyatt commenting on
Tremadog in his book, Where to Climb in the
British Isles 1960.

1960 Apr     **Acropolis** C T Jones, M G H Hanson
The lower section had been climbed as part of
Princess by M J Harris, J Neill in 1953.

1960 Sep     **The Wasp** (5 pts) J Brown, C E Davies
On pitch 1 two slings were used on
chockstones. On pitch 2 a sling was used for
the bulge followed by two pegs in the groove.
This fulfilled Brown's maxim of only two pegs
per route.
Variation start by M Lewis, E Davies on 15
November 1985.

1960     Snowdon South guide published, a quote from
this sums up the feelings of the time. 'Tremadoc
in particular is becoming very popular.
However much mountaineers of the old school
may regret cliffs which are divorced from
mountains, the most doubtful must admit that
rock-climbing as a sport of its own, quite apart
from mountaineering, has come to stay and
flourish. Tremadoc and the other cliffs here
described are no longer relegated to days
when it is too wet for higher things, but are

> *sought out because they provide routes as
> attractive for their own sakes as any in
> Snowdonia. It is hoped that Snowdon South
> will draw off some of the crowds from
> Llanberis; but it should be emphasised that
> nobody need forsake the tops who does not
> want to.'*
> Wilfred Noyce, June 1960.

| | |
|---|---|
| 1960 Dec 30 | **Tro** G Williams, H Morris, D H Jones |
| 1961 Jan 14 | **Corniog** J G Trumper, P Lloyd |

*Variation to pitch 2 by I Lloyd Jones, C
Greatwich on Sep 1 1990.*

1961 Jan 19 **Clapton's Crack** G Clapton and party
*The variation to the last pitch was added by J
Brown, C E Davies in 1961. The route was
originally called Vicuna.*

| | |
|---|---|
| 1961 Mar 24 | **Yogi** G Hodgkiss, M Shannon |
| 1961 Mar 24 | **Boo-Boo** M Edwards, N Crofton |
| 1961 Apr 3 | **Striptease** J Brown, C E Davies |

*Named after the second's leg movements
around the crux overhang when viewed from
the belay.*

1961 June 2 **The Grasper** (5 pts) J Brown, D Thomas
bach
*Several points of aid were used in the final
groove. 'Obviously if more aid is used
the climb will become easier. Perhaps the best
example of this is The Grasper which is quite a
good Extreme with only one sling and one peg
on its top pitch. It is regularly climbed with a
peg on the first pitch and four or five on the top
pitch. With that amount of aid it can't be much
more than normal Hard VS. Some climbers
must get quite a shock when they get onto a
really hard route which they can't put pegs
into!' Pete Crew, Rocksport Aug 1970.*

1961 June 4 **The Fang** J Brown, C E Davies
1961 June **The Neb** J Brown, D Thomas bach
*Pitch 1 was climbed by M H Lewis, H G Davies
in 1968.*
*Neb Direct was first done with aid from
wooden wedges, possibly by B Brewster in the
1960s. It was first climbed free by H Barber.*

| | |
|---|---|
| 1961 June | **Nimbus** (1 pt) J Brown, C Goodey |
| 1961 Aug | **Ek Borge** C T Jones, E Siddall, R F Jones |

| | |
|---|---|
| 1961 Aug | **Kestrel Cracks** C T Jones, C E Davies<br>*Pitch 1 had been climbed by J Brown, D Thomas bach as the start to* The Neb. |
| 1961 Summer | **Mistook** N Gough and party |
| 1961 Sep 16 | **The Toit** (2 pts) J Brown, J R Allen, C E Davies<br>*F.F.A. S Haston 1982.* |
| 1961 Oct | **Sphincter** C T Jones, J H Swallow<br>Sphinx *variation by M Totterdell, S Spalding on 26 June 1980.* |
| 1961 Dec 16-18 | **Bwlch y Moch Girdle** R James, I F Cambell |
| 1961 Dec | **Alcatraz** M Boysen and party |
| 1961 Dec | **Holloway** M Boysen and party<br>*Only the top pitch. Pitch 1 is added later by A Sharp and Pitch 2 by J Moran.* |
| 1961 Dec | **The Plum** (2 pts) R James, D Yates |
| 1962 Mar 24 | **Scratch Arête** (1 pt) B Ingle, R F Jones<br>*Originally the overhang was avoided by climbing the thin crack on the right with a peg for aid.* |
| 1962 Apr 20 | **Vulcan** (15 pts) B Wright, C Goodey<br>*This was climbed as an artificial route. It is reported that B Brewster climbed it free in the 1960s but this seems unlikely. The first free ascent was probably by R Fawcett in Spring 1977.*<br>*'The first few moves seem problematical. Any combatant encountering trouble at this stage would be well-advised to capitulate, for higher up the route takes few prisoners.'*<br>*Phil Burke, Extreme Rock.* |
| 1962 May | **Y Broga** D H Jones, H Morris, G Williams<br>*A frog was found on the upper pitches, hence the route name.*<br>O Brother *variation G Williams, D H Jones June 6 1962.* |
| 1962 July | **Meshach** (1 pt) R James, A Earnshaw, M Petrovsky<br>*Rattlesnake Finish by G Gibson, J Perry, 29 Aug 1978.* |
| 1962 Oct 14 | **Tornado** N Gough, J G Thomas, R E J Gough |
| 1962 Oct | **Falcon** (9 pts) R James, M Petrovsky<br>*F.F.A. J Clements 1964.* |
| 1963 Sep | **R.I.P.** C E Davies, G D Roberts |
| 1963 Dec 9 | **Whirlwind** N Gough, G Williams |

1963 **Cam Fawr** C Paterson, J T Bursnall, D T Bursnall
*A long-forgotten route just right of Belshazzar, it has since fallen down.*

1964 Jan **Mangoletsi** (1 pt) H I Banner, B Ingle
*The finish described was climbed by P Gomersall in spring 1977.*
*Pitch 1 direct by M H Lewis*

1964 Feb **Victimisation** (A2) R James, D A Jones
*Considerable aid was employed on what was later to become Fingerlicker.*

1964 Feb 1 **Groglsen** (S & A1) H Morris, G Williams
*A long forgotten route left of Hound's Head Gully. 'I had a large wooden block with me which was designed to fit chock-wise into the crack. It was too big so I threw it down, it narrowly missed hitting John and Peredur who had just arrived at the botom'. Glanfor Williams's personal log.*

1964 Feb 9 **The Fox** J Harwood, R A Hughes (AL)

1964 Mar 25 **Chinook** N Gough, G Griffith

1964 Mar 31 **Hedera** J Brown, J Cheesemond
*The Latin for Ivy.*

1964 Mar 7 **Tensor** J Brown, C E Davies (2 pts)
*The roof was climbed free by H Barber.*
*'His completely free solo of Tensor in Hush Puppies will take some beating. The thing was typical of Livesey, of his ability, his humour, his competitiveness. He was supposed to be seconding me, a rare occurance and I took the rope in ever faster, until the free unattached end appeared at my feet, to be followed shortly afterwards by Pete'. John Sheard*

1964 Apr 1 **The Croaker** (4 pts) J Brown, J Cheesemond, B Sharp
*First recorded as Cracker, F.F.A. R Fawcett 1976.*

1964 Apr 5 **The Struggler** (1 pt) B Ingle, C T Jones

1964 Apr 25 **Grotto** T Heatherly, A Davies

1964 Apr 25 **Mensor** D Alcock, A Cowburn

1964 Apr 29 **Cursor** (3 pts) D Alcock, S Williams
*F.F.A. A Sharp, D Lewis in May 1978.*

1964 May 22 **Forest View's Shattered Cracks** G Farnsworth, G Barker, B Frost, P Barker, G Pemberton

1964 May 24 **Iolyn** D Thomas bach, G D Roberts

| | |
|---|---|
| 1964 May | **Salix** D Thomas bach, A Cowburn, T W Heatherley |
| 1964 May | **Pellagra** (2 pts) J Brown, J Cheesesman, K I Meldrum |
| | *F.F.A. P Livesey in 1976.* |
| 1964 June 3 | **Diadic** E Penman, A Harris |

'Dismantle Vector Buttress stone by stone and rebuild it in the Pass and you could blow up the rest of Tremadog for all the good it is'. Pete Crew.

| | |
|---|---|
| 1964 July 18 | **The Fly** D E Burgess, J Harwood (AL) |
| 1964 Sep 10 | **Biolet** J Harwood, S Janvrin (AL) |
| 1964 Oct | **Zukator** (7 pts) P Crew, A Harris |

Pitch 1 had been climbed previously by P Crew, B Ingle. The first completely free ascent was by P Livesey, J Sheard in 1976.

'Crew's lack of ability on boulder problems led Harris to say that anything that Pete could do he would follow in winkle-pickers. He was as good as his word on the first ascent of Zukator wearing a cow gown and the appropriate long pointed shoes of the early sixties. Unfortunately Crew used 7 points of aid to complete Zukator which rather flawed the route.' Welsh Rock.

'The ascent of this groove is akin to bridging up a groove in the bottom of an egg, with about as many holds'. Paul Williams.

| | |
|---|---|
| 1964 Oct | **Tiros** (4 pts) R James, D H Jones |

Later to be incorporated into Cream.

| | |
|---|---|
| 1964 | **G String** (1 pt) R James, C Goodey |

Variation by M Lewis, E Davies in May 1985.

| | |
|---|---|
| 1964 | **Molar** (1 pt) D Yates, G Simpkin |
| 1964 | **Mr Ranger** |

Named by R Eden, J Hey in 1981 but regularly climbed by this time.

| | |
|---|---|
| 1964 | **Valor** (3 pts) D Yates, D H Jones |

Pitches 3, 4 and 5 only. Aid was used on pitch 4. Pitch 2 was added later by N Gough and the complete route was first climbed in 1967 by F Cannings, D Peers. Now described in three pitches.

| | |
|---|---|
| 1965 Apr 7 | **Plumbline** C E Davies, G Holmes |
| 1965 Apr 10 | **Integral** (1 pt) J Brown, C E Davies |
| 1965 Oct 17 | **Sisyphus** (1 pt) R Edwards, C Boulton |

The chances of a pendulum are great. "One

> *dank day we were climbing on Craig y Castell and he was on Sisyphus. One moment I could see his face poking around the overhang; the next he was gone, with the tree shaking like a feather duster." Fred Hall.*

1965 Dec 27   **Valerian** (1 pt) H Smith, I Sanderson

1965   **Touche** C E Davies, D W Walker

1966 Feb 9   **Castell High Girdle** (1 pt) R Edwards, C Boulton

1966 Feb 27   **Geireagle** (2 pts) R Edwards, J Edwards
*A name which has had the unusual distinction of having been misspelt in three different ways in its previously printed forms.*

1966 Easter   **The Chateau** R James, J Wilkinson
*The variation was climbed in 1974 by J Rotherham, J Dunwell.*

1966 Apr 9   **Erebus** (3 pts) R Edwards, D Blythe
*The first completely free ascent was by R Fawcett in 1976.*

1966 Apr 12   **Burlesque** R Newcombe, A Campbell
*Now harder since a hold came off in 1981.*

1966 Apr 24   **Astonall** C T Jones, A J J Moulam, N A J Rogers

1966 May 14   **Tarantula** D Yates, I C Lowe, F L Crawford

1966 June 11   **Carlwm Corner** R F Burns, J Harwood

1966 July 31   **Itch** (1 pt) L E Holliwell, L R Holliwell
*F.F.A. A Sharp.*

1966 July 31   **Whistling Rufus** T Gannon, K McCallum

1966 Aug 17   **Via Nimbus** (9 pts/A2) G Farnsworth, C McDonald, G Pemberton
*'Climb the overhanging corner of the cave with the aid of nuts to a wooden wedge at the roof. Peg up cracks above until it is possible to traverse left to the top of the crag'. Later replaced by Void.*

1966   Snowdon South *(Second Edition)* guide published by The Climbers' Club. *'Incredibly, Llanberis seems now to be a fallen idol; and Tremadog, which was the wet weather alternative, has now attained seniority as a major climbing ground for both tigers and apprentice hard men.'* Trevor Jones

1967 Feb 18   **Scorpion** L E Holliwell, L R Holliwell
*Moel y Gest Quarry is developed in a couple*

*of months of frantic activity. Not worth the effort
for most climbers, although in the Peak it would
be a major venue.*

| | |
|---|---|
| 1967 Mar 11 | **Inferior Grooves** & **The Milky Way**<br>F Quigley, D Mossman |
| 1967 Mar 11 | **Penumbra** & **Oblique** (1 pt) L E Holliwell,<br>L R Holliwell |
| 1967 Mar 12 | **Knife Edge** (1 pt) F Quigley, D Mossman |
| 1967 Mar 12 | **The Swinger** (2 pts) L E Holliwell, L R<br>Holliwell |
| 1967 Mar 18 | **Eclipse** (1 pt) F Quigley, D Mossman (AL) |
| 1967 Mar 19 | **Short Wall** F Quigley, D Mossman (AL) |
| 1967 Mar 19 | **The Prow**, **Deception** (3 pts) & **Cut-throat**<br>L E Holliwell, L R Holliwell |
| 1967 Mar 19 | **Gothic Grooves** (1 pt aid) C J Phillips,<br>E Edkin<br>Rookery Nook *variation by J Moran,<br>G Milburn, S Horrox, October 1977.* |
| 1967 Apr 9 | **Fracture** (1 pt) L R Holliwell, D Mossman (AL)<br>P Quigley, L E Holiwell |
| 1967 Apr 15 | **Damocles** (2 pts) L E Holliwell, L R Holliwell |
| 1967 Apr 23 | **Contrast** (2 pts) L E Holliwell, D Mossman, L R<br>Holliwell |
| 1967 Apr 23 | **Puki** C Greatwich, T Cannon<br>*Variation finish C Greatwich, P Kilvert, J Barker<br>on 10 June 1967.* |
| 1967 Apr 29 | **Chwys** (1 pt) M Lewis, H G Davies |
| 1967 May 6 | **Chough** (1 pt) & **Irony** (2 pts) L R Holliwell,<br>L E Holliwell (AL) |
| 1967 May 29 | **Agoraphobia** A Willmott, W Church |
| 1967 June 27 | **Fandango** (2 pts) A Willmott, J Brown<br>*On Avalanche Buttress, Craig Pant Ifan, it fell<br>down in 1981.* |
| 1967 July 2 | **Oughtogo** (1 pt) L E Holliwell, L R Holliwell |
| 1967 Sep 7 | **Huntley** M H Bayliss, P J Bayliss |
| 1967 Sep 8 | **Millipede** M H Bayliss, P J Bayliss |
| 1967 Sep 8 | **Mons Meg** M H Bayliss, P J Bayliss |
| 1967 Oct | **Cawod** M Lewis, D Jones, H G Davies |
| 1967 Oct | **Gestiana** M Lewis, H G Davies |
| 1967 Oct | **Ribidires** M Lewis H G Davies |
| 1967 Oct | **Blas y Cynfyd** M Lewis, D Jones, H G Davies<br>*Mike Lewis unearths some good routes on a<br>buttress left of Craig y Castell. They were never<br>written up at the time and subsequently were<br>claimed by C Greatwich and party in 1990.* |
| 1968 Mar 10 | **Vindaloo** G Tabbner, R Smith |

1968 Apr 15   **Axeminster** M H Bayliss, P J Bayliss, V G
Atkins
*The variation was climbed in 1973 by A
Green, K Latham, C Fryer.*

1968 Apr 27   **Gilljo** B Clarke, D Steele
*Most of this had been climbed before by
various parties.*

1968 May   **Blogg's Route** D K Scott, M Terry

1968 May   **Joe Soap's Route** D K Scott, D Nicol (AL)
*With an A1 section.*

1969 Summer   *'Back in the Welsh heartland there has been a
growing vogue for soloing — hardly new, but
more widespread and serious than in the past.
The main practitioners are Cliff Philips and Eric
Jones. Jones has soloed climbs like Grasper,
Fang and Hardd, the latter two during one
epic 13-route day. The big prize — Vector
which both Jones and Phillips were hoping to
do first, was taken by Alan
McHardy'.* Mountain, July 1969.

1969   **Carlo** M Lewis and party
*Not written up at the time and claimed since by
various teams.*

1970 Mar   **Slipway** R Cane, A de Cousel

1970 July   **Touch Up** K Toms, G Upton
*Little of this was new but it is a better line up
the buttress than the earlier routes that it
replaces, which were: Ek Borge climbed by C T
Jones, J H Swallow and Touche by C E Davies,
D W Walker.*

1971 Jan 13   **Klondyke Meic** M Lewis, R Williams
*Later claimed as Poison Ivy by C Greatwich,
C Lloyd, C Benette. Written up by Mike's
climbing partner in his absence, he had just left
to spend three years working in the Yukon.*

1971 Mar   *Pete Crew and Al Harris produce a guide to
Tremadog published by West Col in direct
competition with The Climbers' Club. The policy
was to rationalize descriptions, combining
some routes and eliminating poor routes and
trivialvariations. The guide was well-received
but was pre-empted by the CC who were*

forced to publish a hastily revised version of
their own guide.

1971 Apr 18     **Silly Arête** J Pasquill, J Nuttall, R Evans
*One of the best routes in the area and a major
find.*
*'The name seems somehow inconsequential,
but in 1971 it was indeed "silly" to conceive
that anyone would scale that magnificent
arête'. Phil Burke, Extreme Rock.*
*'Some people move back left to Pincushion
above the roof and place protection before the
arête, but that to me spoils one of the best
routes in Wales'. A Sharp, Mountain 48.*

1971 Apr 21     **Carborundum** D Alexandra, B Gormley (AL)
*A route right of Belshazzar which has since
fallen down.*

1972 June 15    **Assegai** C L Jones, K Jones, C F Walmsley, M
H L Hewer

1972 July 21    **Dryad** C L Jones, M H L Hewer

1972           **Broadmoor** (1 pt) G Rigby, P Robinson, I
Ross

1972           **Dark Side** (aid) G Upton, K Toms
*Climbed free in 1978 by G Gibson and
renamed A Vengeance.*

1973 Mar 18    **Hindleburg** (1 pt) J de Montjoye, E S
Hindle
*A quote from Glanfor Williams in 1971 having
visited the crag. 'In the lay-by John Gelli was
just going to tell me off when he recognised
me. He explained that he did not allow
climbers on Craig y Gelli as they damaged his
walls and let his sheep stray on to the road'.
Glanfor Williams's personal log.*
*Access problems remain today.*

1973 May 7     **Hogmanay Girdle** (2 pts) J Perrin,
P Basterfield
*'Jim Perrin and Mike Yates put up a route here
which was described as very good. The
highlight is a 30-foot, almost horizontal tension
traverse, so you judge for yourselves'. Alec
Sharp, Mountain 48.*
*Little of this was new. Pitches 6, 7 and 8 had
been climbed in the opposite direction by H
Smith, I Sanderson in 1965 as part of Valerian.
The final pitch had been climbed in 1967 by*

D Yates and party.
*The tension traverse on pitch 4 was freed by R*
*Fawcett by mistake whilst on Psyche 'n' Burn.*

1973 May 26 **Slabby Flues** C L Jones, M H L Hewer
1973 July **Ivy Crack** P Rigg, M Ryan, P Sinclair
1974 Feb 26 **Crocadillo** A Sharp, S Humphries
*Only the first pitch was new. The final crack*
*had been climbed earlier by J Perrin.*
*A local activist was to have a big surprise. As*
*he approached the belay on a warm spring*
*day he nearly fell off the stance when he*
*realised that the belayer was topless, the*
*belayer was the Australian climber, Louise*
*Shepherd.*

1974 Apr 20 **Touched in the Head** D Alexander,
R Williams
1974 Apr 24 **Caravansoreye** G Davies, R Williams (AL),
I Prichard, H Jones
*'Probably a better route than Bramble Buttress,*
*should improve if climbed regularly'. Rocksport,*
*Aug 1974.*

1974 July **Pretzl Logic** A Rouse, B Hall
*Most of this had been climbed before by*
*I Edwards and party.*
*'My own introduction to unroped climbing*
*came when I hitched to Tremadog and got*
*picked up by Eric Jones, whom I didn't know at*
*the time. Since he was obviously a climber and*
*alone, I suggested doing a few routes together.*
*He said fine, but he didn't want to use a rope!*
*After starting with Grim Wall we moved across*
*to The Fang and by the end of the afternoon*
*we had completed a dozen routes and I was*
*hooked'. Alan Rouse, 'Walk on the Wild Side',*
*an article in Crags 11.*

1974 Oct 4 **Dragon** (aid) J Dunwell, J Parry
*F.F.A. was made in July 1978 by M Griffiths.*
1974 Nov **Chain Gang** R Edwards, P Trower
*A poor girdle of Strangeways Buttress which*
*started up Alcatraz and finished up the arête*
*just left of Strangeways, graded VS.*

1975 Apr **Peuterey Girdle** M Gough, M Creasey
1975 May 5 **Vulture** A Sharp, C Dale
*'The layback is not very hard, but feels bold, as*
*your feet continually seem to be about to shoot*
*off the outward sloping ramp. At the top of the*

ramp, no rest is possible while you try to work out the difficult moves into the niche'. A Sharp. Vulture Direct: A Pollitt (unseconded) on 19 September 1982. 'A fine pitch, though less strenuous than Fingerlicker. It has a technical entry into a holdless niche, where a few notables have shot their bolt.' Crags 5.

1975 May 11 **Fingerlicker** P Livesey, J Lawrence
Free climbed what was Victimisation. Livesey developed a tatic for the route which involved falling off and lowering down to start again from the ground. Controversial at the time, some saw it as a disturbing new ethic.
Direct Finish: J Redhead, A Pollitt on 29 May 1982. On the first ascent of the direct finish, Redhead climbing in underpants because of the heat, stopped for 10 minutes in one position. When asked why he pointed to the topless woman sunbathing in the meadow below.

1975 June 1 **The Snake** A Sharp, C Dale
The first free route to venture onto the Vector headwall.

1975 June 16 **Extraction** C J Phillips, M Crook
'Of Vector quality'. First ascent description.

1975 **Void** (1 pt aid ) R Edwards, I Pomfret
F.F.A. R Fawcett in February 1976.

1976 Apr 27 **Venom** I Edwards, W Turner, T Riley
The first pitch was climbed as a direct start to Leg Slip (1 pt aid) by C J Mortlock.

1976 May 1 **Cream** P Livesey, R Fawcett
The final pitch had been climbed with four points of aid by R James, D Jones in 1964 as part of a route called Tiros, whose first pitch lay up the vegetated gully.

1976 May **Terraqua** (aid) S Cathcart
Climbed free in January 1980 by K 'Chipper' Jones.

1976 **Leg Break** N Shepherd and party
A climb taking a similar line, The Last Gasp, was climbed by G Gibson, J Perry on 12 August 1978.

1976 **Soft Touch** P Trower, M Crook, P Deans
The upper part of this had been climbed earlier by K Wilson, D Blackwell.

| | |
|---|---|
| 1977 Jan 1 | **Wanda** J Moran, M Crook, P Deans |
| | *'The block of the final pitch appears to be held together by faith, hope and congealed mud. I'm not going near it again'. J Moran.* |
| 1977 Feb 26 | **Scarecrow** J Moran, D Hollows |
| 1977 Apr 29 | **Steelfingers** J Moran, P Williams |
| 1977 | **Tall Dwarfs** J Moran, M Crook, P Williams |
| | *A trio of routes that were all cleaned from an abseil rope, an approach that was becoming increasingly common in the area.* |
| 1977 Apr | **Tachyphouse** S Cathcart, P Waters |
| 1977 May | **The Mongoose** P Gomersall, A Evans, J Moran |
| | *So-called because it eliminated The Snake which was climbed by A Sharp, C Dale in 1975. A route with an interesting history. Orginally climbed with side runners in Void it was climbed without by P Gomersall in June 1980, then soloed by P Burke and finally soloed down by R Fawcett albeit by an easier variation which went left missing out the crux.* |
| 1977 June 5 | **Marathon Man** R Fawcett, C Gibb |
| | *'Marathon Man, described in the guide as poorly protected, is not quite as serious as is made out. Jim Moran, attempting the second ascent placed nine runners in the top groove — admittedly not all perfect, including a Friend in a flared crack which took several falls'. Crags 19. (It should be mentioned that Friends were not around when Fawcett first climbed the route.)* |
| | *The alternative finish wqs climbed on sight by M Griffiths plucking off fronds of ivy as he went along.* |
| 1977 June 5 | **Pippikin** P Gomersall, E Masson, J Moran |
| | *Only the final groove was new. The direct start to Falcon had been climbed by L E Holliwell and the creaking flakes by J Lamb.* |
| 1977 Oct 2 | **The Olympiad** J Moran, S Horrox, G Milburn |
| 1977 Oct 24 | **Touchstone** J Moran, A Evans |
| 1977 Dec 13 | *'The most severe natural rockfall to date occured between Craig Pant Ifan and Craig Bwlch y Moch. Three large blocks were detached by natural erosion and fell from 150 feet up the hillside on to the first house on the* |

*Tremadog side of Bwlch y Moch Farm. The rear of the house was virtually demolished and the woman who lived there was fortunate to escape with her life. By chance she was pinned beneath her refrigerator as it fell. This undoubtedly saved her, but her injuries included a broken pelvis and internal damage'. Mountain, Jan 1978.*

| | |
|---|---|
| 1977 | **Spare Rib** P Gomersall, E Masson<br>*Pitch 2 only. Pitch 1 by P Gomersall on June 23 1979.* |
| 1977 | **Certain Slip** P Livesey, P Gomersall |
| 1978 Jan 5 | **The Sting** R Edwards, P Williams |
| 1978 Jan 14 | **Groove of Horror** (1 pt) R Edwards, D Roberts, P Williams<br>*'Extremely strenuous and not often repeated, it was typical of the audacious Edwards'. Welsh Rock 1986.*<br>*F.F.A. B Hannon, summer 1978.*<br>*It should be noted that at this time some activists only acknowledged a point of aid when it had been used for upward progress. Rests on gear were not thought to count.* |
| 1978 Jan 15 | **Daddy Cool** D Roberts, P Williams (AL), R Edwards |
| 1978 Jan 24 | **Salamanda** R Edwards, M R Edwards<br>*'On Bwlch y Moch the Belshazzar Buttress has been subjected to some dedicated cleaning. There have been suggestions of Ministry of Agriculture grants for the ploughing involved. There are now five arable routes on what was once pasture'. Mountain, March 1978.* |
| 1978 Jan 24 | **Heartbreak Hotel** P Williams, D Cuthbertson |
| 1978 Feb 7 | **Earthsea** R Edwards, M R Edwards<br>*Much of this was the same as two earlier routes Belshazzar Variation and Cam Fawr. The latter was the original route of the area but has suffered severely in the recent rockfalls. Indeed one wonders how long much of Merlin Buttress will last.* |
| 1978 Feb 12 | **Curved Air** L McGinley, R Hughes<br>*The grade of this excellent route remains unchanged for an on sight ascent.* |

'Comparable to Archangel'. Tremadog Guide, 1989.

1978 Mar    **Anagram** B Wintringham, M Wintringham
So-called as the nearby Neb was an anagram of the first ascensionist's name.

1978 Mar    **Electric Edge** M Griffiths, G Griffiths
'This climb has quality every inch of its 70 feet, taking a steep, sustained line up an arête on tiny crystals, then finishing over an overhang; well worth the expedition needed to find it. Cleaned, climbed and claimed by Mel ('hanging on tinies') Griffiths, it is undoubtedly a classic'. Paul Williams, Crags 24.

1978 Apr 29  **Starship Trooper** P Thomas

1978 Sping   **Bloodsucker** G Gibson, J Perry

1978 July 16 **Freudian Slip** B Wintringham, A D Baker

1978 July 24 **Hot Rats** S Cathcart, G Griffiths

1978 Aug 27  **Heartline** S Cathcart, G Griffiths
It seems that Heartline and Bloodsucker originally took the same line up this area of slab. They have been separated to give two reasonable routes.

1978 Aug 28  **Timeslip** S Cathcart, G Griffiths

1978 Sep 27  **Final Exam** M Griffiths, M Crook

1978 Sep     **Blinkers** P Livesey, A Livesey, A Taylor

1978         **High Kicks** D Cuthbertson, M Duff
May have been climbed earlier by G Gibson, J Perry.

1978         **Titanium Man** K Robertson, I Langston
An interesting route by 'Tractor Arm' man. The first pitch is a variation climbed by G Gibson, I Barker on 24 June 1979 and called Walk on By.

1979 Apr 15  **Bombshell** G Gibson, J Walker

1979 Apr 16  **Integral Direct** D Humphreys, B Sutton, P Williams

1979 May 26  **Föhn** T Hulme, L McKeown, T Wright

1979 May 29  **Sometimes** G Gibson, J Walker

1979 May 31  **Sorry Sally** A Evans, S Tansey, S Beresford

1979 May     **Technical Master** M Griffiths, S Peake
Improved by the collapse of Fandango.

1979 May     **Oblatron** G Gibson, R Hewitt, D Beetlestone
In the last guide for the area, Oblatron appeared twice in the first ascent list; that of July 30 1978, this time by G Gibson, M Hewitt. The route sometimes did the same.

| | |
|---|---|
| 1979 May | **Bucket Rider** M Griffiths, S Peake |
| 1979 June 1 | **One Step in the Crowds** A Evans, S Tansey, S Beresford |
| 1979 June 24 | **Cruel Tone** G Gibson, I Barker |
| 1979 June 24 | **Hey!** G Gibson, I Barker |
| 1979 July 1 | **Back to Nature** G Gibson, J Walker |
| 1979 July 3 | **Magic Mushroom** S Peake, P Walsh |
| | *Top-roped three times before it was led.* |
| 1979 July 5 | **Broken Edge** S Peake (solo) |
| | *'The actual top pitch is quite interesting with only one commiting little move, but in an excellent position'. M Lewis.* |
| 1979 July 21 | **Hurricane** M Crook, D Farrant |
| 1979 July 30 | **New Management** S Peake, G Griffiths |
| | *Eric Jones starts his long reign at the Bwlch y Moch cafe. Still one of the very few camp sites where a mug of tea in bed is standard.* |
| 1979 July | **Laser Crack** M Griffiths, K Robertson, S Peake |
| 1979 Aug | **The Quakermen** D Cuthbertson, M Griffiths, K Johnson |
| | *Variation on pitch 2; Harvey Proctor's Spanking Slap by D Lampard in 1986.* |
| 1979 Oct | **Pulsar** F Crook, K Crook |
| 1979 | **The Jackal** M Crook, M Griffiths |
| | *'Sadly, this route will never become popular as the approach up mud and grass is probably 5b as well'. P Williams, Crags 24.* |
| 1979 | **Fear** S Cathcart, G Griffiths |
| 1979 | **Silly Billy** P Williams, M Griffiths, D Pyecroft |
| | *Williams was called all sorts of names after this offering, not all polite; it remains, however, quite a good eliminate.* |
| 1979 | **Savage Man** S Cathcart, G Griffiths |
| | *'Savage Man is situated on a small buttress high in the undergrowth right of Boo-Boo. If you liked watching the Botanic Man series with David Bellamy then this is the route for you'. Paul Williams, Crags 24.* |
| 1979 | **Solitaire** M Duff, T Dailey |
| 1979 | **Footless Frenzy** S Cathcart, G Griffiths |
| 1979 | **Crazy Diamond** S Cathcart, G Griffiths |
| 1979 | **Turnterror** S Cathcart, G Griffiths |
| | *Tumbledown Variation was climbed by C Greatwich, A Woodward on June 5 1988.* |
| 1979 | **Lysergic Touch** S Cathcart, W Lockley |

1979      **Perilous Journey** S Cathcart, G Griffiths
*Claimed later as The Throwback by N Carson, D Carson.*

1979      **Tea Time Arête** M Griffiths, M Crook

1980 Feb      **The Weaver** P Williams, C Shorter (AL)
*A modern classic, claimed the first ascensionists, most of it had been climbed before by J Brown. One climber was heard to say shortly after an ascent. "Yeah, it's a great route, shame its Paul's, I keep telling him it's eliminate shit and he should be ashamed of himself."*

1980 Mar 2      **The Atomic Finger Flake** J Redhead, P Williams (AL), C Shorter, K Robertson
*Ascended the day previously by Paul Williams with three points of aid. 'A wild foot-dangling move gains the flake itself'. Paul Williams.*

1980 Mar 15      **Sexual Salami** J Redhead, K Robertson, C Shorter
*'He not only surprised the climbing world with the hardness of his new routes but also created a bottom-squirming reluctance to accept his somewhat nauseating nomenclature'. Welsh Rock 1986.*

1980 Mar      **Strawberries** R Fawcett
*A route with an interesting ethical history. On . his succesful ascent spread over two weekends Fawcett pre-placed and clipped runners from his previous days high point. "John (Redhead) would have done it months before if he had used the same tactics." Keith Robertson.*
*A subsequent ascent by J Moffatt was made over two days. Moffatt wanted to rename the route as he said he had made an ascent in 'better style'. This still involved four falls and a yo-yo over two days.*
*The first true free ascent was made by J Woodward in 1982.*
*The first on sight flash ascent S Glowacz, August 1987.*
*'As one well-known Yorkshire climber said "It will be 10 years before that goes." Another Yorkshireman, Ron Fawcett, had different ideas. Later local climbers were horrified to find two bolts had been placed on Strawberries. However, these turned out to*

*have been araldited on to the rock by some
wag. Who says that climbers are too serious
about their sport!'*
Paul Williams, Crags 24.
*There was much discussion at the guidebook
meeting whether the route should be given a
French grade. The E6 grade remains for an on
sight ascent.*

1980 Mar 30 **Bananas** J Redhead, K Robertson
*'Bananas had the distinction of being originally
graded 7a (Britain's first), but a second ascent
by Ron Fawcett and Phil Burke dropped it a
grade. Redhead admitted that it was nearly
impossible to be objective about such a route.
"Just how do you grade a boulder problem in
the sky?" Nonetheless, it is a sensational route,
a gritstone type desperate on the edge of
eternity'.* Paul Williams, Crags 24.
*Redhead took six falls on his ascent.*
*'Make sure the routes aren't harder than 5a, so
I can repeat them'. Eric Jones in the new routes
book of the time.*

1980 Apr **Plastic Nerve** G Gibson, S Keeling
1980 Apr 12 **Ace High** S Reid, A Creaigh
*'Perhaps the best route on Gesail, which isn't
saying much'. First ascent comment.*

1980 Apr **Sultans of Swing** J Redhead, P Williams
*'Mongoose, a controversial route in its original
form as the crux was virtually top-roped from a
high nut in Void, was effectively killed off by
the ascent of this girdle, sorry Pete'.*
Paul Williams.
*P Williams with J de Monjoye had done pitch
1 two days earlier.*

1980 June 6 **Rock on Tommy** S Kennedy, C Roberts
1980 June **Sheer Khan** S Kennedy (solo)
1980 July 30 **Clean Edge** P Elliot, J Cousins, G Dady
1980 Aug 22 **Sonic Sinbin** J Moffatt, S Law
1980 Aug 27 **Tweek** J Moffatt, S Kennedy
1980 Sep 5 **Emily Street** E Masson, P Gomersall,
P Livesey
*'Probably the first time that a woman has led a
first ascent of a route of this standard on British
rock'. Comment in the 1983 Tremadog guide.*

1980 Oct 2 **The Dune Child** M Griffiths, J Moffatt (AL)
*A very technical offering, unrepeated for some*

*time after.*

1980 Nov 30  **Cheap Trick** K Telfer, P Dicken
*The top part was climbed before by Mike Lewis
but never recorded.*

1980 Dec 7  **Cardiac Arête** J de Montjoye, V Thomas

1980  **Penicillin** J Redhead, R Fawcett
*Claimed earlier the same month by Gary
Gibson as Big Bug. When Fawcett and
Redhead tried to repeat the line they got
nowhere. Redhead eventually solved the
problem by going left from the line that was
written up. 'Gary's got a problem!' was a
comment in the new routes book at the time.*

1981 Jan 25  **Gwaed** M Roberts, C Jones

1981 Jan 30  **Pengo's Eliminate** S Haston, M Griffiths,
M Crook

1981 Mar 15  **Lonely Edge** G Gibson, D Beetlestone

1981 Mar 29  **Hitler's Buttock** J Redhead, J de Montjoye,
J Perrin, P Williams

1981 Apr 18  **T.I.S.** M Totterdell, G Bedford

1981 Apr 18  **Life in a Day** G Gibson, D Beetlestone

1981 Apr 19  **Bigger Bug** G Gibson, D Beetlestone

1981 Apr 19  **Silver Crow** M Crook, M Mitchell

1981 Apr  **Ringwraith** M Griffiths, M Crook (AL)

1981 Apr  **Jellystone Park** N Plant, P Hellon
*Almost certainly climbed before.*

1981 Apr  **Quimbo** P Elliot, K Robertson, N Green

1981 May 30  **Jackdaw on the Edge of Time** M Crook,
D Farrant

1981 June 18  **Muscles** C Jones, S Smith
*Straightened out a previous route Apples and
Pears by the same team.*

1981 July  **Psyche 'n' Burn** J Moffatt
*An outstanding achievement. "No-one else but
me can hang on those holds." Jerry Moffatt.
The bitching started almost immediately with
accusations in the new routes book of a point
of aid being used and holds having been
enlarged.*

1981 July  **Re-entry** R Chamberlain, G Thomas

1981  **Space Panic** A Brown, M Rievelex
*The first route in the right-hand bay of Moel y
Gest and easily the best route on the whole
crag.*

1982 Feb 14  **Pert** M Lewis, J G Trumper
*The second revisits a crag where he climbed a*

*new route 21 years previously.*

| | |
|---|---|
| 1982 Mar 13 | **Jill the Thrill** S Reid, S Wilkingson |
| 1982 Mar 13 | **Holly Tree Variation** S Reid, S Wilkingson |
| 1982 Mar 13 | **Brass** S Reid, S Wilkingson |
| 1982 Apr | **Surreal** D Lee, D Lee |
| 1982 May 12 | **The Unreal Finish** A Pollitt, M Wilson. |
| 1982 May 29 | **Sheer Resist** A Pollitt, J Redhead |

*There exists one 'last great problem' just to the left.*

1982 Nov 13 **Blade Runner** A Pollitt, C Parker, H Ford
*The use of a blade peg for protection caused angry exchanges in the new routes book of the time. It's hard to see what all the fuss was about.*

1982

*In 1982 the Nature Conservancy Council, the owners of Pant Ifan, put up perimeter fencing and no entry signs around the site. This was an attempt to cover the council's legal responsibility by protecting innocent parties from straying into a potentially dangerous area. A warden was intially employed to deter climbers, but strangely this didn't work.*
*'The climber must go where his feet take him'.*
*Steve Ashton, Climber and Rambler, July 1982.*

| | |
|---|---|
| 1983 Apr 4 | **Dagrau** M Roberts, D Roberts |
| 1983 Apr 22 | **Pwyll** M Lewis, G Davies, E Davies |
| 1983 Apr 22 | **Pryderi** M Lewis, J G Trumper |
| 1983 Apr 24 | **Non Stop** G Gibson, N Harvey |

*Reclaimed on 16 Oct 1988 as The Shining by C Greatwich, A Woodward with a point of aid, followed by a free ascent of an already free route on 4 January 1990 by N Carson, P G Williams and claimed as Choddy.*

1983 Apr **The Pink Fridge** N Dixon, I Dunn, A Popp
*Many thought that the line claimed was New Management.*

1983 Apr **Emotional Crisis** A Andrew, A Hardcastle
*Much debate in Eric's route book took place concerning the tactics used on the ascent. Accusations of pre-placed slings in a tree was one such comment.*

| | |
|---|---|
| 1983 May 6 | **Marino** M Lewis, H G Davies, B Grimston |
| 1983 July 25 | **Geronimo** M Lewis, J Trumper B Grimston |

*The route name had been painted on to the*

rock, a practice that should be roundly condemned. It has now been removed. The pity is in the fact that scratched graffiti may not so easily...

1983
A mysterious episode of peg removal occured on the Tremadog crags during 1983. Was it someone taking a pure ethical stance or, more likely, using them for other routes. Only one person will ever know.

1984 Feb 26   **Borneo** J Trumper, E Davies, M Lewis
A route for the budding arboriculturist.

1984 Apr 6   **Rio** B Grimston, E Davies
1984 Apr   **The Rampart** M Brothers, M Evans
1984 May 28   **Surreal McCoy** J Moran, R Ashton
1984 June 9   **Dotheboys** M Lewis, J Ells
A long forgotten route on the same buttress had an identical name. This could cause confusion if we get a new V Diff called Strawberries.

1984 July 18   **The Steal** A Bailey, R Haszko
1984 Aug 3   **Stormy Weather** A Bailey R Haszko
1984 Sep 6   **Limited Edition** P Gommersall, E Masson
1984 Sep 7   **Rhych dy Din** M Roberts, C Edwards
1984 Sep 8   **The Sandbagger** P Gommersall, E Masson
'One of the best lines at Tremadog'. A tongue in cheek comment by one of the first ascensionists.

1984 Sep   **The Sword** B Grimston, E Davies
1984 Sep   **Iron in the Soul** M Crook
1984 Oct   **Dream Topping** M Atkinson
Sieged over several days. 'I thought Dream Topping was instant, I didn't know it took eight days to prepare'. Comment in the new routes book.

1984 Oct 19   **Rapunzel** M Lewis, B Grimston, E Davies
1984 Dec 21   **Cerberus** M Lewis, E Davies
1985 Jan 11   **Tam Lin** M Lewis, E Davies
1985 Jan 12   **Saffron Sunset** B Drury, D Jones
Claimed later as Harvey Proctor's Spanking Groove by D Lampard, N Bonnet, A Phizacklea. A route name that just couldn't be binned so it appears later in another guise.

1985 May 6   **Cnychwyr** I A Jones, F Hall, J Pitts
1985 June 28   **Omerta Crack** M Lewis, E Davies
'The crack is more imtimidating than difficult, if

*it were on gritstone it would most definitely be only E2 5c'. Mike Lewis.*

| | |
|---|---|
| 1985 | **Placebo** F Hall, I A Jones |

*The ascent was made whilst trying to follow a previous description for Penicillin.*

| | |
|---|---|
| 1986 June 2 | **Quite Easy for Bigheads** C Smith, I Jones |

*No grade was given when the route was written up 'to save controversy'. Crux climbed by R Fawcett in 1982: "Dead steady!"*

| | |
|---|---|
| 1986 June 14 | **Omo** B Grimston, E Davies, K Neal |
| 1986 Aug 16 | **Dead Rooks Don't Speak** M E Crook, A N Newton |
| 1987 May 5 | **Llanberries** J Dawes |

*A very impressive series of moves. 'Make a dynamic move for a thumb sprag, go up to a faint pod and then out to a sloper. Mantel this (crux) and continue... Too hard for Reginald Perrin'. Pete's Eats new routes book.*

| | |
|---|---|
| 1987 Oct 2 | **The Jewel in the Crown** C Greatwich, G Russell |
| 1987 Dec 25 | **Jumble Tumble** C Greatwich, C Lloyd, C Benette |
| 1987 | **The Agony and the Ecstasy** J Redhead, M Crook |
| 1988 Feb 27 | **Wild Horses** C Greatwich, G Russell |
| 1988 Mar 26 | **Smarter than the Average Bear** T D Hughes, D J Jacques |

*This has certainly been climbed before, but by whom?*

| | |
|---|---|
| 1988 Apr 3 | **Food for Thought** A Woodward, C Greatwich |
| 1988 Jun 5 | **Golfball** C Greatwich, C Lloyd, A Woodward |

*'I was unable to find any E3 5c climbing on this slab. A figment of someone's imagination'. Mike Lewis.*

| | |
|---|---|
| 1988 Oct 1 | **Drug Test** C Greatwich, C Benette |

*Part of the groove on pitch 2 is alos climbed by an earlier route Next of Kin.*

| | |
|---|---|
| 1990 Apr 11 | **Pleasure Cruise** C Greatwich |

*Hopelessly overgraded at E2 5c. "I thought I was climbing well until I got on The Wasp." A local climber at the start of the season.*

| | |
|---|---|
| 1990 Aug 25 | **Shadow Play** P A Targett, A Woodward |

*'Once in the jungle your only hope is to bump into Professor Challenger or Indiana Jones.' On the Edge 1991.*

| 1990 Aug 25 | **Helix** D Dutton, M Wells |
| 1990 Sep 1 | **Souvenir** P A Targett, A Woodward |
| 1990 Sep 1 | **September Blue** I Lloyd Jones, C Greatwich |
| 1990 Sep 8 | **Sourveld** C Greatwich P A Targett, D Dutton |
| 1990 Sep 23 | **California Dreaming** A Woodward, C Greatwich |
| 1990 Nov 3 | **Knight on the Tiles** D Dutton, C Greatwich, C Stephenson |

1990 Nov    **Swift Undercut** G Smith

'Imaginative, historic, 8a+, outrageous, powerful and wild. These are just some of the adjectives being used to describe George Smith's sideways ascent of the underside of the Ochre Slab. When the weather deteriorated and the rest of Wales was dripping wet, the rain shadow of Tremadog was applauding the powerful body swings and heel hooks of the tanned and rippling lean frame of Big Blonde George.' Mick Ryan, On the Edge 21. Tremadog isn't in the rain shadow and George is very embarrassed.

| 1990 | **Trick or Treat** F Hall, I A Jones |
| 1991 May 5 | **No Holds Barred** S Mayers |

A stupendous route that had been 'inspected' before by some misguided individual.

1991 May 5    **Simper Dexter Nil Sinister** I A Jones, F Hall

A spoof motto for the Thatcher dynasty, 'Always right, nothing left'. A route did climb the initial section of this area of rock, only to dodge the main difficulties. It continued on up to take the area of rock left of Venom's top pitch, which was in fact another route called Carlo.

1991 May 5    **Bashi Bazouk** F Hall, I A Jones

A rather wandering route started up the groove but then broke out to take in much of the Nifl Heim area of rock. A route called Falconette may have ascended the groove and rib above in full, unfortunately details are not available.

| 1991 May 5 | **Pizzle Puzzle** F Hall, I A Jones |
| 1991 | **Eleventh Hour** C Parkin, K Robertson (both led) |
| 1993 Feb 14 | **Carbonara** C Greatwich, C Stephenson |

A supplement is published to this area of the crag by Greatwich and his friends. It annoyed a few people at the time as routes that were recorded previously by Mike Lewis and Steve Reid had not been included. They had in fact been claimed *again by Greatwich and others. Despite the criticism the pamphlet sold well and many jaded local climbers visited the area to sample some long-forgotten routes and some very good new additions.*

1993 Mar 13     **Y Dewin Dwl** M Lewis, E Davies
*Mike returns to new routeing.*

1993 May 9     **Rwdlan** M Lewis, E Davies

1993 May 14     **Slip Shod** M Lewis, E Davies

1993 May 22     **Rala Rwdins** M Lewis, E Davies

1993 May 22     **Mursen** M Lewis, E Davies

1994 June 30     **The Root** M Lewis, J Yates

1994 Oct     **Down to Earth** N Berry, I Wright

1994 Nov 22     **Blobby Goes Ballistic** T Keep, B Timms

1994 June 19     **Trivial Pursuits** M Lewis, J Yates

1995 Apr 9     **Basin Street** M Lewis, J Ells
*A long forgotten aid route now free. Probably climbed by members of the Cave and Crag Club in the 1950s. A picture of the route once featured in a tourist guide to Porthmadog.*

1996 Apr     **Llafur** I A Jones P Stott

1996 Apr     **Rip Torn** I A Jones P Stott

1997 Jan 20     **Jude the Obscure** M Lewis, J Yates

1997 Mar 30     **Far From the Madding Crowd** M Lewis, J Yates

1997 Mar 30     **Jess** M Lewis, J Yates

1997 June 6     **Mab y Mynydd** M Lewis, J Yates

1997 July 14     **Mab y Bwthyn** M Lewis, J Yates
*The name means 'son of the cottage', the buttress was originally Cottage Buttress now Fear Buttress.*

1997 Aug 28     **Tree Radical** I A Jones, G Fenton

1997 Aug 31     **Clown of Thorns** I A Jones, G Fenton
*Utilizes the top section of Fandango — the original route in this area — traversed left to come out to the arête about 40 feet up pitch 2.*

1998 Jan 24     **Gwrywgydiwr** I A Jones, R Wightman, D Ferguson

1998 Jan 25     **Strempan** M Lewis, J Yates

1998 Mar 14     **Rhywbeth Bach** M Lewis, J Yates

1998 May     **The Man Who Fell to Earth** M Turner, L Thomas
*Direct Finish S Mayers, T Keep in October 1999.*

1999 May 31     **Wow Factor** M Lewis, K Neal

1998 Aug 4     **Gorwedd Nol a Meddwl, Gelli'r Haul,**

|            | **Llys y Mynydd**, **Perthi Gwyn**, **Cleddyf**, **Cnwc** I A Jones (solo) |
|------------|---------------------------------------------------------------------------|
| 1999 Jan 10 | **Carlwm Arête** M Lewis, J Yates |
| 1999 Aug 28 | **Yellow Fever** C Jordan (roped solo) |
| 1999 Aug 28 | **Sea Fever** C Jordan (roped solo) |
| 1999 | **Goop** M Crook |

# Aberglaslyn, Nantmor and the Gwynant Valley

| 1895 | Aberglaslyn Gorge |
|------|-------------------|
|      | *'There is fairly good practice climbing on both sides of the gorge, but not very steep.'* |
|      | Climbing in the British Isles *W P Haskett Smith*. |
| 1900s | **The Gwynant Crack** The Pioneers |
|      | *'The wall is split by a crack which invites the super-gymnast. The last eight feet are devoid of holds and overhang. The only ascent on record was made by an expert with the aid of five other experts stationed on the top of the rock'.* |
|      | Clogwyn y Fulfran — *'The rocks plunge sheer into the waters of the lake, and a climb is rumoured to have been done on the crag which was begun from a boat. Useful, no doubt, for the climber-fisherman when he tires of the inferior sport.'* A Climber's Guide to Snowdon *H R C Carr* |
| 1908 | **Lockwood's Chimney** A Lockwood |
|      | Known for a long time as The Great Chimney. The following route description comes from Carr's guide published in 1926. *'The party now gathers and examines what it has "come to see". A huge flake has split a few inches from the main mass of the cliff, and has thoughtfully left room in the resulting fissure for the passage of man. Upon passing the entrance, a glimmer of light will be observed through an exiguous hole high up in the interior of the Chimney. A slim and dainty leader will find difficulty with the pitch (20 feet), but less adaptable persons will not succeed without "the windy suspiration of forced breath" in fitting their ampler proportions to the aperture. Having overcome the chockstone, we find ourselves at the bottom of a crypt-like crevasse, lit by a narrow lancet window 40 feet overhead. Those* |

*ambitious of a superior virtue may back-and-knee
with great labour directly upwards, but it is more
usual to sidle along the floor of the passage
which twists, rises and ends 90 feet from the
chockstone. Leaving his companions in the
cellarage, the leader pulls out of the exit to find
himself on a pleasant ledge beside a large belay.
Nothing remains except 30 feet of easy climbing
to the grass ledges at the top of the crag. It may
be of some use to mention that the rope is useless
inside the chimney, and a man is quite likely to
become hopelessly jammed if those above him try
to haul him up. At certain seasons, too, it is as
well to remember that the climb and the descent
from it, are considerably harder and more painful
when done in the dark.'*
Variations by P L Roberts, E O Ransome, F G
Breteul on 18 February 1932.

| | |
|---|---|
| 1934 | **Forest Wall** T C G Tilby, W R Reade |

*Known for a long time as Kirkus's Climb, The
Direct Finish, known as Cave Finish was added
by Menlove Edwards in 1952.*

1935         *'About 1935 P L Roberts made a number of
climbs on Clogwyn y Wenallt and Craig y Llyn.
Details have not yet been obtained of these.'*
CC Journal 1956.

1947 Dec 25   **Christmas Climb** P O Work, E S Trickett
1948 May      **Chimney and Face Climb** P O Work
1948 May      **Llyndy Arête, Llyndy Groove** P O Work
*Two long-forgotten routes; the crag has now
yielded some more modern lines, the pay-off
for trawling through back copies of the CC
Journal.*

1950 Jan 8    **Ordinary Route** D E Pullin, P O Work,
              J Derry
1950 Jan 15   **Direct Route** P O Work, G W Staunton
*'Use the groove to gain a standing position on
the five-inch ledge above, use the crack
beyond for 2 feet of upward progress, then
cross back up the left wall.'* CC Journal 1950.

1950 May 26   **Gash Wall** A J J Moulam, P R J Harding,
              G Dyke
*The rock stars come to Nantmor and find a
route that should not be underestimated, even
today.*

1951 April 17 **Great Chimney Wall** C R Upton

1951 Sep 3     **Canyon Rib** P O Work, T Blackburn (AL)
*An excellent find amongst some fairly undistinguished climbs. Described as being the nearest thing to the Verdon in Wales in the 1989 guide.*

1951 Sep 24    **Tunnel Rib** P O Work, I A Dear
*'Started from the Beddgelert end of the railway tunnel. Graded as "Very Difficult and rather dangerous at present".' CC Journal 1952*

1952 May 20   **Pineways** P O Work, B E Nicholson
*A long-lost route upstream of Canyon Rib. 'Start at a giant boulder by the fisherman's path 200 yards upstream from the Aberglaslyn Bridge'.*

1952 Aug 28   **Corner of Roots** J M Edwards, H C Bryson
*The corner left of Lockwood's Chimney. 'Brush past a fallen tree to a grassy ledge with a small forest'. Earlier, during the war, Edwards had rented a cottage called Hafod Owen on the hill behind Llyn Dinas and overlooking Craig y Llyn. Any climbing exploits from this period are sadly not recorded. 'Hafod Owen is cut off by over half a mile of bog and rough ground from the nearest road. From the small blue-framed windows cut in its white-distempered stone walls you look out on to the empty hillside on one hand, and across to Snowdon and Yr Aran, beyond the woods and waters of Gwynant, on the other. There is no water except from the stream nearby, and any means of lighting or heating has to be carried up from Beddgelert on ones's back. A more ideal place to isolate himself from a world gone mad could not be designed.' Samson G Sutton & W Noyce, 1960.*

1952 Aug 28   **The Tenth Rib** J M Edwards, H C Bryson
*Menlove had met his second, Courtney Bryson, at Harrison's Rocks, whilst he was convalescing with his family in Kent after a suicide attempt.*
Direct Start by M J Harris, E W Dance, J Neill on 26 January 1957.

1952 Aug 31   **Side Entry** J M Edwards, H C Bryson, A Shutt

1953 April 12   **Oxo** J R Lees, G D Roberts, W A Trench
*'Those spurning the use of various, not very substantial bushes will use a piton for a belay'. A fine new crag begins to undergo development, it is described in Carr's 1926 guide as 'a small crag a little north and above the lake, but the*

*rock is reported to be rotten and vegetation very rank'.*

| | |
|---|---|
| 1953 May | **Waney Edge** G D Roberts, W A Trench |
| | *A long forgotten Diff on the right-hand side of Clogwyn y Wenallt.* |
| 1953 June 12 | **Honeysuckle Wall** D H Haworth, J Tester |
| 1953 Nov | **Carol Crack** G D Roberts, J Lines |

1953 Dec 28    *Cnicht — a route was made up the left side of the buttress. 'Not a very good climb, rather artificial and herbaceous. The only major point in favour is that it is the most interesting way we know up Cnicht'. Glanfor Williams's personal log.*

| | |
|---|---|
| 1954 Mar 12 | **Shake** G D Roberts, W A Trench |
| | *Originally graded 'Medium Very Severe'.* |
| 1954 May 23 | **Treasurer's Wall** P Hampson, W V Lamb, E Siddall |
| | *Another variation start to Carol Crack. Not included in the description.* |
| 1954 June 11 | **Gam Bay** A J J Moulam, Mrs E Upton |
| | *A route on the mass of rock north of the Tunnel Rib buttress in the Aberglaslyn Pass.* |
| 1954 Aug 1 | **Bovril** D McKelvey, L Rogerson, Miss M Dutton |
| 1954 | **Vaughan's Crack** P Vaughan |
| | *A hard variation start to Carol Crack. Not included in the description.* |
| 1955 Apr 3 | *Glanfor Williams describes several routes in the Yr Arddu area, especially on 'Lliwedd Bach' climbed with members of Clwb Dringo. May well have been climbed before.* |
| 1955 June 1 | **Verti-Veg** D McKelvey, S Wiseman, B Wright, Miss B Warbrick |
| | *An overgrown excursion right of the gully on Craig y Llyn.* |
| 1955 June 1 | **Umbala** A Cowburn, L Rogerson |
| | *'Round on the right of Craig y Llyn, a square buttress with a block overhang, in the right-hand corner. Climb to an ash and a holly, go up and traverse across the perched block, exciting' CC Journal 1956.* |
| 1955 Aug 27 | **Aquila** (aid) H I Banner, J Neill |
| | *'This climb only escapes an A grading by virtue of the use of inserted pebbles and slings where pitons and etriers would be more comfortable'.* |

*In the old Snowdon South guide the description of the last pitch read; 'climb the wall, beg for aid'. A printing error perhaps, but still very appropriate. The variation start, The Beakin was climbed by C T Jones and A J J Moulam at Easter 1969.*

1955 Sep 25    **Callunacy** D Thomas, J Neill, M J Harris
*The ribs right of an open gully, 80 yards left of Honeysuckle Wall. A clever play on the meaning of calluna — heather.*

1956 Mar 3    **Crystal Rib** G W S Pigott, J Neill
*'The route takes the steep buttress-ridge immediately left of the hanging gully, and follows a sharp little quartz ridge with jolly pinnacles, giving altogether about 200 feet of climbing on good rock with pitches reminiscent of Tryfan East Face'. First ascent description.*

1956 Jan 8    **Gallop Step** J I Disley, Miss D Morin
*Originally graded Severe this fine route really opened people's eyes to the potential of Clogwyn y Bustach.*

1956 Mar 3    **Mistrust** G W S Pigott, J Neill

1956 April 2    **Contempt** D H Briggs, J Neill
*'Not more worthy than the name suggests.' First ascent description.*

1956 April 2    **Rancour** D H Briggs, J Neill

1956 May 28    **Anniversary Waltz** (A2) T D Bourdillon, M H Westmacott
*The second pitch was climbed using several pegs. The same team with M P Ward had first tried the route on 29 May 1954, hence the name.*
*'A previous ascent had been made by the same party plus F Fitzgerald on 8 January 1956, using pitch one of Gallop Step and the easy variant to pitch three.' CC Journal 1957.*
*F.F.A. unknown.*

1956 Sep 9    **Goebbels** J Walmsley, J Neill
*'The nearest climb to the Pinnacle Club Hut'. CC Journal 1957.*

1957 May 19    **Bovine** (1 pt aid) C E Davies, B D Wright, D McKelvey

1958 May    **The Maelstrom** C T Jones, C E Davies, C Pryke
*The Maelstrom proved to be an alarming*

*experience on pumice-like rock. At the end of the traverse was a tree with long roots which came away with a plate of earth. The leader's alarming arboreal descent consequently lessened his faith in the stability of all Nant Gwynant trees.'* Welsh Rock.
*'Reminiscent of Kaisergebirge Wall'.* First ascent description.

1959 Feb 7 | **Ferdinand** J Brown, C T Jones
*'Joe espied a crack in a wall on the left-hand side of the crag, a fierce 80-foot crack in the Brown tradition with only Trevor Jones able to follow. The crux caused Jones such exhaustion that when he pulled over the top he was unable to speak for at least five minutes, a phenomenon not known either before or since. The route was called Ferdinand.'* Welsh Rock.
*'At present this is the hardest route in the valley.'* Snowdon South, 1960.

1959 May | **Torero** (1 pt) J Brown, D D Whillans
*'Next to Ferdinand it is the most formidable undertaking in the valley.'* Snowdon South, 1960. It certainly took a bullfighter's boldness to climb this with the gear of the time.

1960 Feb 26 | **Primus** (2 pts) J Brown, C E Davies
The first attack on a very fierce crag that the Cromlech Club had 'given' to Brown for joining after the break-up of the Rock and Ice. *'At last climbers were breaking free from the strangulation of the Ogwen Valley and Llanberis Pass. Here in the southern part of the mountains they found sunshine, and more important, peace and quiet'.* Wilfred Noyce, Snowdon South, 1960.

1960 Easter | **Hardd** (1 pt) J Brown, G D Roberts, N Drasdo
*"We had been told that Hardd contained the hardest move on British rock and although the author of this statement was hardly in a position to speak with authority, we knew he was a good climber. Rumour had it that Whillans had jumped onto a hold somewhere on the cliff when normal tactics had proved inadequate. Others had raved over the trundling from the cliff's overhanging crest on to the road below. The commonest legend of all*

> was of those who had gone to climb and
> stayed to watch." Dave Cook, 1966.
> Direct Finish *(3 pts)* by M Boysen and party
> on 17 September 1961.

1960 Mar 27    **The Girdle Traverse** (of Carreg Hylldrem)
J Brown, G D Verity
*The Maybelline Finish (2 pts) C Boulton, D
Cook (AL) June 8 1965.*

1961 Sep 17    **Forte Strapiombo** F Corner, B Thompson
1961 Oct 15    **Kellogg Crack** B Thompson, F Corner
1962    **Peachpla** C A G Jones and party

1963    *Showell Styles publishes a guide to rock-climbs
on Yr Arrdu. He describes the area as 'offering
nothing to the tiger, much to the rabbit, and
most to the superannuated mountaineer weary
of the litter of humanity that has nowadays
scattered across the mountains from Aber to
Beddgelert'. These comments remain relevant
today although a few harder routes have been
added, the route names in this guide are
almost entirely his and Styles is the first to
admit that many people may have climbed
there as far back as the 1920s. First ascents
can, therefore, not be reliably recorded. 'The
mountain (Yr Arddu) may be commended to the
wanderer who likes to dally with an occasional
exercise in gymnastics'. A Climber's Guide to
Snowdon H R C Carr 1926.*

1963 June 15    **Tunnel Rib Direct** G Williams and party
*This was an ascent of a route in the
Aberglaslyn Gorge above the tunnel at VS
standard.*

1964 April    **Toreador** R Edwards and party
1965    **Gwynant Needle** S Dwyer, J Henson
*A long-forgotten feature on a crag that has
been rediscovered by various parties. An old
peg adorned the summit at one time, now long
since gone.*

1965    **Excalibur** S Dwyer, J Henson
*Named and claimed by J Appleby in 1996.
The route had been used by various instructors
at Plas Gwynant from the early 70s.*

1966 April 14    **Terra Nova** (1 pt) C T Jones, A J J Moulam
1966 May 13    **Scuffer** (1 pt) G Rogan, B Ingle (AL)

*The right-hand side of the square-cut gully to the right of Aquila.*

1966 May 15    **Femaelstrom** S Wroe, T Howard
*'The wall left of The Maelstrom, the rock is of a similar friable material'.* Snowdon South *1970.*

1966 June    **The Spook** (1 pt) S Tattersall, R Dixon (AL)
*F.F.A. M Griffiths 1981?*

1966 Aug 21    **The Burner** R Evans, I R Esplin

1966 Sep 10    **Poker** L E Holliwell, L R Holliwell

1967 Mar 24    **The Prow** (5 pts) R Evans, E Jones
*Three pegs were used for aid in the chimney. Freed in 1983 and renamed Raging Bull.*

1968 April    **Gwastadanas** C E Davies, G Holmes
*The Direct Finish was added by P Littlejohn and J Cox on 27 April 1998.*

1969 May    **Split Finger** C T Jones, R Conway

1969 May    **Clonus** C T Jones, R F Jones, A J J Moulam

1969 June    **Thirty-Nine Steps** C T Jones, S Williams

1970 Sep 27    **Paranoia** C Phillips, T Taylor

1971 April 14    **Foxtrot** (2 pts) Z Leppert, J Blears
*Unaccountably left out of previous guides to the area.*

1971 April 25    **Samurai Groove** (2 pts) B Wyvill, D Mossman
*F.F.A. P Thomas in 1979. M Griffiths and Thomas both turned up at the same time to free the route. A coin was tossed and Thomas had first go to free the route, which he did. Soloed by M Griffiths.*

1971 Aug 6    **The Deceiver** (2 pts) G Rigby, K Bentham
*The route described incorporates a direct finish added by N Gough, M Creasey in May 1975.*

1972    **Taylor-Made** J Taylor and party

1972    **The Ox Bow Incident** (2 pts) D Cook, A Evans (AL)
*F.F.A. Unknown.*

1973 Mar 25    **Troubador** J Perrin, D Britt (AL)

1973    **Peak Frean** K Martin, J Whittle

1973    **Tarzan** R Evans

1974 June    **King Kong** R Evans, H Pasquill
*A fall on the first pitch invariably results in the flake 'expanding' and locking in cams and nuts.*

1977 April    **The Moon** S Cathcart, P Waters
*'The crag looks as if it has been assembled in a hurry and keeps turning at right angles to*

*itself in a distinctly perturbing manner'.* Welsh Rock.

| | | |
|---|---|---|
| 1977 June | **The Matador** M Crook, S McCartney | |
| 1977 June | **The Death Wisher** M Crook, S McCartney | |

*"The flake is about the thickness of Ryvita."* Fred Hall.

| | |
|---|---|
| 1977 | **Sunset Traverse** B Wyvill, R Evans |
| 1978 April | **Poacher** (1 pt) P Burke, G Kent |

*F.F.A. R Fawcett in 1980.*

| | |
|---|---|
| 1978 June | **Sybilla the Pun** P Gomersall, P Livesey |
| 1978 June | **Chance Encounter** P Livesey, P Gomersall, E Masson |
| 1978 Aug 25 | **Wailing Wall** P Livesey, C Crawshaw |

*'It was left to Livesey to produce one of the longest pitches in Wales. It was to be a thin, bold pitch up the main unclimbed part of the crag. It was the sort of place to which Livesey naturally gravitated'.* Welsh Rock.
*"This will sort out the men from the boys."*

| | |
|---|---|
| 1979 Aug 30 | **Biggles** M Griffiths, R Camberlain |
| 1979 Aug 31 | **Caligula** M Griffiths, R Camberlain |
| 1979 Aug 31 | **Picador** M Griffiths, R Camberlain |
| 1979 Sept 29 | **Perdido Street** W Wayman, D Walsh |
| 1979 Sept | **The Gamekeeper** B Chamberlain, M Griffiths |
| c.1979 | **Erotickos** Unknown |
| 1980 June | **The Fugitive** M Crook, M Griffiths |
| 1981 Jan | **The Wildebeest** S Haston, G Tinning |
| 1981 Mar | **The Weirpig** S Haston (solo) |
| 1981 April 17 | **Marshall Hearts** S Cathcart, M Cameron |
| 1981 May | **Danger Days** S Cathcart, P Stott |
| 1981 Aug 20 | **Sleeping Beauty** C Shorter, M Creasey |
| 1982 Nov 20 | **Death Can Be Fatal** A Pollit, P Bailey |

*Climbed in mistake for* The Moon. *Aptly named and seriously bizzare.*

| | |
|---|---|
| 1983 April | **First Blood** M Crook, M Griffiths |
| 1983 May 25 | **Raging Bull** M Griffiths, R Griffiths |

*"The hardest off width in Britain?"* First ascensionist's comment. This was in fact a fine free ascent of an earlier aid route called The Prow.

| | |
|---|---|
| 1983 June 2 | **Compromising Positions** C Gore, S Haston |

*'If the end of the block came off it may squash a badly positioned belayer, so beware'.* Chris Gore.

| | |
|---|---|
| 1983 June 5 | **Prince of Darkness** M Crook, A Newton |

*"Super Glue is a good idea for this route"*
Martin Crook.
*The Enlightenment variation was added by*
*P Littlejohn and A Gold on 1 May 1998.*

1983 July  **Bychan** J Brown, D Jones
*Joe returns to Gwynant Valley new routeing*
*after a break of 24 years.*

1983 July  **Ryan's Son** M Griffiths, E Jones

1983 Nov 22  **Beyond the Cosmos** M Crook, D 'Smiler'
Cuthbertson

1983  **Tower Groove, Pink Wall** P Watkin (solo)

1984 April 28  **Psychedelic Cult** M Crook, M Brothers

1984 April 31  **The Wolf** A Newton (unseconded)

1984 May  **Raving Lunatic** P Littlejohn, M Campell

1984 May 2  **Fishbox** J Redhead, D Towse
*'Strenuous but good pro'. First ascent*
*description.*

1985  **The Killing Fields** J Silvester

1986 June  **Flatulence** S Haston, R Kay, C Dale
*Described as 'overprotected but cerebral'.*

1986 June  **The Tawg: In Homage to a Hound**
J Silvester (solo)
*Named after John's dog who had died shortly*
*before the ascent.*

1986 Aug 8  **Honorary Grit** J Dawes
*Climbed in June but not led, it took another two*
*months to get the redpoint.*
*'Provides the best move in Wales'. First ascent*
*comment.*

1986 Aug 17  **Left Groove** and **Right Groove** A Newton
(solo)

1986 Aug 17  **29 Not Out** A Newton, M Crook

1986 Aug 17  **Cat Woman** M Crook, A Newton
*This may have been climbed before, an old*
*peg was found en route.*

1987 Aug 1  **Gwyddbwyll** R Griffiths, E Jones
*This the Welsh name for chess.*

1987 Sep 8  **Total Bull** G Smith P Hawkins

1987  **Bleed for the Dancer** A Greenwood (solo)

1987  **The Witching Stick** J Silvester, S Howe

1987  **Cunnyson** J Silvester, C Dale

1988 Mar 13  **The Big Six Fun Box** P Pritchard, T Hodgson

1988 April 20  **One Fine Day** P Littlejohn, T Jepson

1988 May 11  **Bay of Pigs** P Littlejohn, J de Montjoye

1988 May 26  **Welsh Water Subversion** P Littlejohn, J de
Montjoye

*Originally called* Rain Shadow.

| | |
|---|---|
| 1988 May 26 | **Going for Gold** P Littlejohn, J de Montjoye |
| 1988 May 29 | **Dion** R Griffiths, G Jones |

*Named after Dick's son.*

| | |
|---|---|
| 1988 June | **Flare Up** J de Montjoye, P Littlejohn |
| 1988 June 1 | **Spooks** P Littlejohn, M Hardwick |
| 1989 Jan | **Hong, Kong** M Crook (solo) |

*Two short routes side by side.*

| | |
|---|---|
| 1989 Jan | **Kennedy's Mile** M Crook, A Bierd |

*Another fine 'Crag X' is developed in a long-forgotten area.*

| | |
|---|---|
| 1989 Feb | **Crocodile Goose** D Kendall, M Crook |
| 1989 Feb | **Zeitgeist** M Crook, D Kendall, J Redhead |

*The name can be translated as 'the spirit of the times'.*

| | |
|---|---|
| 1989 June | **My Dear Holmes** D Holmes, J Tombs |
| 1989 June | **Wild Orchid** M Crook, J Tombs |
| 1989 June | **The Pig Elf** M Crook, J Tombs |
| 1989 June | **Honcho Foot Path** M Crook, J Irvine |
| 1989 | **Get Weaving** M Crook, G Smith |
| 1989 | **The Thing of Shapes to Come** M Crook, J Irvine, N Walton |

*A very hard addition which took several visits to complete. 'Stem the groove and ride the ripples'.*

| | |
|---|---|
| 1990 May | **Caleb** G Hughes, A Bierd |
| 1990 July 2 | **Wagtail** N Carson, D Carson |

*A good new crag with much potential found by a local strong team (of brothers).*

| | |
|---|---|
| 1990 July | **The Hayward Slot** O Hayward |
| 1990 Sep 26 | **Chute Up or Chute Off** N Carson, D Carson |
| 1990 Oct | **The Hanging Tree** P Littlejohn, P Judge |
| 1990 Oct | **Sharky** P Littlejohn, P Judge |
| 1990 Nov 11 | **Skyline** P Littlejohn, P Judge |
| 1990 Nov 11 | **End of an Era** P Littlejohn, P Judge |

*Climbed on the day Margaret Thatcher resigned as Prime Minister.*

| | |
|---|---|
| 1990 | **Left Flank** P Littlejohn, P Judge |
| 1990 | **Early Riser** P Littlejohn (solo) |
| 1990 | **Sunrise** P Littlejohn (solo) |
| 1991 Mar | **No Sheep Till Buxton** M Crook, J Tombs |
| 1991 Mar 31 | **Cracking Up** D Carson, N Carson |

*'Don't crack up on this one'. D Carson*

| | |
|---|---|
| 1991 Mar 31 | **Cookie Munster** N Carson, D Carson |
| 1991 April | **Phuddi Crack** M Anthoine (solo) |

1991 April   **Big Fin Reef Squid** G Smith, M Crook
1991 April   **Off All the Bars in All the World** G Smith
*'Good route George, I couldn't find any bars though'. Steve Mayers.*

1991 May 1   **Smashing, Fantastic, Lovely** G Odds, B Pritchard
*The central crackline right of Wagtail on Craig Nant y Fedw, cleaned a few days before by P Lovelock but it rained before he could climb the line. 'I think you two owe me a pint for this one'.*

1991 June   **Sad Cow** B Pritchard
*Allegations of chipped holds were made, but not against the first ascensionist. The crag was known locally as Craig y Frank Carson, after the brothers who discovered it. 'Frank says... it's the way you chip 'em'. Comment in new routes book.*

1991 Aug 30   **Stub** A Bierd, P Lovelock
1991 Oct   **The Chimp in Me** G Smith
1992 April   **Fin Bar** G Smith (unseconded)
1992 Aug   **Rattle and Roll** P Baxter, P Bradbury
*'Steve — please don't retrobolt this mega classic'. a reference to the retrobolting of Castle Inn Quarry, Baxter had removed the bolts in line with the BMC guidelines of the time.*

1993 Feb   **Steep for 5 minutes** G Smith, M Topkins
1993 April   **Hugh Walton's Legendary Flying Arête** M Crook, J Tombs
*'Named because Hugh had mentioned he'd seen a clean arête somewhere in Gwynant, but couldn't say exactly where. This is a short route with massive exposure, due to the steepness of the hillside from which it protrudes. A pinnacle leaning against the start has recently attempted to toboggan down towards the lake'. Martin Crook*

1993 May   **Ripcurl** O Hayward, J Anthoine
*'Massively overhanging and sequency, a slightly scary clip-up'. First ascensionist's comment.*

1993 June   **The Bear of Tralee** M E Crook, B McMurray, G Robbins
*McMurray, who had only ever done sports routes before that day was heard to utter "No*

way man, you've placed a nut, tops, I've never seen that before."

1993 Oct 10   **Alt Stazione** P Jenkinson, M Smith
*Finished off in a downpour, the second could only be seen when he fell off and swung into view. The other member of the first ascent team ran off back to the car when he saw heavy rain approaching.*

1993 Nov 15   **Don't Look Now** P Littlejohn, M Diggins .

1993 Nov   **Personal Problems** P Littlejohn, M Charlton

1993   **Stampede** G Smith

1994 April   **Priapic Worship** M Crook, J Perrin
*'I'm sure the pinnacle had been climbed before by an easier route round the back but can't find any records. My route starts up the most obvious line and on the first ascent a large flake came off in my hand at about 15 feet, the crux of the route in fact, except for the the final step back onto land from the top of the pinnacle. Abseiling from the top of the flake constitutes failure'. Martin Crook.*

1995 April   **Tronsience** G Smith, M Crook
*Named due to the second removing his trousers to accomplish the squeeze chimney. The leader forgot all about belaying as he was laughing so much. Trôns is the Welsh for underpants.*

1995 April   **Liposuchfun** A Wainwright, C Waddy

1996 April 11   **Trout Fishing in America** J Appleby, P Livesey

1996 May 5   **The Hangman's Favourite Daughter** J Appleby (unseconded)
*'If the Gwynant Needle is Wales' answer to Napes Needle, then this could be its Kern Knotts Crack'. J Appleby.*

1996 May   **Braveheart** S Sturgess, J Keightley, A Leary

1996 May   **First Night** S Sturgess, J Keightley, A Leary

1996 May   **Not Tonight Dear I've Got Sore Elbows** M Eade, A Leary

1996 May   **Last Knight** M Eade, A Leary
*A new crag developed from necessity. A combination of split shifts at the Youth Hostel allowing a few hours free in the afternoon and no transport meant that Al had a very limited choice of venues.*

1996 Aug 7   **Red Star Belgrade** J Appleby, L Appleby

| 1996 Sep 23 | **The Caretaker** G Huxter, A Leary |
| 1996 Sep 23 | **Urban Cookie Collective** A Leary, G Huxter |
| 1996 Oct 16 | **False Destiny** A Leary, G Huxter |

*The first pitch was climbed earlier on 29 September. Named after the Stone of Destiny, which was returned to Scotland having been taken by the English in 1296. However, the real stone was hidden so it was only a copy that made its way to London.*

| 1996 Oct 23 | **To Pick a Pocket or Two** A Leary (solo) |

*The on sight solo was scuppered by the 'stopper' move at the top.*

| 1996 | **Eclipse** D Lampard, P Jenkinson |
| 1997 April 9 | **Willy Wobbles But She Don't Fall Off** A Leary, J Wilson |

*An interesting foray onto a wall that many climbers had looked at but couldn't be bothered to walk to.*

| 1997 April | **Power Snob** M Crook, J Tombs |

*This route has one of the shortest crag walks in Snowdonia, one minute from the car. Probably not attempted before because it was obscured by rhododendrons, until a purge on the shrub was undertaken a few years ago.*

| 1997 April | **Manta Ray Hone Hang** M Crook, A Brudawicz |

*'A bizzare parody of Hoop La Buttress at Frodsham in size and severity'.*

| 1997 May 2 | **Cymru Heb Geidwadwyr** A Leary, S Sturgess |

*Climbed just after the General Election, the Welsh for 'Tory-free Wales'.*

| 1997 May 19 | **Irn Bru** A Leary, S Sturgess, J Wilson |
| 1997 June 2 | **Christmas Climb Direct** J Appleby, L Appleby |
| 1997 Oct 19 | **Christmas Cracker** T Storry, C Storry |
| 1997 Oct | **Lost Tango** T Ralphs, P Littlejohn |

*Done before as an aid route and may well have been climbed free before this date.*

| 1998 Jan 24 | **Heddwch** P Littlejohn, E Hughes |

*The start of a sprint for print.*

| 1998 Jan 24 | **Eloquence** P Littlejohn (unseconded) |
| 1998 Jan 26 | **Punky's Dilemma** J Appleby (unseconded) |
| 1998 Jan 26 | **Route 66** J Appleby, S Lloyd |
| 1998 Jan 26 | **Obscurer** J Appleby, S Lloyd |
| 1998 Jan 31 | **Twister** P Littlejohn, J Littlejohn |

| | | |
|---|---|---|
| 1998 Jan 31 | **Magnum** P Littlejohn, J Littlejohn | |

*Climbed while checking the script for the guide, a long forgotten crag yields some more secrets.*

1998 Jan 31    **Joy Division** J Appleby, H Drasdo
1998 Feb 14    **Stone the Crows** J Appleby, H Drasdo
1998 Feb 14    **King Crimson** J Appleby, H Drasdo
1998 Feb 17    **Irene Handel** D Ashworth, B Woodley
1998 Feb 17    **Dark and Bim** B Woodley, D Ashworth
1998 Mar 5    **Twister** J Appleby, L Appleby
1998 Mar 5    **Steelworker** J Appleby, L Appleby
*Almost certainly done before as an old peg was found on the last pitch.*

1998 Mar 5    **Mur Bach Pinnacle** J Appleby, L Appleby
1998 Mar 31    **Cat's Paw** P Littlejohn, T Jepson (AL)
1998 April 18    **The Precipice Walk** P Littlejohn, J Littlejohn
1998 April 30    **Camel Whip** A Ekins, C Slinn, D Ferguson
*The variation finish J Appleby L Appleby 22 June 1998.*

1998 April 30    **Reservoir Frogs** C Slinn, A Ekins, D Ferguson

1998 April 30    **Second Death** D Ferguson, C Slinn, A Ekins
*A large block came away on the final quartz overhang to give the second a bit of a fright. The line had been mentioned before; 'The central part of the crag is crowned with a quartzy forehead and a route might go direct up and over it'. CC Journal 1950.*

1998 May 3    **Qualen** I A Jones, R Wightman
1998 May 3    **Brewer's Troupe** I A Jones, R Wightman
1998 May 3    **Bank Holiday Bliss** P Winbush, B Woodley, D Ferguson
1998 May 3    **Wizard** P Littlejohn, N Biven
1998 May 16    **Lurking Libido** T Taylor, G Morgan
1998 May 16    **Test on Your Own** T Taylor, G Morgan
1998 May 16    **Teaching Organon** T Taylor, G Morgan
1998 May 31    **Saeth** P Littlejohn, J Littlejohn
1998 June 22    **Vasco** J Appleby, L Appleby
1998 June 22    **Tao of Stone** J Appleby, L Appleby
1998 June 22    **Orbita** J Appleby, L Appleby
1998 June 29    **Oakum** P Littlejohn, A Gold
1998 June 29    **Bwa** P Littlejohn, A Gold
1998 July 7    **Stonecrop** J Appleby, L Appleby, H Hobson
1999 June 23    **The Prowler** P Littlejohn, E Williams, M Glaister, S Monks

# Index

# Accident Procedure

## First Aid

If spinal or head injuries are suspected, do not move the patient without skilled help, except to maintain breathing or if this is essential for further protection.

If breathing has stopped, clear the airways and start artificial respiration. Do not stop until expert opinion has diagnosed death.

Summon help as quickly as is compatible with safety. Do not hesitate or delay.

## Rescue

In the event of a serious accident where assistance is required, a message giving all the factual information about the person(s) location (crag, climb, pitch etc.) should be passed on to the North Wales Police by dialling 999. The Police will contact the respective Rescue Team/Post, and as co-ordinators will obtain further assistance (e.g. helicopter) as directed by those effecting the rescue.

The Police and/or the Rescue Team involved will require the names and addresses of the persons climbing with the injured party. Avoid making rash or unconsidered statements to the press; refer any journalists to the mountaineer who has overall charge of the rescue

## Helicopter Notes

In the event of a helicopter evacuation ALL climbers ON or OFF the cliff should take heed. A helicopter flying close to the cliff will make verbal communications between climbers difficult, and small stones etc. will be dislodged by the rotor downdraft. All loose equipment must be secured and climbers in precarious positions should try to make themselves safe. A smoke grenade may be dropped from the helicopter to give wind direction.

The persons with the injured party should try to identify their location. NO attempt should be made to throw a rope at the helicopter, but assistance should be given to the helicopter crew/personnel if requested.

A helicopter will always be flown into the wind to effect a rescue and on landing there are three danger points: the main rotor, the tail rotor and the engine exhaust. The helicopter should not be approached until directed to do so by the aircrew.

Strumble Head

Saint David's Head

Saint Govan's

Milford Haven ●

Gower

● Swansea

River Usk

Chepstow
●